CRE▲TIVE
HOMEOWNER®

CREATING BEAUTIFUL
BATHROOMS

DESIGN TIPS ▪ REMODELING IDEAS ▪ BUILDING PROJECTS

JERRY GERMER, RA

CREATIVE HOMEOWNER®, Upper Saddle River, New Jersey

COPYRIGHT © 2001

CREATIVE
HOMEOWNER®

A Division of Federal Marketing Corp.
Upper Saddle River, NJ

Publisher: Natalie Chapman
Editorial Director: Timothy O. Bakke
Art Director: Monduane Harris
Creative Director: Clarke Barre
Production Manager: Kimberly H. Vivas

Associate Editor: Paul Rieder
Assistant Editor: Dan Lane
Copy Editor: Ellie Sweeney
Editorial Assistants: Dan Houghtaling,
   Sharon Ranftle
Photo Editor: Stanley Sudol
Technical Consultants: John Spitz, National Kitchen and Bath Association; Charles L. Rogers, Technical Skills Development Services
Indexer: Sandi Schroeder/Schroeder Indexing Services

Designer: Scott Molenaro
Cover Design: Clarke Barre, Robert Strauch
Cover Photography: Tim Street-Porter/Beate Works
Illustrations: Ian Worpole
Principal How-to Photography: Freeze Frame Studio, Hackensack NJ
Photographers: Chris Craig, Glenn Teitell
Photo Assistants: Craig Grothues, Jonathan Kingston, Margaret McGill

Manufactured in the United States of America

Current Printing (last digit)
10 9 8 7 6 5 4 3

Creating Beautiful Bathrooms
Library of Congress Catalog Card Number: 2001086957
ISBN: 1-58011-077-0

CREATIVE HOMEOWNER®
A Division of Federal Marketing Corp.
24 Park Way, Upper Saddle River, NJ 07458
Web site: **www.creativehomeowner.com**

Photo Credits

All photographs not credited here are by Freeze Frame Studio, Hackensack NJ.

p. 1: Mark Lohman **pp. 6–7:** Tria Giovan **p. 8:** Tria Giovan **p. 9:** Nancy Hill (top); Mark Samu (bottom) **p. 10:** davidduncanlivingston.com **p. 11:** Mark Samu (top); davidduncanlivingston.com (bottom); **p. 12:** davidduncanlivingston.com **p. 13:** davidduncanlivingston.com **pp. 14–15:** Mark Lohman **pp. 16–17:** Crandall & Crandall **p. 18:** davidduncanlivingston.com **p. 20:** Brian Vanden Brink **p. 21:** Melabee M Miller/Elizabeth Gillin, designer **pp. 22–23:** davidduncanlivingston.com **p. 24:** davidduncanlivingston.com **p. 25:** Mark Samu (top); Melabee M Miller/Doyle Budden, designer (bottom left); Phillip H. Ennis (bottom right) **p. 26:** Melabee M Miller **p. 27:** Phillip H. Ennis (left); Melabee M Miller/Geraldine E. Kaupp, designer (right) **p. 28:** Mark Samu (top); Janet Henderson (bottom) **p. 29:** davidduncanlivingston.com (top); Kohler (bottom) **p. 30:** Brian Vanden Brink **p. 31:** Mark Samu **p. 32:** Mark Samu (top); Phillip H. Ennis (bottom) **p. 33:** Saunatec **pp. 34–35:** Brian Vanden Brink **p. 36:** Tria Giovan (top); Mark Samu (bottom) **p. 37:** Richard Gross **p. 38:** davidduncanlivingston.com **p. 39:** davidduncanlivingston.com **p. 40:** Phillip H. Ennis **p. 41:** Mark Samu **p. 42:** Brian Vanden Brink **p. 43:** Brian Vanden Brink (top); davidduncanlivingston.com (bottom) **pp. 44–45:** Brian Vanden Brink **p. 46:** davidduncanlivingston.com (top); Scott Dorrance (bottom) **p. 47:** Brian Vanden Brink (top); Crandall & Crandall (bottom) **p. 48:** BathEase, Inc. **p. 49:** Smedbo **pp. 50–51:** Peter Tata **p. 52:** Crandall & Crandall (top); Mark Samu (bottom) **p. 53:** Mark Samu (top 2); davidduncanlivingston.com (bottom) **p. 54:** Mark Samu **p. 55:** Brian Vanden Brink (top); davidduncanlivingston.com (bottom) **p. 56:** davidduncanlivingston.com (both) **p. 57:** davidduncanlivingston.com (top); Tria Giovan (bottom) **pp. 58–59:** Mark Samu **p. 60:** davidduncanlivingston.com (both) **p. 61:** Phillip H. Ennis **p. 62:** Bill Rothschild **p. 63:** Richard Gross **p. 64:** Brian Vanden Brink (left); davidduncanlivingston.com (right) **p. 65:** Brian Vanden Brink (top); Phillip H. Ennis (bottom) **p. 66:** Mark Samu (left); davidduncanlivingston.com (right) **p. 67:** davidduncanlivingston.com (top); Melabee M Miller (bottom) **pp. 68–69:** davidduncanlivingston.com **p. 73:** Clarke Barre (bottom) **p. 76:** Clarke Barre **p. 77:** John Parsekian **p. 78:** Clarke Barre **p. 79:** John Parsekian **pp. 80–81:** Tria Giovan **p. 89:** John Parsekian **p. 91:** Clarke Barre (bottom left), John Parsekian (bottom right) **p. 94:** Clarke Barre **pp. 96–97:** Mark Lohman **p. 98:** John Parsekian **p. 102:** John Parsekian **p. 109:** Velux **p. 110:** Velux (top left, middle right, bottom) **pp. 114–115:** Tria Giovan **p. 120:** Brian C. Nieves **p. 124:** Merle Henkenius (bottom left) **p. 125:** John Parsekian (top 2) **p. 128:** Clarke Barre **p. 132:** Kohler **p. 152:** Sloan/Flushmate **pp. 154–155:** Melabee M Miller/tile by Crossville Tile **p. 156:** Brian C. Nieves **p. 158:** Brian C. Nieves (right) **p. 158:** Clarke Barre (left) **p. 159:** Brian C. Nieves **p. 169:** Brian C. Nieves (top 4) **p. 169:** Clarke Barre (bottom) **p. 174:** Clarke Barre **p. 175:** Brian C. Nieves **p. 177:** Brian C. Nieves **pp. 178–179:** Mark Samu **pp. 186–187:** John Parsekian **p. 188:** John Parsekian **p. 190:** Kohler **pp. 196–197:** Mark Lohman **p. 199:** John Parsekian **pp. 208–209:** John Parsekian **p. 210:** John Parsekian

Safety

Although the methods in this book have been reviewed for safety, it is not possible to overstate the importance of using the safest methods you can. What follows are reminders—some do's and don'ts of work safety—to use along with your common sense.

❖ Always use caution, care, and good judgment when following the procedures described in this book.

❖ Always be sure that the electrical setup is safe, that no circuit is overloaded, and that all power tools and outlets are properly grounded. Do not use power tools in wet locations.

❖ Always read container labels on paints, solvents, and other products; provide ventilation; and observe all other warnings.

❖ Always read the manufacturer's instructions for using a tool, especially the warnings.

❖ Use hold-downs and push sticks whenever possible when working on a table saw. Avoid working short pieces if you can.

❖ Always remove the key from any drill chuck (portable or press) before starting the drill.

❖ Always pay deliberate attention to how a tool works so that you can avoid being injured.

❖ Always know the limitations of your tools. Do not try to force them to do what they were not designed to do.

❖ Always make sure that any adjustment is locked before proceeding. For example, always check the rip fence on a table saw or the bevel adjustment on a portable saw before starting to work.

❖ Always clamp small pieces to a bench or other work surface when using a power tool.

❖ Always wear the appropriate rubber gloves or work gloves when handling chemicals, moving or stacking lumber, working with concrete, or doing heavy construction.

❖ Always wear a disposable face mask when you create dust by sawing or sanding. Use a special filtering respirator when working with toxic substances and solvents.

❖ Always wear eye protection, especially when using power tools or striking metal on metal or concrete; a chip can fly off, for example, when chiseling concrete.

❖ Never work while wearing loose clothing, open cuffs, or jewelry, and tie back long hair.

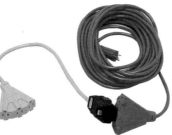

❖ Always be aware that there is seldom enough time for your body's reflexes to save you from injury from a power tool in a dangerous situation. Everything happens too fast. Be alert!

❖ Always keep your hands away from the business ends of blades, cutters, and bits.

❖ Always hold a circular saw firmly, usually with both hands.

❖ Always use a drill with an auxiliary handle to control the torque when using large-size bits.

❖ Always check local building codes when planning new construction. The codes are intended to protect public safety and should be observed to the letter.

❖ Never work with power tools when you are tired or under the influence of alcohol or drugs.

❖ Never cut tiny pieces of wood or pipe using a power saw. When you need a small piece, saw it from a securely clamped longer piece.

❖ Never change a saw blade or a drill or router bit unless the power cord is unplugged. Do not depend on the switch being off. You might accidentally hit it.

❖ Never work in insufficient lighting.

❖ Never work with dull tools. Have them sharpened, or learn how to sharpen them yourself.

❖ Never use a power tool on a workpiece—large or small—that is not firmly supported.

❖ Never saw a workpiece that spans a large distance between horses without close support on each side of the cut. The piece can bend, closing on and jamming the blade, causing saw kickback.

❖ When sawing, never support a workpiece from underneath with your leg or other part of your body.

❖ Never carry sharp or pointed tools, such as utility knives, awls, or chisels in your pocket. If you want to carry these tools, use a special-purpose tool belt that has leather pockets and holders.

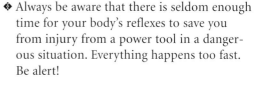

Contents

Designing the
Bathroom
CHAPTER 1

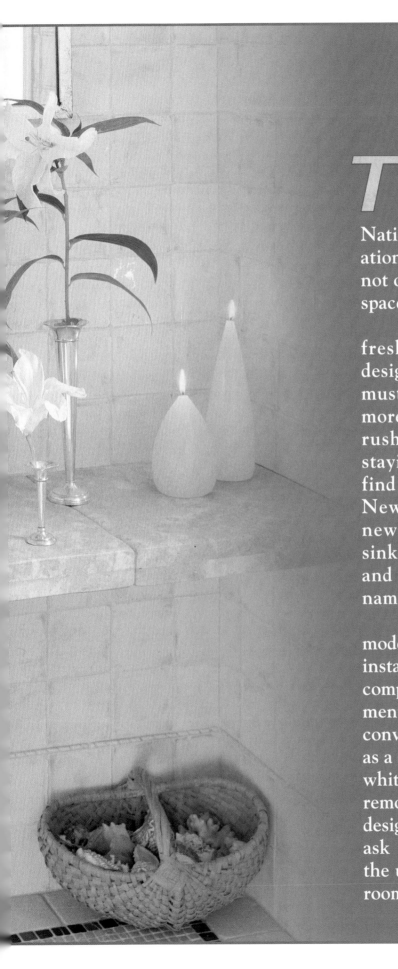

The bathroom is the most frequently remodeled room in the house, according to the National Kitchen and Bath Association (NKBA). Homeowners want not only more bathrooms with more space but also more amenities.

Changing lifestyles call for fresh approaches to bathroom design. Bathrooms in older houses must now accommodate two or more adults during the morning rush. With more young adults staying at home longer, families find they need additional space. New lifestyle patterns demand new design approaches: more sinks, separate tubs and showers, and separate dressing rooms, to name a few.

To cope with the stresses of modern life, homeowners are now installing spas, whirlpool tubs, steam compartments, even exercise equipment. These items challenge the conventional notion of the bathroom as a small utilitarian room with three white fixtures. But before you begin remodeling your old bathroom—or designing a new one—you need to ask yourself what services (besides the usual ones) you want your bathroom to provide.

What Do You Want from Your Bathroom?

A good way to start is to write down your bathroom's shortcomings. You probably know your bathroom's problems well; others in the household probably have their own gripes. A detailed list of each person's complaints can be a valuable guide in your planning. Here are some questions to help spark discussion:

• Are the bathrooms conveniently located?

• What's wrong with the mirror above the sink? Is it too small? Poorly placed?

• Are all electrical outlets in bathrooms protected with ground-fault circuit interrupters (GFCIs)?

• Does anyone regularly wash or dye hair in the bathroom sink? If so, is the faucet suited to this?

• Do you have enough storage space in your medicine cabinet?

• Can drugs and other substances be stored where small children can't get to them?

• Do members of your household prefer to wash in a tub, shower, or both? Are there enough of each?

• Do any fixtures leak?

• Do you see any effects of moisture? Is there mildew on tiles, curled vinyl flooring, or loose paint or wallcovering?

• Do you have adequate ventilation to remove odors and moisture?

• What is right and wrong with your bathroom's lighting fixtures?

This bathroom design provides plenty of room for two adults to get ready in the morning, with two sinks, two mirrors, and an abundance of accessible storage space.

Make a Scrapbook

Use your list of problems to begin a scrapbook or file folder of improvement ideas. You might include
• Ideas for improving efficiency— whether it might be better to improve the present bathroom for use by two persons or to add another bathroom
• Pictures of fixtures from magazines and promotional literature
• Ideas for storage of towels, washcloths, and personal hygiene items
• Ideas for floor and wall finishes
• Business cards, newspaper ads, and names and addresses of designers, suppliers, and builders

Don't Pour Money down the Drain

It's hard to resist the urge to remodel when you see a magazine article that shows how to transform a bathroom with three plain fixtures into a room that's a pleasure to inhabit. Even though the typical bathroom is smaller than the other rooms in the house, it is packed with expensive systems. So before you pick up a paintbrush or adjustable wrench, decide why you want to remodel and which changes you need.

If you have a good sense of design, a few small changes to an older bathroom can make it look new without costing you a lot of money.

Increasing Your Home's Resale Value

Getting your money back may not be your first priority when you ponder bathroom improvements. Should it be? People move more frequently today than ever before. If it seems likely you'll sell your home in the next few years, you should weigh any remodeling investment more carefully than if you think you will stay long enough to recoup your money in the form of a greater benefit.

Ideally, you should aim to spend no more on total remodeling costs for your entire home than you can get back at sale time. One rule of thumb: Don't add more than 20 percent of the value of your home in total improvements. At most, don't spend more on improvements than the difference between the price you paid for your home and the

You don't necessarily need a contractor to give your bathroom an entirely new look: painting, tiling, and replacing existing lighting and vanities can be done by the patient DIYer.

average sale price of other homes in the area.

It will also help to find out what kind of bathroom facilities home buyers expect to find in your area. Speak with a local real estate agent, and ask how many bathrooms buyers are seeking and which kinds of amenities they want.

Improving an Existing Bathroom

Whatever buyers want, bringing an existing bathroom up to modern standards is usually money well spent. You can expect to recoup almost all of the cost if you do the work yourself, but only 40 percent or so if you hire someone. Perhaps more important than the money is the chance that the work will help your home sell more quickly.

With this in mind, play it safe with colors, textures, and fixtures. An outdoor deck adjacent to the bathroom might be great in sunny San Diego, but won't be much of a draw in Buf-

The large, old-fashioned bathtub is a stylish but unusual addition to this bathroom, creating a contrast with the very modern-looking decor.

falo. Also, choose a style that will blend with the character of your house. A modern bath in a Colonial-style home looks out of place. With care, you can have up-to-date amenities and still retain the traditional decor of your home.

Whether you do it yourself or hire specialists, use high-quality materials that are good-looking and wear well. For work that you plan to do yourself, be sure you are capable of professional-quality workmanship.

Adding a New Bathroom

Deciding whether to add another bathroom is a tough call. If your house has fewer bathrooms than other houses in the neighborhood, adding one can be a good investment. But if you have two bathrooms in a neighborhood of two-bathroom houses, you probably won't recoup your expenses by adding a third.

Where you locate the new bathroom also plays a part. Adding a new bath in an unused or underused room next to an existing bathroom or laundry area is relatively cost efficient. It takes much more money to put a bathroom in a part of the house that is remote from existing plumbing or to add another room onto the house.

Remodeling for You

You may decide you need to make improvements even though you may not recover the costs when you sell your house. Maybe it's just time to get the bathroom that you have always wanted, even if the improvements don't add your home's resale value.

No argument here. After all, your home is your personal space, and any change that doesn't make your bathroom better for you and your family misses the real mark. If you can meet your own goals and add real value to your home, so much the better.

However, if you have to compromise, it's probably better to hedge on the side of satisfying your present needs rather than trying to outguess the tastes and desires of unknown future buyers.

How Much?

Whatever your investment strategy, before getting tied down to a plan of action, it's a good idea to determine just how much you can spend. You can set limits on what you ought to spend from the guidelines discussed earlier. What you can afford will be set by one or more of the following factors:

- Available cash
- The amount of financing you can obtain
- The amount of your monthly loan payments
- Your overall financial goals

An idea of the actual costs of improvements can help you set a budget. The total cost of your project depends on the extent of the remodeling and how

These cubbyholes make good use of otherwise dead space behind the tub; this project is also easy for a do-it-yourselfer to complete.

much of the work you plan to do yourself. Obviously, the more work you do yourself, the more you stand to save on the total costs of your improvements. If you do all of the work yourself and pay only for materials, you may do the job for about half the cost of hiring someone to do it for you.

DIY or Hire?

As you make plans, you will have to decide whether to do the work yourself or hire a contractor—or maybe a little of both. Doing your own work can save money and give you the satisfaction that comes from creating something of value. But not everyone can undertake every task. To help you decide, consider these issues:

Skills. You'll know that you can do a job if you have done it before, of course. But there's a first time for everything: maybe plumbing is something you would like to learn. If you're really starting from scratch, perhaps you could do the task working alongside an experienced friend or neighbor.

Also, if you haven't done a task before, find out its physical demands. To replace a faucet, you need dexterity in both hands. More extensive remodeling of plumbing requires strength and a good back. If you're unsure, do a little research before committing yourself. Pros make installing drywall look like a snap, but a 4-by-8-foot sheet weighs 50 to 70 pounds.

Time & Money. By doing it yourself, you'll obviously save the cost of labor. If you don't mind spending a few weekends painting, it's money well saved. But if you've never worked on plumb-

If you're turning a spare room into a bathroom, don't forget to leave space for decorative elements and lots of room to move around.

ing, it's going to be difficult to estimate how long it will take you to figure out how to solder pipe on your first shot. You might save some money on a plumber, but you probably don't want to shut down the water to the bathroom for two weeks instead of half a day.

Safety. There are also local building-code restrictions and the safety factor. Some cities and towns allow only licensed pros to work on wiring and plumbing. Even if you're permitted to do all or some of the work, you still have to meet code requirements—and be able to do the job without endangering yourself. If you don't think you can attain these standards, you're better off hiring a professional.

Whom Do You Need to Hire?

Depending on what you are planning for your bathroom, you may need the services of a design or construction professional.

Architects. If you are planning significant structural changes in your bathroom, an architect is the best choice. While all licensed architects are schooled in both residential and commercial design, one who regularly designs baths for residences is the best candidate for your project.

Certified Bath Designers. These people are certified by the National Kitchen & Bath Association as professionals who deal specifically in bath design and remodeling. Because they are specialists, they know the latest in bath products and trends and can help you choose the best layout and materials for your particular job. The NKBA offers a listing of certified designers on their Web site, www.nkba.org.

Interior Designers. Interior designers can help you create style in your new bath and integrate it into the overall look of your home. You may want to contact an interior designer if you are making significant cosmetic changes to your bath rather than structural changes. Some states require licensing by the American Society of Interior Designers.

Design-Build Remodeling Firms. These firms retain both designers and remodelers on staff. They are extremely popular because of the convenience of having all the necessary services within one company. If something goes wrong, you only have to make one call.

Remodeling Contractors. Some contractors offer design as part of their remodeling services, or they partner with a design professional. A contractor is a good choice if you have already hired an architect to design the bath or if you are not changing the structure of your bath substantially. Always work with a licensed contractor.

Finding the Right Pro

Hiring a professional builder, plumber, electrician, or other licensed contractor guarantees that the provider has satisfied the state's requirements to perform a certain service. It makes no guarantee, however, for the quality of the service. How do you find the best person for your job?

Start with the recommendations of your friends and business associates. If you can't find leads there, look in the Yellow Pages. When you phone prospective providers, ask if

This bathroom, with its open plan and French doors leading to a courtyard, is not for the timid. It's beautiful, but may make your home more difficult to sell.

they have worked on projects like yours and whether they would be interested in looking over the plans.

Internet sites also provide names of dependable contractors in your area. One site, ImproveNet (www.improvenet.com), has a national database of 600,000 selected contractors. Just submit the details of your job and your zip code, and you will receive a list of contractors, pre-screened to eliminate those without a clean legal and credit record. You'll usually get a response within 48 hours.

You will need, at least, a floor plan and a written specification sheet describing your fixture selection, cabinetry choices, electrical items, and finishes. For all but ordinary designs, drawings of each wall (elevations) and cross sections are helpful.

Do You Need a Permit?

Permits and inspections are a way of enforcing the building code. A permit is essentially a license that gives you permission to do the work, while an inspection ensures that you did the work in accordance with the codes. For minor repair or remodeling work, you don't usually need a permit, but you may need one if you add or resupport walls, extend the plumbing, or add an electrical circuit. You will nearly always need one if your new bathroom is in a new addition to your house. Some municipal codes allow work by a homeowner on his or her house, even wiring and plumbing, if a permit is obtained first. Some won't let anyone but a licensed contractor work on wiring or plumbing.

Depending on the scope of the work, your permit application should include the following items:
• A legal description of the property. You can get this from city or county records or from a deed.
• A site-plan drawing. This shows the position of the house on the lot and the approximate location of adjacent houses. It should also show the location of the well and septic system, if any.
• A drawing of the proposed changes. This needn't be drawn by an architect, but it should clearly show the structural changes you plan to make and identify all materials. Most building departments will accept plans drawn by a homeowner as long as they're clearly labeled.

Inspections

Whenever a permit is required, you'll probably have to schedule time for an inspector to examine the

If you want to install a sink in a new spot, you will need to get a permit. You may also need to get a plumber—some municipalities restrict who can install new plumbing.

work. He or she will check to see that the work meets or exceeds the building code. When you obtain your permit, ask about the inspection schedule. On small projects an inspector might come out only for a final inspection; on a larger project you might have several intermediate inspections before a final inspection.

Zoning Ordinances

If you are planning to add a bathroom, zoning ordinances might require you to enlarge your septic system. If the bathroom is an addition that increases the "footprint" of your house (its outline on the ground), you must be sure it complies with zoning restrictions. For example, most zoning ordinances require that any addition to your house be set back a certain minimum distance from your neighbors' properties and from the road. Though most bathroom projects won't run afoul of zoning ordinances, it's always a good idea to check with local officials before you start.

Arranging the
Space
CHAPTER 2

hether you want to explore ways to make an existing bathroom more useful or you want to design a new one, you can do your planning most easily in two dimensions. In this chapter you'll see how to translate your ideas into scaled drawings from which you or your contractor can build.

Planning bathroom improvements begins with a drawing of the room as it exists—the base plan—and ends with a scale drawing of the layout as you want it to be. Between these "before" and "after" plans, you'll probably make a few sketches on tracing paper to explore different ways to arrange your space.

The arrangement of space plays an important role in how well a bathroom functions. A bathroom addition to the outside wall of the house offers the most possibilities for more floor space, but it's also the most expensive option. Sometimes a small amount of space can be stolen from a closet or adjacent room. If the existing floor plan works for you, all you have to think about is updating old fixtures, installing new tiles, and perhaps replacing the cabinetry.

Making a Base Drawing

For your base drawing, you'll need a piece of graph paper with grids marked at ¼-inch intervals and a measuring tape. Mount your pad of paper to a clipboard, and use it to make a rough freehand sketch of the existing plan of your bathroom and any adjacent areas you want to consider. The purpose of your drawing is to record the physical layout of the space as it now exists.

Now start taking measurements. If the room is small and you have a good steel measuring tape, you may be able to hold the tape yourself, but it's always easier to have a helper hold one end of the tape.

Start with the big picture, and work down to the details. First, record the length and width of the room. Then, from one corner, measure the location of windows, doors, and walls; be sure to show the swing of doors. Note each dimension in feet and inches to the nearest ¼ inch.

After you have measured and recorded the room's main features, record the cabinetry and plumbing fixtures. Measure to the centerline of sinks, toilets, and bidets, but be sure you also list the overall widths and lengths. Lastly, note electrical and mechanical items, such as heat registers, light fixtures, and outlets.

Make a Base Plan

Next, transfer your measurements from rough form to one you can use to plan the layout of the space.

A certified bath designer (CBD) can be helpful in arranging your bathroom's fixtures in a way that makes the best possible use of the allotted space.

You can sketch the base plan by hand, making it to scale. A convenient scale for planning a bathroom is to make ½ inch equal to 1 foot; in other words, each ½ inch on your drawing represents 12 inches of floor space. If you are using graph paper with a ¼-inch grid, each square represents a 6-inch square. Anything less than 6 inches you can approximate.

Use a point at one corner of a square to begin laying out the room's walls. Follow the same sequence as you did when measuring. Begin by drawing the outer walls in the proper locations, add the windows, doors, and other features, and then show the minor details.

When you have completed your base plan, make several copies so that you can explore different options.

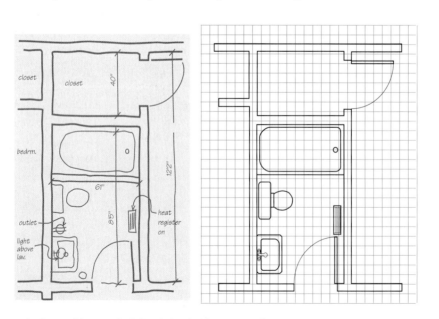

Begin by making a sketch of the bathroom as it now exists by recording the room dimensions. Include any adjacent areas that might be used for expansion.

Planning the New Layout

Fixtures make bathrooms different from other rooms in the house, so your planning should revolve around them. By now, you probably have a pretty good idea of the fixtures you want. To serve your goals effectively, the fixtures will have to be located efficiently with respect to one another other and with enough space in and around them to make them convenient to use. But the fixtures themselves are only part of the picture. The part you don't see is the network of hot- and cold-water supply pipes and waste pipes. Unless you are ready to gut the entire room and completely rework the plumbing (sometimes the best tack), keep these guidelines in mind for economical fixture location:

- Don't move the toilet unless you have to.
- Keep the plumbing fixtures on the same wall.

Make Templates

Paper templates of fixtures and cabinets are an easy way to experiment with different layouts. First draw the fixtures on graph paper, using the same scale as your base plan. If you have collected pictures and spec sheets in a scrapbook, use the dimensions given. If not, use the dimensions for fixtures shown in this book as a guide. When cutting out tem-

2 Arranging the Space

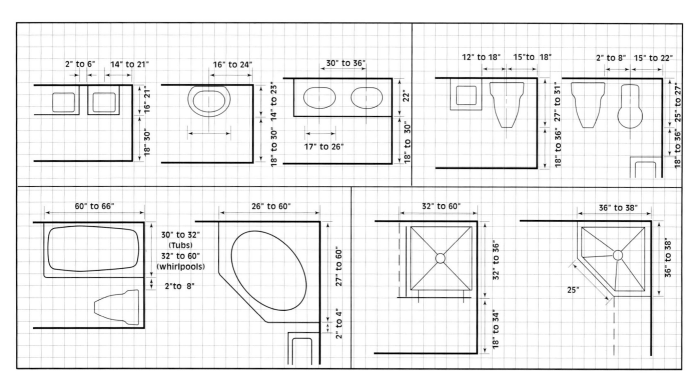

To experiment with different layouts, make templates using the measurements of your fixtures. Keep in mind the minimum clearances between fixtures shown here. You should also consult your local plumbing code.

plates, include both the fixture and its required front and side clearances—that way you won't get caught short.

Knowing what fixture clearances to use is as much art as science. While each fixture requires a minimum distance from a wall or another fixture, usually set by plumbing codes, bathrooms planned to these minimum clearances are cramped and inconvenient to use. Two fixture clearances are shown in the drawings on page 17. The first figure in each pair is the minimum required by code, and the second figure allows for a more generous layout. For an efficient but convenient arrangement, shoot for somewhere between the two numbers.

Basic Bath Arrangements

Bathrooms are defined by the combination of essential fixtures they contain. By fixture count, there are three basic types of bathrooms:

• Half baths (powder rooms) contain a toilet plus a sink.

• Three-quarter baths contain a toilet plus a sink and a shower.

• Full baths contain a toilet plus a sink and a tub.

Half Baths. In a half bath, the sink and toilet may be located on the same wall, adjacent walls, or opposite walls. If your house has only one bathroom, you can reduce the morning rush by adding a half bath. Placed on the main floor, it can also serve as a facility for guests.

Three-Quarter Baths. A bath with a shower instead of a tub is a wise second bathroom for big households. Relying more on a shower and less on a tub will cut water consumption and the cost of heating water. It will also help minimize bathroom gridlock. And, as noted earlier, stall showers are safer and more convenient to use than tub showers.

Full Baths. Possibly the most common bathroom in America is a 60 × 84-inch or 60 × 96-inch space with a sink, toilet, and tub/shower plumbed along one wall. The door is usually located in the short wall, but sometimes placed in the long wall,

This bathroom makes good use of a finished attic by placing an extra-large bathtub underneath a gable window.

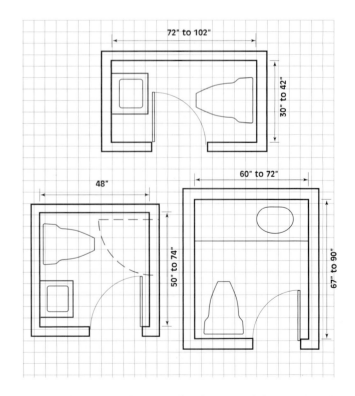

A half bath (or powder room) makes a useful second bathroom. You can fit one into an unused closet or extra hallway space (top) or a larger rectangular space (bottom).

opposite the fixtures. In this layout, the tub wall, frequently the only outside wall, contains a window—a safety hazard if you wind up having to stand in the tub while trying to muscle a stuck window open or closed. If the window is long and narrow, it probably also catches water on the sill and thwarts privacy. Consider replacing the existing window with a casement or awning type. The new window should be half the size of the original and located in the upper half of the opening.

Luxury Baths. Including a bidet or second sink (or both!) in a full bath adds luxury and convenience. When planning for additional fixtures, consider who will use them and what level of privacy will be needed. Should you try to organize everything into one space, or perhaps subdivide the space into smaller compartments that would be isolated for privacy?

Placing Fixtures in the Proper Order

Some fixtures are used much more often than others. In a full bath, the sink is the most-used fixture, the toilet comes next, and then the tub or shower. The most efficient way to plan this kind of bath is to locate the sink closest to the door, with the toilet being next in line and tub most remote.

It shouldn't come as a surprise that this is the most common layout for bathrooms in the 60 × 84-inch size range. If you have any leeway in your floor plan, try to locate the toilet so that it won't be seen when the door is open. Even in small rooms, the door swing direction can help shield the toilet from view.

In many families, several people often have to use the facilities at the same time as they get ready for work and school. One way to ease the traffic jam is to place the sink and vanity outside the main room that contains the toilet and bathing fixtures. When floor space is big enough, the toilet is often contained within a separate stall.

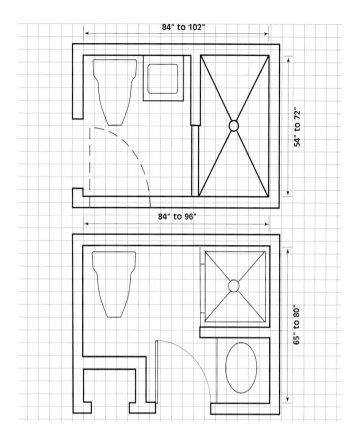

Use these basic layouts to help you plan a three-quarter bath. The in-line layout at top allows for a larger shower and better use of space than the one at right, where plumbing also needs to be roughed-in behind two walls.

2 Arranging the Space

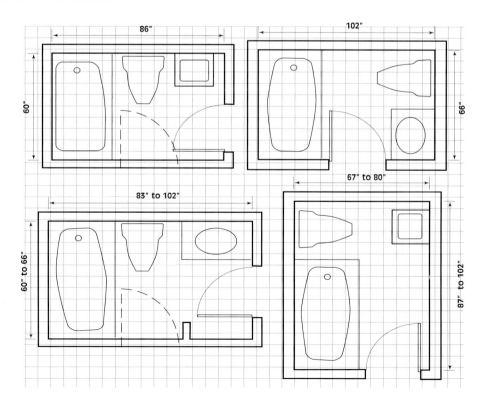

Above are the layouts required for full baths. Increasing the depth of the small room at left by 16 in. and the width by 6 in. allows for more storage and greater convenience.

Expanding outward with a small bump-out addition is an effective but expensive way to turn a small powder room into a spacious full bath.

Improving Your Layout

Chapter 1 suggested that you start your bathroom planning with a list of shortcomings of the present room. Note your list of gripes on the base plan to give you a good starting point for changing the layout. Next, see what changes you can make to solve each problem. Use your templates to explore alternatives.

Expanding into Adjacent Space

If you can't improve the layout without adding space, take a look at the rooms adjacent to your bathroom. Begin by looking for unused spaces, such as the area below a stairway. If closets are nearby, ask yourself whether some or all of the space can be used for the bath. Maybe you can take 2 feet of floor space from a large abutting room without reducing its usefulness.

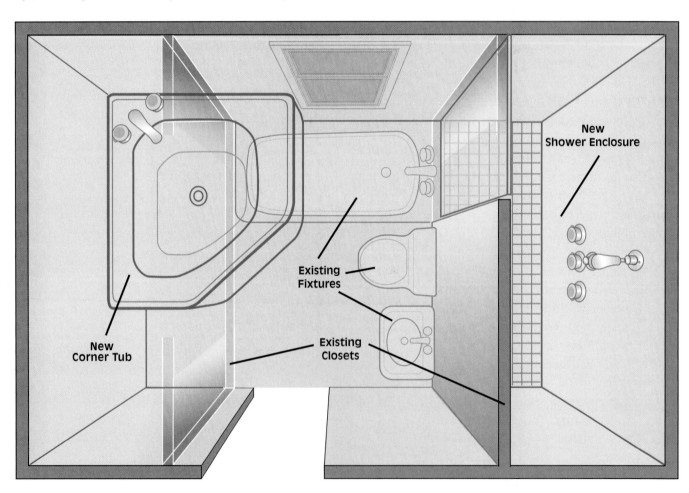

New Shower Enclosure

Existing Fixtures

New Corner Tub

Existing Closets

By expanding into the closet at left, there is enough room to replace this existing tub with a large corner tub while still leaving plenty of room for storage and generous floor space between the fixtures. A similar closet space seen at right allows a large shower compartment or, if you wish, a long vanity with double sinks.

You can expand into an adjacent space or expand outward on cantilevered joists to gain more storage space or just to make the bathroom roomier. By putting the toilet in its own separate room, you can open up the rest of the bathroom for use by more people during busy mornings.

Enlarging Outward

A bump-out bathroom addition to an outside wall offers the chance to gain floor space. However, additional foundation work makes this the most expensive option. It may be possible to extend the outer wall out by 3 feet or so without building a new foundation, by extending the floor structure out over the foundation with cantilevered joists.

If the existing bathroom floor joists run perpendicular into the outer wall, you would add a "sister" to each joist, which would cantilever out and overhang the foundation. If this looks possible, get the help of an architect or engineer to make sure the structure is sound. You will also need to be sure that you will not be encroaching into the setback required by the local zoning ordinance.

Using Vertical Space

You also need to think about how vertical surfaces can be used for storage or for mounting accessories. Building shelves or extending a countertop over a toilet makes storage space on an otherwise empty wall. Another option is to use the cavities between the studs in interior walls for shallow storage alcoves.

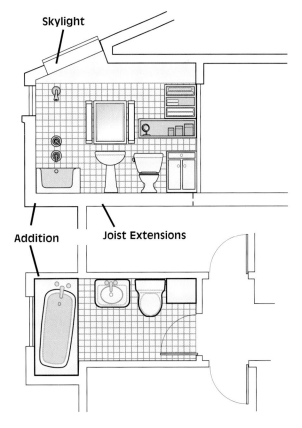

By extending the floor joists out a few feet, you can enlarge your bathroom without having to construct a foundation. The roof can be similarly extended and enhanced with a skylight.

Selecting Fixtures

One of the first things you'll notice when you start poring through bathroom catalogs and product literature is the vast number of choices of fixtures and accessories available today. Gone are the days of the purely utilitarian bathroom furnished with three white fixtures jammed in side by side. Now you can breathe new life into your bathroom with a rainbow of colors, a multitude of styles, and a host of amenities stretching from whirlpools and bidets to saunas and steam baths.

The products you select for your new bathroom will affect both your design and your budget. Factors that influence the cost of new fixtures include updated technology and type of finish. The more advanced the device, the more you'll pay for it. Likewise, the fancier the finish, the higher the price tag. But cost does not necessarily reflect quality or satisfaction, the two most important factors to consider when selecting fixtures.

How can you tell whether a product is reliable and will endure the daily wear and tear of water and moisture? To find out, you can do a little research. Shop around, visit some designer showrooms, read a few books, and always ask questions.

Metal sinks are associated with the kitchen, but this Asian-inspired model is a centerpiece of this bath's design.

Sinks

Sinks are often called lavatories or basins by the industry. With standard fittings, they accommodate shaving, washing, and brushing teeth. You can also adapt a sink for shampooing by adding a sprayer attached to a short hose. Sinks come as ovals, rectangles, circles, and other shapes. Manufacturers have gone to great lengths to give sinks appeal by sculpting their forms, but the simpler shapes are both more practical to use and easier to keep clean. Sizes vary from a 12 × 18-inch rectangle to a 33-inch-diameter oval.

Sinks used to be made either of glazed vitreous china, or porcelain over cast iron or steel. These sinks' finishes proved impervious to water, mold, and mildew; they dulled only after years of abrasion. Fiberglass and acrylic sinks, modern innovations, open endless possibilities for shapes, colors, and patterns, but are much more susceptible to scratches than vitreous china and porcelain.

Freestanding Sinks

A good place to begin your sink selection is to decide whether you want a freestanding fixture or one built into a countertop. Freestanding sinks—including those designed specifically to go in corners—can be mounted either directly on the wall or on

Some ceramic sinks, called vessel sinks, are designed to be displayed rather than dropped into a countertop. This design also features an unusual wall-mounted faucet.

legs or pedestals. Freestanding sinks are available in colors, shapes, and sizes to suit any taste. They come with flat tops or raised backsplashes that meet the wall. If you choose a freestanding sink, be sure you allow enough space in your design. Wall-mounted units will look and feel cramped if they abut a wall or other fixture with minimal clearance at the sides. While you can stuff a pedestal sink into a space as narrow as 22 inches, it will look better with generous open space on each side. Also keep in mind that you're losing under-sink storage with a freestanding sink, which may affect the rest of your bathroom layout.

Vanity-Mounted Sinks

Vanity-mounted sinks became popular when bathrooms shrank to the tiny size that marked much of the housing built after World War II. For extra storage, the space under the fixture was enclosed in a cabinet; any extra space above could be used to hold accessories such as drinking glasses, toothpaste, or soap. Combination vanities and sinks may not be much wider than the sink, or they may be as wide as the room. If you are stuck with a bathroom measuring 50 square feet or less, a vanity-mounted sink may be the only way to get enough storage space.

Sinks mounted on a countertop are self-rimming (where the bowl forms its own seal) or rimmed (where the bowl is installed with a metal trim piece to join it to the countertop). Self-rimming sinks can also be installed from below, with the countertop overlapping the rim of the sink; however, the edges of the countertop must be able to withstand moisture. Molded solid-surface countertops, solid marble, and ceramic tile work well for this kind of application. Plastic laminate, which has a seam at the edge, will not hold up.

The way the sink is mounted in the countertop has both aesthetic and practical consequences. The exposed edge of a self-rimming sink sits atop the vanity surface. Though attractive, the edge prevents water splashed onto the counter from draining into the sink. Metal rims overcome this drawback by aligning the edge of the sink with the countertop, but the metal trim creates a less-elegant look than the self-rimming model. Sinks mounted below ceramic-

White china pedestal sinks are the perfect match for this traditional bathroom design.

tile, solid-surface, or stone countertops provide a pleasing separation between countertop and sink.

Integral Sinks

One-piece sink/countertop units are molded from a single material, such as solid-surfacing material or faux stone. The look is seamless, sleek, and sculptural. Many of these units contain preformed backsplashes, built-in soap dishes, and other useful design features.

This unusual vessel sink, which resembles a glass punch bowl, makes a striking addition to a spare wall-mounted countertop.

Drop-in sinks installed in a laminate countertop don't have to be ordinary, as this example shows.

Toilets & Bidets

Toilets come in a great variety of styles, shapes, and colors—though colors other than white usually cost more. Vitreous china still prevails as the most common material.

You can choose between toilets that contain the tank and base in a single molded unit and toilets that have a separate tank. The most common type puts the tank directly behind the base. Another version, which raises the tank high on the wall, is available for people who want a Victorian look.

When selecting a toilet for a small room, it will help to know basic toilet sizes. Tank widths vary from 20 to 24 inches. Toilets with the tank mounted high on the wall are around 15 inches wide. Toilets project out from the wall 26 to 30 inches, requiring a minimum room depth of 44 and 48 inches, respectively. Scaled-down toilets—even toilets that fit into a corner—are available for tiny apartment bathrooms or small powder rooms, such as those tucked under a stairwell.

Low-Flush Toilets

Regardless of its color or style, you want a toilet that will function dependably and quietly. Another factor to consider is water conservation. Until recently, toilets required 5 to 7 gallons for each flush, making them the largest single daily user of household water. But with water becoming scarce in many parts of the United States, conservation has become a top concern. The federal government enacted a national standard that limits the water used by residential toi-

This traditional white toilet is discreetly hidden from view in an alcove that was once a linen closet.

lets made in the United States after January 1, 1994, to 1.6 gallons per flush (gpf). Manufacturers are meeting the challenge with improved versions of standard gravity toilets and new designs that use air pressure.

Water-conserving toilets cost more than the older 5-gallon units, but the money you save in water use (and, for well users, electricity and septic maintenance) will eventually make up for the difference.

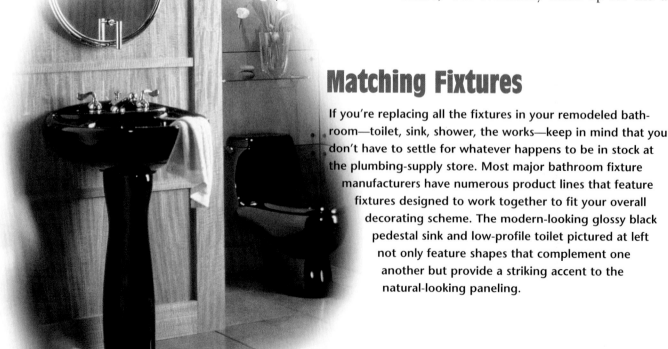

Matching Fixtures

If you're replacing all the fixtures in your remodeled bathroom—toilet, sink, shower, the works—keep in mind that you don't have to settle for whatever happens to be in stock at the plumbing-supply store. Most major bathroom fixture manufacturers have numerous product lines that feature fixtures designed to work together to fit your overall decorating scheme. The modern-looking glossy black pedestal sink and low-profile toilet pictured at left not only feature shapes that complement one another but provide a striking accent to the natural-looking paneling.

A low profile and black finish give this toilet a sleek but unobtrusively modern look.

Toilets with an old-fashioned design are still being made to suit current standards for efficient water use.

Gravity Toilets

The traditional gravity toilet has been improved to reduce the water required for flushing. Taller and narrower tanks, steeper bowls, and smaller water spots (the water surface in the bowl) account for most of the improved design. While users report general satisfaction with 1.6-gpf models, 1-gpf models sometimes require more than a single flush to clear the bowl.

Pressure-Assisted & Pump Toilets

Some toilets use the water pressure in the line to compress air. The compressed air then works with a small amount of water to empty the bowl. One model draws as little as one-half gallon per flush, but it costs two to three times more than the standard gravity-operated toilet.

In more recent toilet design, a small pump pushes water through the toilet. You can set the amount of flush water at either 1 or 1.6 gpf with the press of a button. This unit's list price makes it the most expensive of all low-flush toilets.

Bidets

A bidet is used for personal hygiene. It looks like a toilet without the tank or lid. Sitting astride the bidet, the user can conveniently cleanse the pelvic region. Water is supplied by a sprayer mounted on the back wall or bottom of the bowl.

Bidets have only recently made much of an appearance in American bathrooms. Now they are made by all major fixture manufacturers in the same colors and styles as other fixtures. Like a lavatory, they require a hot- and cold-water supply line and a drain. You should allow at least 30 inches length and width in your plan.

The bidet—shown here with matching toilet—is becoming increasingly common in North American homes.

3 Selecting Fixtures

Showers

Begin by deciding what kind of shower you want. Will it be small and utilitarian or ample and luxurious? Your choice depends not only on space but on your budget and how much you're willing to work (or pay) for your installation. Usually at least one bathroom in a house has a bathtub (or tub shower). For second or third bathrooms, a shower unit alone would be a less expensive choice.

Tub Showers

Showers combined with tubs save money and space, but not without trade-offs. Because bathtub bottoms are narrower and curved, tub showers are less safe and convenient than separate showers. Another drawback is the way the shower spray is kept from spilling out. Shower curtains have to be long enough to overlap the inside rim of the tub to work. They crowd the already tight space needed for standing. Sliding doors, better for keeping water off the bathroom floor, are in the way when you want to use the tub for bathing.

Separate Showers

If you are like most people these days, you shower more often than you bathe, so you should consider ways to include a separate shower in your remodeling plans. A separate shower offers more space and is safer to use than a tub shower. It keeps water inside with curtains, sliding or hinged doors, or even no doors if space allows. You can choose a prefabricated shower or custom-build one into one end or the corner of the room.

Prefab showers and shower-bath combinations are available as single units molded of fiberglass or cast acrylic and as PVC wall and floor components that you assemble in place (referred to as "knock-down," or KD). Single-unit showers come in widths of 32, 36, and 48 inches, with a standard depth of 36 inches and height of 73 inches. Don't choose a one-piece model without first making sure you can

If you're putting in a custom shower, you can use the spaces between the studs for customized storage shelves.

This glass compartment combines the convenience of a shower stall with the luxury of an extra-large bathtub. The floor tiles are continued onto the tub platform for a pleasing, unified design.

get it through your house and into its destination. Measure the widths of doorways and hallways and any points where you will have to turn corners or negotiate stairs. If clearances are insufficient, consider a knock-down type.

Both types of prefab showers come with glass or plastic doors and various built-in accessories—for example, soap holders, grab bars, and brush and washcloth hooks.

Building Your Own Shower

Custom-building your own shower demands more time and expertise but allows you choices not available with prefab units. For starters, you can build the shower into the space available. You can also choose your floor and wall materials as well as the type of door and accessories. Even with this freedom, you should start with a space at least 30 inches wide and 36 inches deep so that you can move around without knocking your knees and elbows into the walls.

Floors of a custom shower can be site-installed tile over a rubberized shower pan or a prefab base of fiberglass. Choosing a prefabricated base eliminates the hassles of constructing a

Shower seats are a smart addition if there's someone in your house with limited mobility. If you're redoing the inside of your shower, you can buy an aftermarket seat kit and then tile it to match your decor.

Shower Head Options

Shower faucets fall into three categories. Fixed sprays, which are mounted on the wall or ceiling, can be fitted with more than the usual shower-massage head; you can opt for a cascade of water delivered by a waterfall spout or a rain bar that lets you relax in a soft rainlike rinse. Handheld sprays are convenient devices for directing water where you need it; they're usually found in combination with fixed spray heads. Combine a handheld spray with a stationary shower head, and add a massager with as many as eight settings and a body brush, and you've created a custom shower environment that rivals any spa. Jet sprays are like those used in whirlpool tubs: they are installed behind the shower walls, as many as 16 per unit. Just set the jet sprayers at your desired intensity, and enjoy a therapeutic hydromassage.

watertight floor but limits your shower to the size and shape of the base. Prefab bases come in squares, typically 32, 34, or 36 inches; rectangles of various sizes up to 60 inches long; and as corner units, with the two wall sides typically 36 or 38 inches long.

Special Features. Spectacular spray options and spa features can make showering as relaxing as the most luxuriously appointed bathtub. Top-of-the-line features include massaging hydrotherapy sprays, steam units, a foot whirlpool, built-in seat-ing, even a radio or CD player. Amazing technology can let you enjoy the equivalent of a full-body massage on a miserly amount of water.

Bathtubs

Soakers, whirlpools, classic claw-footed models, tubs for two, spas for four, contour shapes, ovals, squares, rounded tubs, streamlined or sculptured models, tubs with neck rests and arm rests, tubs in a variety of colors, freestanding tubs, tubs set into platforms, tubs you step down into—it's your soak, so have it your way.

Every household should have at least one bathtub. Even if you prefer to take showers, you may have to accommodate small children or elderly persons who can't use a shower. Also consider the value of a tub on the resale of your house. Whether you long for a Victorian claw-foot tub or want a more modern model, there's probably one that's just right for your bathroom.

Before choosing a tub style, ask yourself: How do I like to bathe? Do I prefer a long, linger-ing soak or an invigorating hydromassage? A popular trend is the sunk-in whirlpool tub, which comes with an array of therapeutic and relaxing options in the form of neck jets, back jets, side jets, multiple jets, or single jets that are installed in the walls behind the tub.

Generally, modern bathtubs are made of one of the these three materials:

Fiberglass. Lightweight and moldable, a fiberglass tub is the least expensive type you can buy. But it's prone to scratching and wear after about a dozen years. Some come with an acrylic finish, which holds up against wear longer.

Solid Acrylic. A mid-price-range product, it is more durable

Many prefabricated shower units are made for corners. Even a large shower stall such as this one leave plenty of floor space for a handy bench and other furnishings.

A **large bathtub** can take up a lot of room in a small bathroom. This home-owner maximizes space by placing the storage above the tub but still in reach.

The days of the cast-iron tub in the middle of the house may be long gone, but if you want the luxury of a large soaking tub and lack room for a separate shower stall, a tub with a handheld sprayer may be for you.

than fiberglass and less prone to scratching because the color is solid all the way through. Whirlpool tubs are usually made of acrylic because it can be shaped easily. It's also lightweight, an important feature for large tubs that can put damaging stress on structural elements under the floor.

Cast Iron. A porcelain-enamel-coated cast-iron tub will endure as long as your house stands. It's a heavyweight, though, and not recommended for a large soaking tub. As with sinks, the heat-fused finishes of metal-based tubs stand up to much more abuse than the newer plastic alternatives, but plastic is lighter and allows manufacturers to offer a wider variety of forms and surface features.

Tub Sizes

The most common size for tubs that back up to a wall is 32 × 60 inches. Widths from 24 to 42 inches are generally available. If someone in the family is tall, no problem: You can purchase a standard tub that's up to 72 inches long. Corner units come in at around 48 inches on the wall sides. Size your tub according to the floor space available, your height, and the level of luxury you desire. For example, if the tub is to serve two people together, the width inside should be at least 42 inches.

Claw-footed and other freestanding tubs need adequate clearance on all sides to look their best. Unlike prefab showers, tubs don't come in knock-down models, so check the tub's dimensions against your doorways, hallways, and stairways to ensure that you will be able to maneuver it into the bathroom.

Other Considerations

Tubs can be placed at floor level, raised on a platform, or sunk into the floor. If raised, provide steps up with treads at least 11 inches deep and risers not exceeding 7 inches. Provide grab bars for both raised and sunken tubs to help you climb into and out of them.

This large whirlpool tub fits easily into the corner of a spacious bathroom, and requires only a minimum of new plumbing work. Note the dual faucets and generous amount of storage space behind the tub.

This enormous whirlpool tub essentially functions as a hot tub. With its large picture windows and spacious layout, this bathroom has essentially been designed to fit the tub.

Whirlpools & Spas

Whirlpools and spas offer the ultimate in relaxation: the chance to soak your cares away in deep, hot water. It's easy to understand their appeal, considering the stresses of modern life.

Whirlpools, like ordinary bathtubs, get drained after each use; spas retain their water. Indoor spas are a variation of outdoor hot tubs, which are usually made of redwood or cedar. Deeper than whirlpools, spas—whether heated by gas or electricity—can be used indoors or out. Because they cannot double as bathtubs, spas are usually better adapted for outside installation—or for very large bathrooms that can accommodate a spa and a regular bathtub.

Whirlpools are made of the same materials and in the same colors as tubs. Rectangular sizes start as small as a standard bathtub and range up to 48 × 84 inches. Like tubs, they can be installed at floor level, recessed into the floor, or raised on platforms.

A whirlpool contains a pump that circulates the water through jets positioned around the sides of the unit. If the unit doesn't come with an in-line heater, it will draw hot water from your home's hot-water supply lines. The pump is located under or adjacent to the unit. Such equipment should be accessible through an access panel at the side, front, or rear. If you have the space and the budget for a whirlpool, you can choose among a number of optional accessories, such as a telephone or controls for room lights and other appliances.

A sauna is not everyone's taste, but if you find their intense heat and steamy air rejuvenating, you might consider installing one in a small unused room. Saunas don't require plumbing, so they can be located anywhere, even as a separate building.

Home Health Clubs

If a whirlpool doesn't deliver enough luxury for your taste, you may want to consider the next step up: a sauna room with wooden benches and an electric heater, or even a unit containing an entire health club in a single enclosure. Some of these units combine whirlpools topped by an enclosure with glass doors on the front. Inside, not only do you have the option of soaking in the turbulent hot water of a whirlpool, but you can call up any environment you desire. By pushing a button, you can be baked by the dry heat of a sauna or steamed by a Turkish bath.

For installation, a sauna will require new wiring and additional insulation. A home health club will also need new hot- and cold-water supply and waste lines and one or two GFCI-protected electrical circuits. If you want to consider a luxury unit, visit a bath specialty store to see what's available—be prepared for the cost, which generally runs into the thousands of dollars. When you make your selection, study the product data for installation requirements.

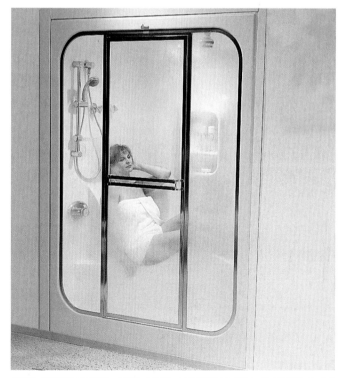

This home-health-club unit combines the functions of shower and steam room in one enclosed fixture.

Designing for Light & View
CHAPTER 4

Electrical lighting and mechanical ventilation make a bathroom without windows serve basic needs quite well. But opening the wall or ceiling to the outside makes the space come alive. Properly located windows or skylights cheer the room with sunlight, give views to the outside, and provide natural ventilation, all without sacrificing privacy.

Of course, windows may encourage longer stays, something you may want to deter during the morning rush hour. But wouldn't it be nice if you had a place where you could relax while you showered, soaked, or shaved? This is the room where you should strive to make the most of a skylight or window.

You can create an opening to the outside world in an interior bathroom that sits directly under the roof (or the attic) by adding a skylight. Obviously, you won't have access to the outside in a bathroom located under a room and with no wall facing on the outside of the house. In this case, make the room as functional and cheerful as you can by carefully selecting and locating your light fixtures.

Designing the Opening

A well-designed skylight or window should
• Let in ample sunlight
• Permit views to the outside
• Inhibit views to the inside
• Open for natural ventilation
• Be properly sealed from the cold when closed
• Be safe to operate

If you are considering a skylight or roof window, your installed unit should
• Let in as much natural light as possible
• Distribute the light evenly inside the room without creating glare
• Open for ventilation
• Inhibit heat loss in the winter and heat gain in the summer

How well your window choice meets these objectives depends on how the unit is made, the way it opens, and where it is located in the wall or ceiling. A good place to begin is by matching the window frame and glazing materials to your needs.

Window Materials

Today's residential window frames are made of wood, metal, or plastic. Wood frames may be solid or made of pressed wood particles. The most common residential metal windows are made of extruded aluminum, but steel units are also available. There are also plastic (usually PVC) and fiberglass frames.

When choosing among finishes, first consider whether you want to repaint the window frames from time to time or whether you prefer a finish that requires almost no maintenance. Wood windows are clad in aluminum or vinyl and need no upkeep, or they may come primed for painting or staining. Aluminum windows are surfaced with a per-

These opaque windows provide a bounty of natural light while still maintaining privacy.

If you don't need to worry about passersby, a large picture window is a great addition to a bathroom. The transparent glass shower doors in this bathroom add to the feeling of open space.

manent finish of baked enamel. Steel windows come primed for painting. The plastic finish, usually the same material used in the frame, never needs painting.

Glazing

During cold periods, even the best windows waste more heat to the outside than does a solid wall. Fortunately, today's windows are better sealed against leakage and better insulated against heat loss through the glass. Select doubledglazed windows (two separated panes) wherever you live. If you live in a cold climate, you'll get even better energy efficiency with windows protected with a low-emissivity (low-E) film, either on the glass or as a separate film, and argon gas in the space between the two panes.

Curved windows require special flashing, but many homeowners feel that their old-fashioned elegance is worth the trouble.

Window Types

Because space may be tight in your bathroom, you need to consider the way your windows will open and close as well as the shapes and sizes of the units. Here are the most common types of residential windows and the pros and cons of using them in bathrooms.

Fixed Windows

As the name implies, fixed windows do not open. They come as glass sheets you install into a finished opening or as ready-to-install units enclosed in wood, metal, or plastic frames. Another way to create a fixed window is with glass block. Because it lets in light but distorts images, glass block is an excellent way to achieve privacy while brightening an interior.

Because fixed windows don't provide ventilation, they are feasible in the bathroom only in combination with operable windows or mechanical ventilation. An advantage to fixed windows is that they are readily available in many shapes and sizes.

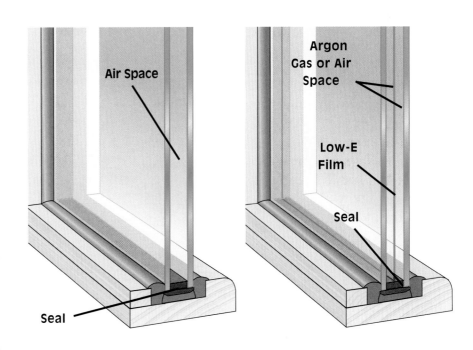

Double-glazed windows (left) provide some insulation, but Low-E glazing (right) can more than double this with a reflective film and argon gas between the panes.

Double- & Single-Hung Windows

The most common type of window used in homes is probably the double-hung window, which has upper and lower sash that ride up and down in their own channels. With newer types, you can tilt each section to the inside for easier cleaning. Prolonged contact with high bathroom humidity may cause a wood sash and guides to swell, making the window hard to open. If placed above a tub or shower, the

Where a large window isn't practical, you can use glass-block insets and a roof window to provide natural light.

extra force needed to open a stuck window could lead to slips and falls. Another possible downside of these windows is their vertical shape, which affords views through the lower half that may compromise your privacy.

Single-hung windows are like double-hung types, but only the lower sash moves. Before choosing a single-hung window, decide whether you will ever want or need to open the upper half.

Casement Windows

Casements range in shape from vertical to slightly horizontal. They are hinged along one side and open outward by use of a crank mounted on the sill. Because the entire window opens and the opened sash directs breezes into the room, casement windows provide better ventilation than double-hung windows. But there are some disadvantages. Exposure to rain is greater than with other types of windows, and the out-hanging sash may obstruct people from walking past a ground-level open window.

Sliding Windows

Sliders are like double-hung windows turned sideways. As horizontally oriented windows, they offer greater privacy while freeing up wall space below the sill. But the wood sliders may stick and become hard to operate when continually exposed to a high-moisture environment such as a shower or tub stall.

Awning Windows

Turn a casement on its side, and you have an awning window. These windows also open outward and are controlled by a sill-mounted crank. Awning windows are the best type to deflect rain. Like casements, the full opening is exposed for ventilation, though the open awning window doesn't catch breezes quite as well as a casement window.

Perhaps the best thing about awnings in bathrooms is their horizontal shape. High placement also allows you to see out—at least while standing—but limits views from the outside to only the ceiling area.

Fixed **Double-Hung** **Casement**

Sliding **Awning**

Five types of windows: fixed, double-hung, casement, sliding, and awning. Horizontal windows like awning units are good choices for tubs and showers.

This second-floor bath makes dramatic use of a roof window with a light shaft to illuminate the large soaking tub.

Skylights & Roof Windows

An opening in the roof is an excellent way to flood a bathroom with natural light without taking up wall space. If you choose a unit that opens, you can also get additional ventilation.

People often refer to any glazed opening in the roof as a skylight. That was fine in the 1950s when the only option for homes was a plastic bubble. These are still available, but today you can buy roof windows, which resemble wall windows. Some even pivot inward to allow cleaning of the outer pane.

Flat-profile roof windows change your home's outside appearance less than bubble-dome skylights. Bubble-domes make good sense on a flat roof, however, because they shed rain better. Fixed skylights are the most economical choice, followed by venting skylights, with operable roof windows at the top of cost scale.

Light & Glare. All roof windows and skylights are efficient sources of outside light. Even small units, if placed near the center of the ceiling, can flood all corners of the room with light. To avoid glare from overhead sunlight striking a wall window or mirror, you

can order a roof window already equipped with adjustable horizontal blinds.

Heat & Ventilation. Unlike wall windows, roof windows and skylights pose more of a heat-gain than heat-loss problem, particularly if located on a south- or west-facing slope of a roof. To minimize both heat gain and loss, choose insulated (double-pane) units with low-E coating. You can purchase either roof windows or skylights that open, but operating windows that are out of reach require a remote crank or electrically operated control. If you rely on a portable crank, you'll need a place to store it. Before you buy anything, ask the supplier about the control options.

Light Shafts. The distance between the roof opening and ceiling below can range from the thickness of the rafters (for cathedral ceilings) to several feet when the house has an attic. The construction of the shaft that bridges the gap affects how much light gets down into the room and how it is distributed. Splaying the shaft walls out from the roof opening to the ceiling distributes daylight to all corners. You can angle just one or two walls—usually the walls at the top and bottom—or angle all four for the best effect. To promote light distribution, finish the shaft walls with drywall and paint them white or off-white.

A straight vertical shaft is easier to build. Because working within the roof space is tough, you may not want to make it any harder than you have to. The end result, however, isn't likely to be as pleasing as angled walls.

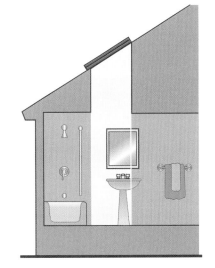

Skylights and roof windows bring sunlight into rooms that don't have windows. Splayed shafts (right) distribute the light more than straight ones (left).

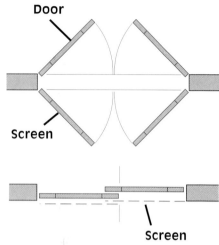

Only a homeowner with the most private of backyards could consider French doors or floor-to-ceiling windows without curtains.

Doors leading outside from the bathroom can be hinged (top) or sliding (bottom).

Exterior Doors

Opening your bathroom to a garden courtyard will require doors in place of, or in addition to, windows. Sliding glass doors or French doors are usually chosen because they allow in light and provide a view at all times.

Sliding Doors

Sliding glass doors come in pairs with overall widths of 60, 72, and 84 inches, and in heights of 84 inches (standard) and 96 inches. You can choose to have a door that has one or two separate glass panels. When open, sliding doors require no additional space inside or outside to house the open panel. On the downside, sliding doors are hard to seal against drafts, and cold drafts are the last thing you want from a door next to a tub or shower.

French Doors

Two hinged doors with glass panes are called French doors. You can choose to have one or both doors in the pair open, and they can be hinged either inward or outward. In any case, there must be a clear path for the doors to swing when in use, and a place for the doors to rest when open. The most common arrangement is to have the doors swing inward so that screens mounted on the outside can swing outward. The inconvenience of a door that swings compared with one that slides is offset by the advantage of a better seal against drafts.

French doors are glazed with single-sheet or insulating glass, in one panel or several small panes. In northern climates, choose insulating glass for the best comfort and energy efficiency.

Window Accessories

After you choose your windows and decide where they will best work in the walls or ceiling, you may need additional measures to control glare, reduce winter heat loss, block unwanted summer heat, and create privacy—all while preserving the view. This tall order calls for flexible controls that respond to the time of day, season, and outside weather.

Window accessories take many forms:
• Storm windows of glass or plastic that you add to the inside or outside of the window
• Awnings or shutters mounted on the outside
• Pleated shades, blinds, and curtains mounted on the inside

Most window treatments can be adjusted, seasonally or daily. Choose a system that will enhance your comfort and help bring together your design ideas. Take your first cue from the climate. Window treatments for a hot climate should block direct sunlight. Next, consider privacy. If your bath window is visible from the yard or neighbor's house, choose a device that you can close easily to block all views to the inside. Your selection will have to accommodate the type and size of windows, appearance, and budget. Here are a few of your choices:

Storm Windows. If you live in a place with cold winters and have old, leaky windows, you can either replace the windows with more energy-efficient ones, tighten them by caulking and weatherstripping, or add a storm window to the inside or outside. Just be sure you can open and close the storm window without removing the entire unit, particularly if it is located above the ground floor.

Blinds. Adjustable blinds are a good way to control glare and create privacy, though they don't add to energy efficiency. You can direct the sunlight where you want while keeping a view to the outdoors. Horizontal miniblinds (venetian blinds) with aluminum or vinyl slats are best for south-facing windows; they shut out the higher sunlight that comes from the south. They are also the best way to ensure privacy. You can angle them upward to let in light or close them tight to completely block it.

For windows facing the east and west, vertical blinds work best by blocking out the low-angle sun that adds heat on summer afternoons. Available in various colors, fabrics, and widths, vertical blinds

can be rotated to direct sunlight where you want it, closed completely, or drawn open like curtains.

Shades. Shades let in some light even when closed. The simplest, cheapest models are rolling shades. To keep your bathroom from looking cheap, check out the classier versions that use different fabrics and ride in side tracks. These are available at window-accessory stores.

Pleated shades stack, rather than roll up, and ride up and down in tracks. Single-layer pleated shades fold up like an accordion. Another type is made of two layers of fabric and forms honeycomb shapes when the shade is pulled shut. The air entrapped within each honeycomb cell helps cut heat loss. Pleated blinds are elegant and allow in filtered light while ensuring complete privacy.

Curtains. Curtains control glare and create privacy. Insulated curtains will provide some control over heat loss and gain. The softness of curtains can personalize a window while making the interior feel elegant. Horizontal units, such as sliding and awning windows, look best with curtains that close over the entire window. Curtains hung the full length of a vertical window, such as a double-hung or casement, can look awkward at the bottom. The folds are fullest there and are likely to take up precious space in a small room. Consider curtains over only the lower half of the window—this will allow privacy without the excess fabric at the bottom of the window.

Awnings & Shutters. Awnings block direct sunlight from entering the window. They work best on south-facing windows, though. To keep late-afternoon sunlight out of west-facing windows, you'll need awnings that nearly cover the full depth of the window, or shutters, which are hinged at the sides. Choose awnings or shutters for your bath windows only if you want to fit the other windows on the house similarly; otherwise your bathroom windows will look out of place.

For privacy, you may want to consider interior wood shutters instead of fabric window treatments. You can easily mount them to an entire window unit or the bottom half of a double- or single-hung window.

For this bathroom, simple wooden shutters painted white provide the necessary privacy while blending well with the overall style.

Bathroom Lighting

If parts of your face are in shadow when you stand in front of the bathroom mirror, you need better lighting. Good bathroom lighting puts light just where you need it. A superb lighting scheme also enhances the mood of the room. You've seen how well-chosen windows and skylights can cheer up a bathroom by bringing sunlight inside. But sunlight is hard to control and not always present, so it pays to get the most from your artificial lighting.

Types of Artificial Light

Two kinds of lighting are needed: ambient lighting, to illuminate the room in general and to create the desired mood, and task lighting, to throw a focused beam onto a specific spot.

Ambient Lighting. The room's general lighting should illuminate the entire room. Lighting can also be expanded to include sources that can be adjusted to create various moods through optional switching and dimmer controls.

The light fixture around a vanity mirror may provide enough light for the entire room if the room is relatively small and open. Larger bathrooms or bathrooms with toilet or shower compartments need additional lighting. Don't try to get by with a single lighting fixture mounted dead center in the ceiling. It will cast shadows in the wrong places on any mirror.

If you locate ambient light sources on the ceilings or walls, choose fixtures that don't project into door swings or obstruct the path of foot traffic.

Task Lighting. Task lighting illuminates a specific area for a particular job, such as putting in contact lenses, reading in the tub, shaving, or applying makeup. The main areas for task lighting are the mirrors intended for grooming. Theatrical lighting around vanity mirrors is an excellent example of task lighting. It provides cross-illumination, while avoiding the distorting shadows that overhead lighting often produces.

Light from the sides of a mirror is best. Place the fixtures at least 30 inches apart so that the light doesn't shine right into the user's eyes. To avoid shadows on the user's face, don't rely on a single light above the mirror. Many medicine cabinet/mirror units have lighting fixtures at each side, or you can add strip fixtures to the sides, top, or both.

Accent & Decorative Lighting. Often the most forgotten in the bath, but always the most dramatic, accent lighting draws attention to a particular element in the room, such as a handsome architectural feature or a work of art. For example, small uplights placed inconspicuously under a potted plant create an interplay of light and shadows on the wall and ceiling. Lights recessed into a soffit above a vanity cast a downward glow of illumination over a countertop.

Where accent lighting draws attention to another object or surface, decorative lighting draws attention to itself. It can be kinetic, in the form of candles or a fireplace, or static, such as a fixed wall candelabra. Because it commands notice, it can attract attention to or distract it from something else. In this sense, it can be functional. You can use decorative lighting in the bath to draw the eye upward

Fluorescent lights on each side of the mirror make personal grooming easier. Be sure to pick warm white bulbs that mimic natural light.

Strip lighting can be installed over the mirror for a decorative effect. To avoid casting shadows on your face, install lights on each side as well.

Simple fluorescent fixtures help illuminate the mirror in this room.

toward a cathedral ceiling or to distract attention from the toilet and bidet, for example.

Lighting for Mirrors. You'll need even, shadow-free lighting for applying makeup, shaving, or caring for hair. This lighting should illuminate both sides of the face, under the chin, and the top of the head. Plan to use at least a total of 120 incandescent watts. Never aim lighting directly into the mirror. Decorative sconces installed at face height on either side of a small mirror do the job nicely. Place them no higher than 60 inches above the floor and at least 28 inches—but not more than 60 inches—apart, unless you pair them with another vanity light source. Ideally, you can combine wall sconces with a ceiling or wall-mounted fixture above the mirror.

If fluorescent side lights are mandated by local code, you'll be happy to know that they come with a special coating that reduces glare and diffuses the light to minimize shadows. Install them up to 48 inches apart for sufficient lighting, and supplement them with recessed or surface-mounted ceiling fixtures. Also, use the deluxe warm white fluorescent bulbs that more closely resemble natural light.

Shower & Tub Lights. Light around the tub and shower area has to be bright enough for safety, adjusting water temperature or shower heads, and reading (if you care to read while you soak). Recessed downlights or any other fixtures designed for wet areas are fine. Shielded fixtures eliminate glare, and shatter-resistant white acrylic diffusers are the safest. Any fixture installed in a wet or damp area has to be protected properly so that water cannot accumulate in wiring compartments, lamp holders, or other electrical parts. An electrician will know how to handle the situation and can recommend the proper fixture.

Planning for Special Needs

CHAPTER 5

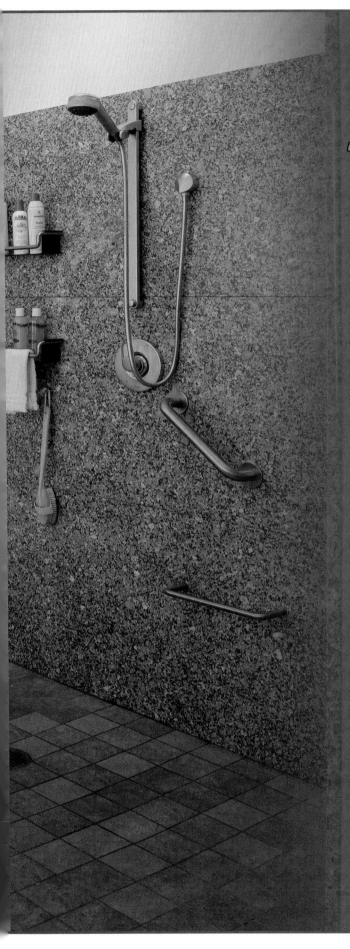

The standard bathroom in most homes cannot be comfortably used by people with disabilities. In fact, people in wheelchairs may find some bathrooms impossible to use. Unfortunately, making bathroom facilities accessible to one household member who has an impairment can be costly. And some changes may make a facility actually harder to use for another family member.

For example, the recommended toilet-seat height for wheelchair users is 17 to 19 inches, which is too high for small children. The trick here is to make compromises so that everyone can safely and easily use the bathroom. And remember, small children will eventually get big enough to use the higher toilet.

To make sure any changes you make meet all your needs, consider these points:

• What difficulties do the standard bathroom facilities create?

• Is the family member facing temporary or permanent disability?

• If permanent adjustments are necessary, would it be more convenient to remodel only one bathroom, or are changes needed in all of them?

Individual Needs

The first step in making special accommodations is to assess the specific physical limitations of the person who will be using the bathroom. This will help you tailor the layout and fixtures to meet his or her needs.

Limited Use of Limbs

Some decrease in the ability to reach and bend is experienced by most people as they age, although young people can certainly have these limitations, too. Adaptations that can make bathrooms easier to use include raised toilet seats, tub seats, and grab bars around the tub/shower and toilet.

If your family member has trouble reaching high objects, provide storage for personal hygiene and medicines at a level between 36 and 60 inches from the floor. A handheld shower is useful for people who must sit while showering.

Limited Use of Hands & Fingers

To make life easier for someone who has difficulty turning faucets on and off, consider replacing a faucet that has knob-type handles with a lever-type faucet. Replace the light's toggle switch with a large rocker plate. Instead of small glass knobs on the vanity drawers, use easy-to-grip C-shaped handles. Provide shallow, open shelves and racks wherever possible, rather than deep storage behind doors.

Reduced Sight

Any changes you may make to improve bathroom access for someone with poor eyesight will make the room easier for

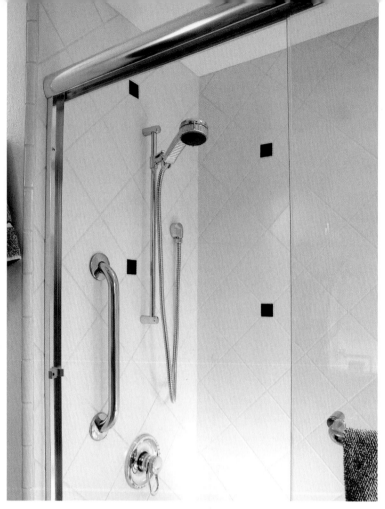

This shower has been modified simply and inexpensively with the addition of a grab bar and a large lever-type faucet control.

This accessible bathroom design has allowed for plenty of space for a wheelchair to maneuver, carefully placed grab bars, and an extra-wide wall-mounted sink accessible to a seated person.

This large sunken tub shows how accessible design—in this case, parallel grab bars that act as a handrail—can be part of a stylish design.

all to use. Start at the floor, and eliminate sudden changes in elevation. Be sure to use an extra-long nonslip mat on the tub or shower floor.

You can also mount the light switch on the outside of the entrance door, and use the type that glows. Provide brighter levels of lighting in the bathroom than you might otherwise install. And make sure there are no unlit corners, such as in the tub/shower area.

Wheelchair Accessibility

Accommodating wheelchairs in a bathroom can be difficult. In addition to including specially designed plumbing fixtures, the layout must include space for the wheelchair user to get in and out of the room and, once inside, to turn around.

Any doors in the pathway to the bathroom should have at least 32 inches clear width—that is, between the stops. Provide at least 60 inches in front of an in-swinging bathroom door. Better still, avoid swinging doors altogether, if possible. They always pose an obstacle to wheelchair users. Consider substituting a pocket door. In some cases, such as a private bath off a bedroom, you might even consider skipping the door altogether.

The floor inside the bathroom should have a

clear circle measuring 60 inches across to allow the wheelchair user to turn around.

Bathing and showering also require special planning. Remember that the shower and adjacent area for maneuvering can consume a lot of floor space.

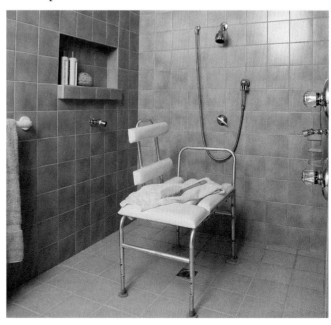

This well-designed shower stall provides plenty of space for a wheelchair user to enter and exit. The padded seat can be used for all or part of the shower.

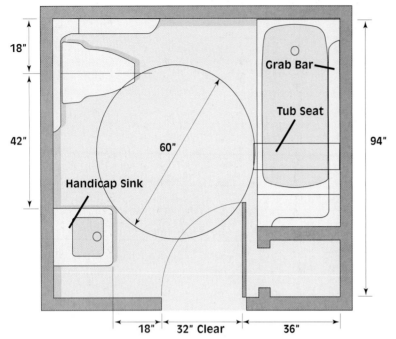

These are the **minimum clearances** and accessories required for wheelchair access in a bathroom with a tub. The 60-in. clear circle allows a person in a wheelchair to turn inside the room.

Permanent versus Temporary Changes

It doesn't make sense to construct permanent physical changes to accommodate a family member whose limitations are temporary. After determining what the person can and can't do, look for ways to make temporary adaptations to the bathroom.

For example, add grab bars that clamp onto the side of the tub or surround the toilet. Extensions are available to raise the height of a standard toilet seat. Visit a medical products supplier to see what's on the market. You may even be able to rent some of these products.

If a household member is permanently disabled, lasting changes may be warranted. You need to determine whether it is possible to adapt an existing bathroom or whether a new bathroom must be added. If a larger room is needed for wheelchair use, consider adapting an unused or underused bedroom or bumping the bathroom into an existing closet, as was discussed in "Improving Your Layout," pages 20 and 21.

If the family member's limitations make for longer bathroom time, you may want to try to add a second full or three-quarter bath to ease the morning rush and make it possible for all of you to be on time for work or school.

Barrier-Free Fixtures

You can adapt existing fixtures by either adding grab bars and various devices that adjust heights or replacing them with fixtures specifically designed for people who use wheelchairs or who have limited mobility. Here are some of the options.

Sinks

Sinks for wheelchair access must allow for knee space below and project out far enough to allow the user to reach the faucets. Insulate exposed

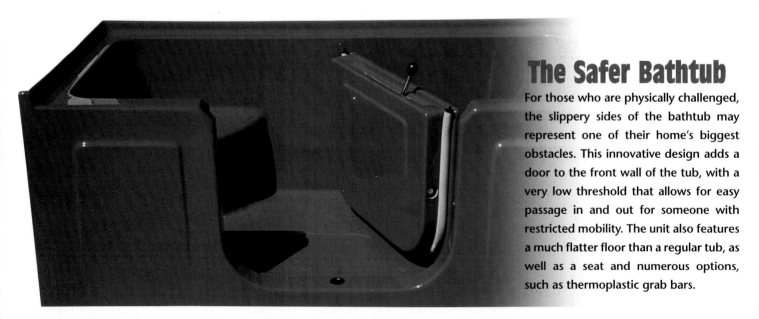

The Safer Bathtub

For those who are physically challenged, the slippery sides of the bathtub may represent one of their home's biggest obstacles. This innovative design adds a door to the front wall of the tub, with a very low threshold that allows for easy passage in and out for someone with restricted mobility. The unit also features a much flatter floor than a regular tub, as well as a seat and numerous options, such as thermoplastic grab bars.

Grab Bars

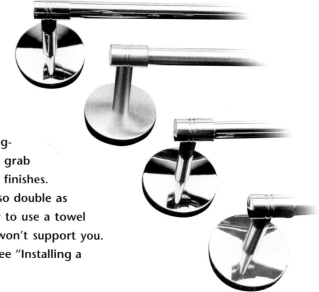

Grab bars are fast becoming standard accessories in bathrooms. Even if you don't need them now, you may in the near future—even if it's while recovering from an injury or in the last few months of pregnancy. Many manufacturers offer grab bars in a variety of styles and finishes. These stylish grab bars can also double as towel racks—but never try to use a towel rack as a grab bar; it won't support you. For proper installation, see "Installing a Grab Bar," page 210.

hot-water pipes beneath the sink to prevent users from burning their legs, and adapt fittings to the user's needs.

Wheelchair-accessible sinks measure about 20 inches wide and project out from the wall 18 to 27 inches. Mount the sinks 34 inches from floor to the underside of the front edge. One model can be mounted on an adjustable wall bracket, allowing users to choose the most convenient height. For wheelchair access to a sink, allow 36 inches of clear width at the floor level.

Showers

There are two types of showers for people who use wheelchairs. One contains a seat: the person wheels up to the shower and uses grab bars to hoist himself or herself onto the seat. Constructed out of fiberglass or acrylic, these units measure 36, 42½, or 56 inches wide by 37 inches deep by 84 inches high. They come equipped with handholds, soap ledges, and adjustable hand-held showers. In the second type, the user can wheel into the compartment and shower while remaining in the wheelchair.

Toilets

Toilets for wheelchair users are basically the same as standard toilets, but the seat is 17 to 19 inches above the floor instead of the more usual height of around 14 inches. Grab bars, preferably at the back and one side, are essential for maneuvering between the wheelchair and toilet. Allow at least 36 inches

of clear width for access around the fixture.

You can adapt a standard toilet by placing a portable extension seat over the existing toilet. This approach is useful if the fixture must also be used by small children, who may have trouble reaching a higher seat. Some extension seats come with grab bars attached to the sides. Look for these items in medical products supply stores. (Check with a doctor or nurse if you have trouble locating this handy device.)

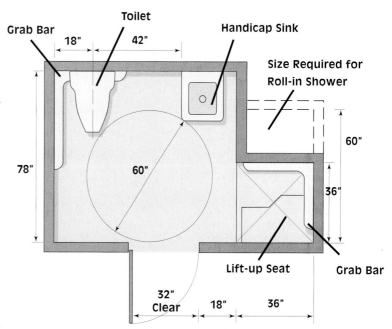

Two types of showers are geared to wheelchair use. People who can leave the wheelchair can move onto the seat of a small square shower. If the person must remain in the wheelchair, a roll-in shower must be installed (indicated by dashed lines).

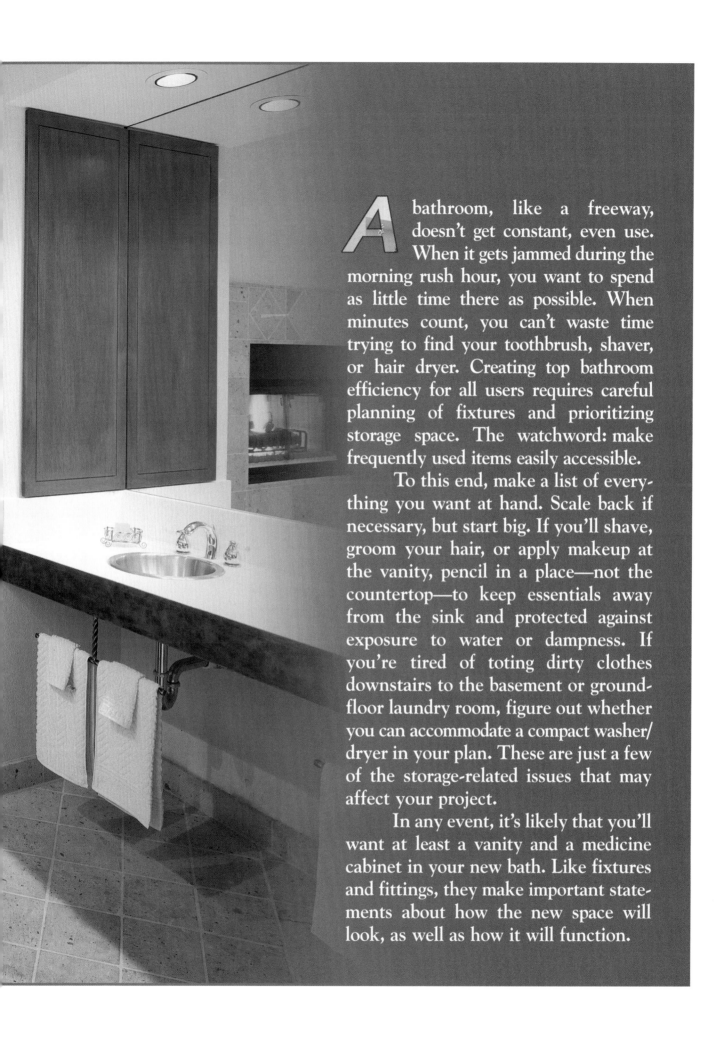

bathroom, like a freeway, doesn't get constant, even use. When it gets jammed during the morning rush hour, you want to spend as little time there as possible. When minutes count, you can't waste time trying to find your toothbrush, shaver, or hair dryer. Creating top bathroom efficiency for all users requires careful planning of fixtures and prioritizing storage space. The watchword: make frequently used items easily accessible.

To this end, make a list of everything you want at hand. Scale back if necessary, but start big. If you'll shave, groom your hair, or apply makeup at the vanity, pencil in a place—not the countertop—to keep essentials away from the sink and protected against exposure to water or dampness. If you're tired of toting dirty clothes downstairs to the basement or ground-floor laundry room, figure out whether you can accommodate a compact washer/dryer in your plan. These are just a few of the storage-related issues that may affect your project.

In any event, it's likely that you'll want at least a vanity and a medicine cabinet in your new bath. Like fixtures and fittings, they make important statements about how the new space will look, as well as how it will function.

Creating a Storage System

Have you ever wondered how so much stuff ends up in such a small room? Let's scan a list of items commonly stored in the bathroom and examine how to safely store them:

Medicines

Store medicines where you'll find them quickly and easily. They must be stored where adults can get at them but where children cannot. If you can't effectively store medicines in a bathroom cabinet where they will be out of the reach of small children, consider another location, such as in a high kitchen cabinet. To be really safe, install a childproof latch or even a lock on the medicine cabinet—but be sure you can open it quickly in emergencies.

Dental-Care Accessories

Locate toothbrushes and toothpaste within easy reach of the sink. A narrow shelf above a free-standing sink works well, as does a position at the rear or side of a vanity top. Keeping your dental-care accessories visible makes sense, even if you have to watch the toothpaste tube getting steadily uglier with each squeeze. Electric toothbrushes, becoming increasingly popular, need a place near an outlet for their chargers; pay attention to where the cord will end up.

Shaving Gear

Keep shaving gear near the sink but out of sight (and out of the reach of children). The lower shelves of a medicine cabinet with doors fills this bill nicely, as does a bin or tub under a vanity or in a vanity drawer.

　　If you use an electric shaver, you need a way to locate it near a GFCI-protected outlet and a mirror. For maximum convenience, you might keep the razor plugged into the outlet, hung on a nearby hook or narrow shelf. But because cords tend to get in the way of other activities in a cramped space and outlets usually have to be shared with other appliances, a shallow drawer below the vanity might be better.

Not all storage is strictly practical—this design has plenty of drawer space for personal items but leaves plenty of room for decoration.

This shower stall uses a small alcove built into the wall framing to form an elegant storage shelf for shampoo and soap.

This simple shelf is kept from looking cluttered with a careful selection of products.

First Aid

Every house should be equipped with basic first-aid items, and the bathroom is a logical site to store them, because administering first aid usually requires ample clean water. When your child is screaming with a cut hand, the last thing you want is to have to grope around for that long-missing box of bandages or bottle of disinfectant. The answer is to locate everything in one, easy-to-get-to place. Designate one drawer for first-aid items, and be sure nothing else ends up in that drawer. Besides the convenience of having all your gear in one place, you will be able to pull the whole drawer out and move it to the site of the patient, if necessary.

Personal Grooming Accessories

You can relieve bathroom gridlock by providing space outside the bathroom for grooming routines not requiring water, such as makeup application and hair-drying. In addition, a dressing table with several shallow drawers in an adjacent area or bedroom can do much to unclutter the bathroom. Those items that need to be used near a water source can be handily squirreled away in shallow drawers in a vanity near the sink.

Hair Dryers

If you choose to use a hair dryer in the bathroom, store it near a GFCI-protected outlet. A deep drawer in a vanity cabinet is a good place.

With a little space stolen from an adjacent closet, the designer of this bathroom replaced wasted wall space with an abundance of storage space for towels.

You have many options for adding storage space. Home centers, department stores, and storage specialty stores offer a wide range of products, such as this wire hamper.

6 *Storage & Amenities*

Soap & Shampoo

You need two kinds of storage for wet-grooming items. Items you use every day need to be within easy reach. Store infrequently used items in a cabinet or on a shelf. Soap is most convenient in a soap dish or pump bottle at the side or rear of the sink. Built-in shelves and soap dishes or hanging bags and plastic-coated racks can give you easy access to items used in the shower or bathtub.

Towels & Washcloths

Place towels and washcloths within easy reach of every sink, bidet, shower, and tub. Plan towel racks with a separate towel bar for each member of the household (for better harmony) and a few additional bars for guests. Fresh towels and washcloths stored on open shelves or in bins in the bathroom can become part of the room decor, or you may want to store them in an adjacent linen cabinet in or near the bathroom.

Most bathrooms don't provide space for dirty washcloths and towels. A bathroom hamper is one solution; a hamper bin built into the vanity is another.

Cleaning & Maintenance Supplies

The odd-shaped space below the sink in a vanity cabinet is ideal for storing cleaning supplies, an advantage that freestanding sinks don't offer. Fit one side of the cabinet with adjustable shelves for small items; keep the other side open for tall items such as scrub brushes and plungers. If you have small children, be sure to install a childproof latch on any cabinet that houses potentially dangerous cleaning chemicals.

The Means of Storage

Whether you buy your bath storage in the form of prefabricated cabinetry or custom-build your own, the most practical storage facilities are suited to the items stored and make use of space not needed for other functions. Each type of storage device has pros and cons.

Drawers

Drawers offer two advantages: items stored are out of sight when not in use, and all items are equally accessible—that is, if you don't pack things one on top of each other. To avoid this pitfall, select shallow drawers for small items such as cosmetics, and reserve deep drawers for larger items such as hair dryers.

Shelves & Trays

Shelves, whether open or enclosed, offer easy access and make good use of shallow spaces on or in walls. You can display decorative items, such as bottles, colored soaps, and towels on open shelves. On the downside, open shelves invite dust and clutter.

If the shelves are mounted on adjustable clips, their height may be changed to fit new uses. Shelves can be shallow or deep, but a greater number of shallow shelves are apt to be more useful than a lesser number of deep shelves. (Items that end up at the rear of deep shelves tend to be forgotten there.) Open shelving for brightly colored towels and decorative bottles and soaps can add to your decor as well as provide storage. If you like the openness of shelves, accentuate this feeling by installing glass ones. Shelving for cleaning materials is better located out of sight behind hinged doors.

Instead of one big mirror above the long vanity, this bathroom uses the space between the sinks for a practical, decorative shelves.

Cubbyholes make for interesting towel storage—not necessarily space saving, but practical for a large family.

Trays can slide out on guides, like drawers, or pivot off of a pole. Either way, they provide a lot of shallow storage space for small objects.

Tubs & Bins

Mount plastic tubs on guides in the odd-shaped leftover space below the sink. Use these tubs to house cleaning products. Spills or leaks will be easy to clean up and will not soil your cabinetry.

Bins hinged near the floor or mounted on drawer guides in vanity cabinets make excellent bathroom hampers.

Pegs, Hooks & Bars

Wet washcloths and towels need a place to dry out. Locate pegs, hooks, or bars made of wood, ceramic, plastic, or metal on walls near the tub or shower. One or two hooks inside the tub/shower area can hold bathing accessories, but locate them where they won't be in your way.

6 Storage & Amenities

This interesting design uses shelves built right into a partition wall—the bottom ones are within easy reach of bathers; the top ones are for purely decorative purposes. Note the circular towel rack around the tub's rim.

If your bathroom has ample storage for all your towels and personal products, you can devote some of the space to displaying artwork or collectables, such as the pottery and decorative mirror on this built-in unit.

This bathroom's Victorian look is accentuated with the addition of an old print and an antique upholstered chair.

Amenities

The right kind of storage facilities for the many accessories used in your bathroom can make for a functional, efficient space. But a submarine is also functional and efficient. Something else is needed to make the space special. You can add that extra touch by opening the room to sunlight, incorporating decorative objects, and finishing the space with colors and textures that complement each other and enhance the area. Here are some possibilities:

Plants

Plants thrive in humid bathroom air as long as they have a source of outside light. The challenge, particularly in small rooms, is to place plants where they won't get in the way. A wide window ledge is an ideal site, as is an unused corner of the vanity. If space permits, plant shelves can be built adjacent to tubs and showers. You might even hang a single Boston fern from a ceiling hook in a corner of the room not used for foot traffic.

If you live in an area with a mild climate, consider adding an enclosed garden courtyard outside your master bath. One or two French doors or sliding glass doors could open onto a wooden deck surrounded by plants. The courtyard need be no larger than the area required for a chaise longue and can be kept private by a high wooden fence. Even when it's chilly outside, sunlight streaming into the bath through the outdoor plants will help cheer the inside space.

Bottles & Vases

While decorative bottles and vases add a touch of luxury to the bath, they must be positioned where they won't be knocked over accidentally. Ledges and windowsills may work if they are out of the line of traffic; a special high shelf is another possibility. Take care where you locate glass items if children use the room. A glass bottle toppled onto a tile floor will shatter into dangerous shards.

Soaps

Pretty scented soaps please the senses whether heaped in bowls or baskets or displayed on ledges surrounding the tub and sink area. You can even hang them in baskets from the ceiling.

Pictures

Like plants, pictures add interest and warmth to the room. Unfortunately, bathroom wall space is usually in short supply even in large bathrooms. Mirrors often take up any spare wall space in small bathrooms. But mirrors are more useful in some places than others, as you'll see later in this chapter. The wall space above a toilet or bidet, if not needed for shelves, can make an excellent site for pictures.

Mirrors

Mirrors give the appearance of expanded space and serve personal grooming needs, but to do either well, they must be located properly.

Locating Mirrors for Grooming

To see your reflection, you'll want a mirror on the wall over the sink. If you also want to see the sides and back of your head, add side mirrors that hinge toward a central mirror. Any medicine cabinet placed directly behind the sink should have a sliding or hinged mirror.

If you want your medicine cabinet to be off to the side, install a unit that comes with a mirror

Large, well-lit mirrors above both sinks make personal grooming easier and help this narrow bathroom seem wider and brighter.

that hinges toward the central mirror. For wheelchair users, consider a fixed or adjustable mirror that tilts toward the floor.

Try to reserve a space on one wall or door for a full-length mirror.

Using Mirrors to Widen the Room

You can visually double the apparent width of a narrow bathroom by cladding one of the long walls with mirrors. Adding mirrors to the opposite side as well can make the space seem even wider, though you risk overkill with a confusing series of multiple reflections.

Mirrors behind plants and decorative objects can magnify their effect. If you are lucky enough to have a garden courtyard outside your bathroom, place mirrors on the abutting end walls to draw the garden into the room.

You don't need to install mirrors on an entire wall to achieve a room-enlarging effect, but if you do, you will save money by using mirror tiles instead of a single extra-large mirror. Mirror tiles come in 12 × 12-inch squares and can be easily attached to the wall with self-adhesive tabs.

A series of small mirrors framed in wood trimwork complements this room's old-fashioned look.

Selecting Finishes

efore grabbing the hammer and saw, you should consider one important part of your project: the finishes. Even in well-ventilated bathrooms, heat, steam, and moisture can take their toll. So it's important to select materials for the walls, floors, and countertops that can hold up to water.

Paint is the least expensive choice for walls and ceilings and the easiest to use; but surfaces still need preparation to ensure that they will not fail due to heat and dampness. Paint (and vinyl wallcoverings) also have the advantage of being easily changed to fit a new decor. Plastic laminate for countertops and vinyl for floors are good choices that come in different price ranges, depending on quality. Generally they are the most affordable as well. Ceramic tile, which can be installed on floors, walls, and counters, falls into the middle of the spectrum. Tile installation is costly, so doing it yourself will save a big part of the expense. Natural materials such as wood or stone are at the high end of the price scale.

If you intend to apply these finishes yourself, you will want to know something about the substrate, cost, and skills required of each. Review the options in this chapter, and take time before making your selections.

Making Colors & Textures Work for You

Do you see your bathroom as a sensual place for relaxing or one that serves with machine-like efficiency? The colors you select affect the mood of the room. Red excites, mauve calms. Here are some colors and their associated moods:

Yellow   Happiness, warmth

Red   Warmth, energy, excitement, anger

Green   Refreshment, nature

Blue   Coolness, restfulness, peace

You probably won't use primary colors full strength on walls and ceilings; you'll be more likely to choose blends, tints, and hues to create different moods. If your bathroom is small, it can be easily overpowered by strong colors. You might want to keep walls and ceiling in the off-white or pastel range and reserve strong colors for fixtures and accents.

Textures also trigger associations. Soft, yielding textures broadcast luxury and relaxation. Hard, smooth surfaces suggest no-nonsense efficiency. Because of the importance we place on bathroom surfaces being easy to clean and resistant to water penetration, smooth surfaces on walls and cabinets are generally preferred.

How Color & Shade Can Affect the Space

Whether you paint your walls and ceiling in light or dark colors affects the visual, if not actual, size of your room. Light surfaces tend to recede; dark ones foreshorten. You can "square" a long bathroom by selecting dark colors for the end walls and light colors for the side walls. The same trick—painting the ceiling darker than the walls—visually lowers a high ceiling.

The shade of the walls and ceiling also affects how light diffuses in the room. Light colors reflect light; dark colors absorb it. Light-colored walls will make any daylight that comes through windows more useful for seeing inside the room. To visually enlarge a very narrow space without moving walls, consider full-length mirrors.

The red amaryllis, bright red trim on the cabinet, and antique rug provide this room's colorful accents.

Floor Covering Options

All sorts of finish materials cover bathroom floors, but not every material meets every challenge. Take tile, for example. It sheds water well, but it is slippery to walk on when wet. You won't slip easily on carpet, but carpets are prone to mildew and can pick up odors from entrapped moisture. So, what makes an ideal bathroom floor covering? You'll naturally want a surface that's pleasing to the eye. Whether you prefer a hard or soft surface, look for these characteristics in a floor covering:

• Ability to withstand moisture

• Safe to walk on when wet

• Easy to clean

Let's see how some finishes found on bathroom floors meet these tests.

Resilient flooring is a popular floor covering choice for bathrooms because it is inexpensive and easy to maintain.

Natural wood tones help to brighten and soften the interior of this small bathroom.

Resilient Flooring

Thin floor coverings composed of resilient materials such as vinyl, rubber, cork, or linoleum are attractive and durable. While softer than tile, resilient flooring feels hard compared with carpeting. Its surface resists water, but it can be slippery when wet. Offset this hazard with throw rugs placed strategically next to tubs and showers.

Resilient flooring comes in a wide range of colors and patterns in both tiles and sheets. Tiles come in $\frac{3}{32}$- and $\frac{1}{8}$-inch thicknesses and are usually 12 inches square; sheet flooring comes in rolls 6 or 12 feet wide. Easier, by far, to install than sheet flooring, tiles are never as resistant to water because of the number of joints that can open if the substrate expands. For the best water resistance, set resilient tiles in a troweled-on adhesive. Self-adhesive tiles, while easy to install, can pull up at the corners over time. Resilient tiles are easily cut by scoring them with a scribing tool or utility knife and snapping them in two. Sheet flooring can be cut with a utility knife.

All resilient flooring is easy to maintain, needing only occasional waxing. The shiny surface layer of so-called no-wax floor covering eventually wears down. In time, you'll need to wax to restore the original luster. While resilient floor covering ideally is installed over a substrate of underlayment-grade

An Oriental rug on top of low-nap wool carpeting gives this bathroom a contrast in styles and textures, as well as a warm place for bathers' feet.

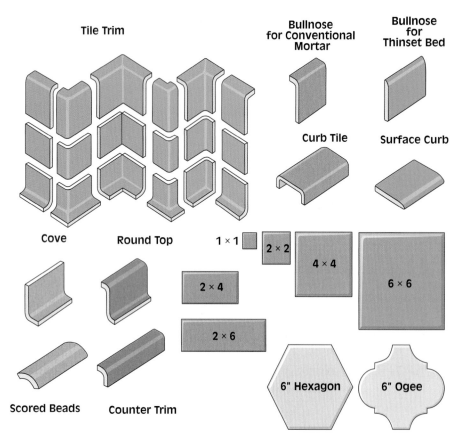

Ceramic tiles come in many sizes and styles that you can use to create your own designs. Trim tiles are available for inside and outside corners, curbs, and edges, but you won't find all of the shapes shown here for every style, color, and type of tile.

plywood, you can also apply it over existing resilient flooring, but only if the existing floor is tightly adhered and smooth.

Ceramic Tile

Ceramic tiles have long been preferred for bathroom floors because of their ability to withstand water. But glazed tiles are slippery when wet, and all tiles can be cold underfoot. To reduce the hazard of slipping, select floor tiles with a matte rather than a glossy finish. Never use wall tiles on a floor because they will crack. You can cushion the hardness of a tile floor with a throw rug, but make sure the rug is backed by a surface that grips the tiles.

Ceramic floor tiles are available in various pastel and deep colors, in sizes from 2×2 inches up to 12×12 inches. If you like the look of small tiles, the ones that come attached to fabric mesh sheets are easiest to install. Quarry tiles come in rectangular shapes in sizes from around 4 inches up to 12 inches on a side; they also are available in hexagons, octagons, and other shapes in a range of sizes. Colors run from the earth tones (buff, browns, and reds) to various grays.

For level floors not subject to constant water, the easiest way to install tiles is to embed them into troweled-on thinset adhesive over a solid subfloor, such as underlayment-grade plywood and cement-based backer board. Regularly wet or sloping floors, such as in showers and their adjacent drying areas, are better tiled by setting the tiles into a bed of mortar (thickset). Whether thinset or thickset, fill all joints between the tiles with grout.

Wall-to-wall carpeting can be a risky choice in a bathroom, but this design wisely keeps the tub's edge far from the carpet.

Stone

Stone adds real class to a bathroom floor. Durability, ease of cleaning, and slipping hazard vary depending on the material and its texture. One thing you can depend on, though, is that this is the most expensive floor you can choose.

The least expensive way to achieve a stone floor is with tiles cut from real stone. Marble, granite, and slate are available in ⅜-inch-thick tiles measuring 12 × 12 inches or 12 × 24 inches. They are installed much the same way as ceramic tiles.

Real stone pieces 1 inch or thicker must be set in mortar, and the combined load of stone plus the setting bed may be more than your floor can safely support without structural reinforcement. To cut stones, you'll need a diamond-tipped wet-saw blade, skill, and a lot of strength. If you are attracted to a stone floor, you should have your subfloor's structural capacity analyzed by an architect, structural engineer, or builder. Then, if the subfloor and joists are deemed strong enough, you should probably consider hiring a specialist to do the installation.

Carpeting & Rugs

The soft feel of carpeting under bare feet makes it an appealing choice for bathroom floors. Unfortunately, carpeting holds moisture, which can lead to mold and mildew, not to mention rot in the underlying subfloor. For these reasons it is best to avoid carpeting in areas that are subject to water spillage, adjacent to tubs, showers, toilets, bidets, and basins. That doesn't leave much spare floor in most bathrooms. If you like the softness of carpeting underfoot, stick with a tile or vinyl floor, but add throw rugs with nonslip backing for a cushiony feel.

If your room is large enough to include a portion of carpet in a dry area or you want to carpet an adjacent dressing area, you have a wide choice of materials, colors, textures, patterns, and underlayments. Prices vary widely, with nylon or polypropylene at the bottom end and wool at the top.

Put a pad under the carpet to increase the softness and to provide the feel of luxury. You can install carpet over almost any subfloor with tackless strips or by gluing the carpet to the subfloor. Tackless strips are thin strips of plywood embedded with hundreds of bent tacks that poke up to grip the carpet and keep it from sliding. The strips are nailed around the outer edges of the room. A simpler way to install carpet in a small room is to simply trowel on an adhesive and "glue" the carpet to the subfloor. The downside is that if and when you have to remove the carpet, you're in for a grueling task.

Wood Flooring

Wood, though hard, imparts a warm, homey look to any room. Properly sealed, it can be fairly resistant to moisture. (Witness the popularity of wood in kitchens.) Nonetheless, it still isn't a good bet for areas adjacent to tubs, showers, toilets, or bidets, which are exposed to almost continuous moisture.

For portions of the floor away from wet areas, you can choose among unfinished and prefinished flooring. Unfinished wood flooring comes as random-length planks or strips with tongue-and-groove edges. Strip flooring normally measures 2¼ inches wide and 2½₂ inches thick; planks come in standard dimensions from 1×4 to 1×10. Oak and maple are available almost everywhere; walnut, fir, and southern yellow pine are less common.

Prefinished wood flooring, an option if your tools, skills, and time are limited, comes in planks that you can glue or nail to the subfloor and as 12 × 12-inch parquet tiles that you glue to the substrate. Installing parquet is easier than cutting, placing, nailing, and finishing raw-wood flooring.

An old-fashioned flowered wallcovering and claw-footed bathtub complement this bathroom's simple country-style decor.

A brightly colored ceramic-tile wainscot with diamond-patterned border tiles makes for an arresting design statement.

Wall & Ceiling Finishes

You should make bathroom walls and ceilings easy to clean and resistant to moisture. Here are the best candidates:

Ceramic Tile

Ceramic tile is an expensive but unbeatable choice for walls in wet areas. (See page 62.) Properly installed, tile will last indefinitely. If and when problems occur, they will usually involve cracked grout joints or cracked and loose individual tiles. Fortunately, you can restore grout and replace cracked tiles. Glazed wall tiles are easiest to keep clean.

Wall tiles vary in size from 2 × 4 inches up to 12 inches square. You can select smaller tiles in a contrasting color to create accents, patterns, or stripes.

Paint

Paint is the most economical and easiest wall finish to apply. Oil- or alkyd-based paints, long preferred for walls and ceilings subject to moisture, are now being phased out in favor of acrylic or latex paints. Because the latter use water as a solvent, they are less harmful to your health and the environment.

When selecting paint, remember that the higher the gloss, the better the finish withstands moisture. The porous surfaces of flat (satin-sheen) paints grow mildew and are hard to clean with water and detergents. Choose acrylic gloss enamel (best) and semigloss (next best) for walls and ceilings. Be forewarned that glossy finishes show surface imperfections more readily than flat ones, so getting a smooth, even finish requires extra attention to surface preparation.

Wall Coverings

Don't call that material you buy in rolls "wallpaper." Though many wallcoverings are backed with paper, they are faced with washable vinyl, making them a good material for bathroom walls. For each of the hundreds of patterns available for the wall, there are an equal number of borders.

You can install roll-stock wallcoverings yourself on almost any smooth, dry substrate that has been sized (coated with a solution that controls the bond). If your walls already have a wallcovering, you'll have to strip it off and apply a solution to remove the adhesive. Walls painted with glossy paint should be dulled by sanding for a good bond.

Many wallcoverings now come prepasted with a self-adhesive coating on the back. Choosing this type will save you the time and effort required to mix a powdered paste and coat each strip separately, but keep in mind that prepasted wallcoverings often don't adhere to the wall as well as the unpasted types.

You can create your own wood wall finish by nailing up solid boards of pine, fir, cedar, or redwood

Wood Walls

Wood adds warmth to bathroom walls but may absorb moisture, depending on the finish. Aim for smooth-textured surfaces with as few joints as possible, and avoid wood altogether in continuously damp areas such as behind toilets. You can get wood veneer paneling in 48 x 96-inch sheets, prefinished or unfinished. Imitation wood veneer, consisting of a particleboard core printed with a wood pattern, is also available. It's cheaper than wood, but it doesn't have the classy look of the real thing.

in various patterns. Check your lumber supplier to see which sizes and species are regularly stocked. Softwood tongue-and-groove boards are commonly available in a nominal 1-inch thickness (actual thickness being ¾ inch) and nominal widths of 6, 8, and 10 inches (actual widths being 5½, 7½, and 9¼ inches respectively).

Paint over Wood

Applying gloss or semigloss paint over two coats of primer makes wood surfaces as scrubbable and water resistant as painted plaster or drywall. While paint hides the grain, it allows any joints to show through, so it can even be a good choice on wall paneling or boards.

Natural Finishes

If you aim for the look of wood, start by selecting a species that has the color and grain you like. Oak and fir have strong grain, while the grain in birch and maple is more subtle. If you want a dark wood, choose walnut, cherry, or redwood. (Bear in mind that too much dark wood in a small room will make it feel closed in.) Semidark woods include cedar and red oak. Pine, maple, fir, spruce, and birch are naturally light woods.

Prefabricated cabinets such as vanities usually come prefinished with highly durable coatings, so you will be able to judge the final effect before you buy. You will have to finish any wood cabinets you custom-build in place and any raw wood you use on walls. It's important to use a finish that's both easy to clean and moisture resistant.

The best moisture-resistant finish is a polyurethane or some other varnish-type finish that you apply in layers on the surface. Penetrating oil finishes, which sink into the wood pores, give a more natural look but offer less protection from water. All finishes darken the wood somewhat. For a different color, you can stain the wood. Alternatively, you can use a finish coating that contains a stain, though this approach doesn't look quite as good because the colorant stays on the surface with the finish rather than penetrating into the wood.

Penetrating oil finishes are simple to apply. You brush or wipe them liberally on the surface, let them sink in for a while, and then wipe off with a cloth. These finishes are also quite easy to repair. Surface finishes are difficult to spot-repair as well as more difficult to apply. The water- and solvent-based varieties are put on differently, so be sure to follow the manufacturer's instructions when applying.

Tumbled stone tiles in pale earth tones give the walls of this room a Mediterranean, almost fresco-like appearance.

Countertop Choices

Laminated Plastic

Plastic laminate is hard to beat for a bathroom countertop. It's economical, easy to maintain, and resists moisture superbly. Hundreds of colors and patterns are available. Plastic laminate comes in sheets 48 × 96 inches that are 1/16 inch thick. Installing plastic laminate to a countertop (described in "Laminate Countertops," pages 184 and 185) requires cutting the sheets and bonding with contact cement, then trimming with a router.

Ceramic Tile

Ceramic tile makes a countertop that stands up well to moisture and use. A ceramic tile countertop will cost more than one finished in plastic laminate but less than a solid-surface top. Costs range widely, however—you can bust your budget on custom-designed hand-formed tiles from Mexico, or you can save a bundle with a generic mass-produced domestic tile.

Your choice of tiles for a countertop runs the gamut from floor to wall tiles. In addition to "field" tiles—those used on the countertop surface—you can choose various edge-trim tiles in colors and shapes to fit your decor. Your local tile-supply store may have some made-up countertops on display and literature that can show you some of the design possibilities.

Setting tiles on a countertop is something you can probably do if you have the desire, time, and patience to do each step right. After selecting field and trim tiles, you'll need to plan the pattern, cut the tiles to fit, and apply them, as described in "Ceramic Tile Countertops," pages 186 and 187.

Solid-Surface Material

Not too long ago if you wanted the look of marble or granite, you were in for high costs. Now you can add the class of real stone at less cost with a lighter synthetic material that can be cut, drilled, and shaped in much the same way as wood. This material, sometimes referred to as synthetic marble,

Stainless steel and laminate make a colorful combination in this modern, mirror-walled bath.

This unusual wood countertop would be a poor choice in a busy bathroom but works well in this guest bath when combined with a vessel sink.

consists of stone dust or chips cast into an acrylic or polyester resin. Unlike plastic laminate, solid-surface material can be repaired by sanding out any defects and filling them with plastic.

Solid-surface material comes in ½- and ¾-inch thicknesses, widths of 30 and 36 inches, and lengths up to 12 feet. Figure on spending three to five times as much for a solid-surface countertop as you would for plastic laminate. Also, though lighter than stone, solid-surface material is still heavy and difficult to install, so consider having the installation done by a specialist. In addition, you should be aware that some manufacturers of solid-surface material will not honor their warranty if you install it yourself.

Ceramic tiles on a vanity top don't need to be small. These 12 x 12 floor tiles make an interesting, sturdy choice.

Countertops made from hard plastic—whether solid or laminate—are a practical and sturdy choice. Choose a custom color, a backsplash, and designer sinks to fit in with your overall design.

Remodeling Floors

CHAPTER 8

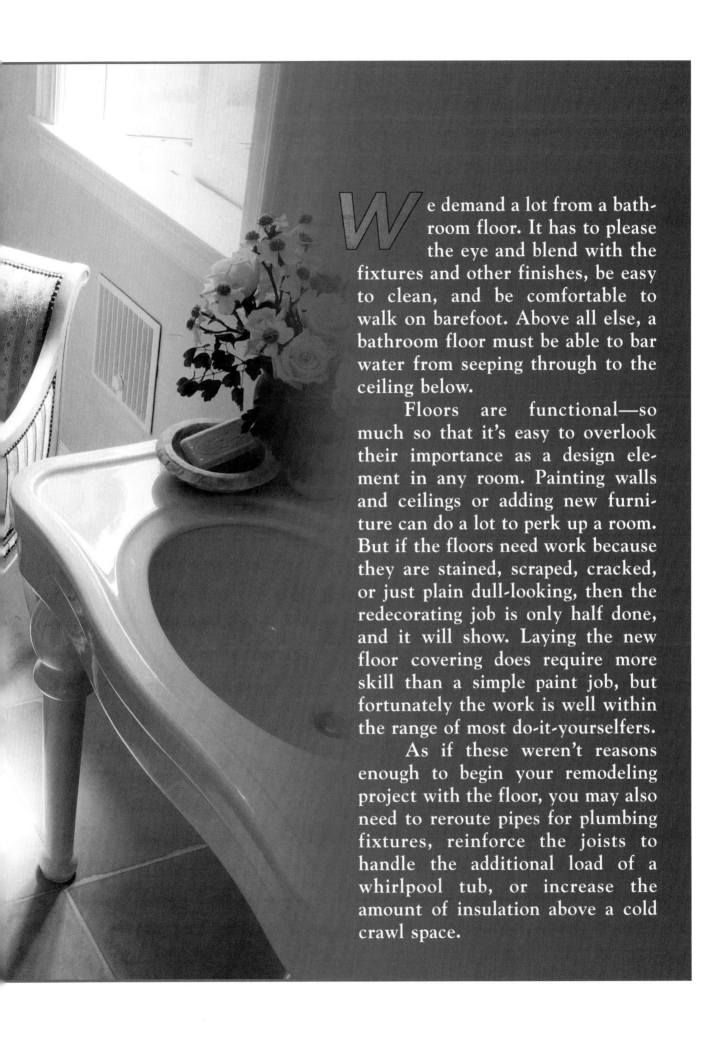

We demand a lot from a bathroom floor. It has to please the eye and blend with the fixtures and other finishes, be easy to clean, and be comfortable to walk on barefoot. Above all else, a bathroom floor must be able to bar water from seeping through to the ceiling below.

Floors are functional—so much so that it's easy to overlook their importance as a design element in any room. Painting walls and ceilings or adding new furniture can do a lot to perk up a room. But if the floors need work because they are stained, scraped, cracked, or just plain dull-looking, then the redecorating job is only half done, and it will show. Laying the new floor covering does require more skill than a simple paint job, but fortunately the work is well within the range of most do-it-yourselfers.

As if these weren't reasons enough to begin your remodeling project with the floor, you may also need to reroute pipes for plumbing fixtures, reinforce the joists to handle the additional load of a whirlpool tub, or increase the amount of insulation above a cold crawl space.

A Bathroom Floor Dissected

Depending on the situation, your floor may require extensive or minimal remodeling. But before you start to tear apart your floor, let's look at the composition of a well-constructed bathroom floor.

Coverings. The surface that you look at and walk on is called the floor covering. Vinyl and ceramic tile rank as the most popular coverings, but other materials such as wood and stone are also used in bathrooms. Just below the floor covering is some sort of water-resistant underlayment, which provides a smooth, flat surface to support the floor covering. The underlayment may be made of a variety of materials, depending on the floor covering. (Never use particleboard, because in a bathroom environment it will absorb moisture and swell.)

Framing. Below the underlayment is the structural part of the floor. For wood floors, this consists of a subfloor—usually plywood or wood planks—supported by joists and beams below. Concrete slab floors are floor structure and subfloor rolled into one, though a plywood subfloor can be installed over a concrete floor that is continually damp, such as in a basement.

Insulation. You may need other materials to insulate the floor from heat loss and to keep water and moisture out of the structure. You can add thermal insulation between or below the floor joists or above a concrete slab, as we'll see later in this chapter. Plastic vapor barriers go between the thermal insulation and floor-covering material.

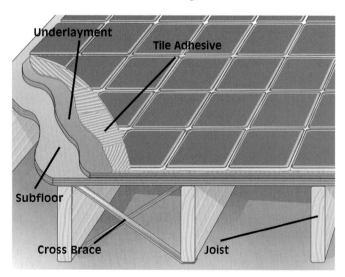

Below the floor covering in most modern homes is a layer of plywood or other panel material (the underlayment); below that, a plywood subfloor; and finally, the framing.

Labels: Underlayment, Tile Adhesive, Subfloor, Cross Brace, Joist

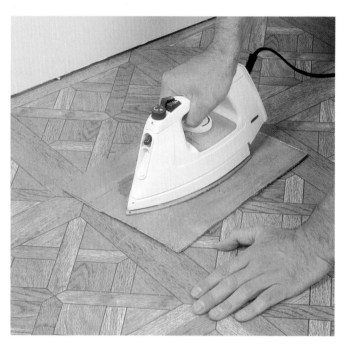

To remove resilient floor tiles, such as these parquet tiles, first heat them with a clothes iron to loosen the adhesive. A piece of thin fiberboard or plywood distributes the heat.

Taking Up the Old Flooring

If you're planning to install new flooring, you may be able to apply it directly over the old covering, saving time and money. New resilient floor coverings (sheet vinyl and vinyl composition tiles) or ceramic tile can be installed over existing vinyl or linoleum if the old flooring (and the underlayment below it) is in good condition. But a curled or chipped edge, usually found around toilets and near tubs and showers may indicate water damage below. If there is damage, you'll need to pry off the trim and pull up the old flooring. Peeling up a few tiles or a part of the sheet should reveal the condition of the underlayment and show you whether it also needs replacement. If the underlayment is severely damaged, peel it back to see whether you need to replace part of the subfloor.

Removing the Trim

Use a pry bar or rigid paint scraper to pull the baseboard and base trim away from the walls. *(1)* As you pry each portion outward, insert a wood shim behind it to keep the trim away from the wall so that you can insert the scraper in the next position. If you intend to reinstall the trim, use a pencil to label each piece. On a room plan sketched on graph paper, keep track of where each piece goes.

Removing Vinyl Flooring

Using a utility knife or linoleum cutter, score lines across the surface to divide the flooring into strips that are 6 to 18 inches wide. *(2)* For resilient tiles, use a clothes iron, hair dryer, or heat gun to melt the adhesive on the back of tiles. If you use an iron, start with the lowest temperature, increasing the heat as needed. (See photo at left.)

Using a pry bar or rigid paint scraper, loosen a tile or sheet-flooring strip. *(3)* Grip and pull up the released flooring as you continue to loosen the remainder of the tile or flooring strip. Because tiles are brittle, you may have to pry them off in chunks. Scrape off any adhesive residue left on the floor using the putty knife, or sand it off with an random-orbit sander.

If the floor covering will not come up, either remove the underlayment and floor covering or install an appropriate underlayment right over the existing floor. The latter option will result in a slightly raised floor—if you're installing tile, perhaps as much as an inch above the old floor surface. In this case, you may also need to plane down the bottom of the bathroom door and install a transition piece, such as a wood or tile threshold, where the new floor will intersect adjacent flooring.

Removing old sheet flooring

Difficulty Level:

Tools & Materials: Pry bar ❖ Shims or scrap wood ❖ Utility knife ❖ Clothes iron, hair dryer, or heat gun ❖ Paint scraper or wood chisel ❖ Random-orbit sander

1 Pry the base trim from the baseboard with a pry bar or paint scraper, inserting wood shims as you go. If you use a pry bar, protect the wall with a piece of scrap wood.

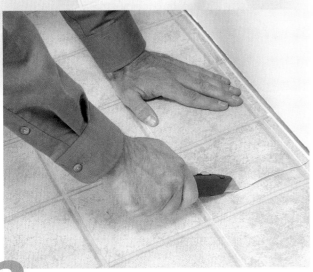

2 Score sheet flooring into strips using a utility knife or linoleum cutter. The strips should be about 6 to 18 in. wide to facilitate easy removal.

3 Loosen each tile or strip of sheet flooring with a pry bar or paint scraper. Pull on the free end as you continue to loosen the back.

Tearing Up Damaged Underlayment

Bathroom floors are constantly subjected to intense moisture and water spillage. If moisture penetrates the finished floor, it will inevitably saturate the subfloor. The first sign of a problem will be sponginess in the floor as you walk on it.

A curled edge on resilient flooring is also a sign that moisture is seeping underneath it and damaging its adhesive. If the problem is limited, you may need to take up only a small portion of the floor covering and replace the damaged section of the subfloor. Nevertheless, if damage is extensive, be prepared to replace the entire subfloor and possibly some of the floor joists.

Removing the Toilet

Water damage often occurs near a toilet. In humid weather, when water condenses on the fixture, droplets run down the surface, seeping into floor cracks. To remove a toilet, first shut off the cold water to the fixture. Once you have disconnected it, set the toilet aside or dispose of it if you intend to replace it. *(1)* (See "Mounting the New Toilet," page 153, for replacement.) Stuff a rag into the drain hole to prevent sewer gas and odor from seeping into the room.

Removing the Underlayment

Set the blade on your circular saw to cut just through the layer you want. Determine this thickness by pulling out a floor grille, if there is one, or by drilling a ¾-inch-diameter hole through the

Removing damaged subfloor

Difficulty Level:

Tools & Materials: Plumbing tools (for toilets & sinks) ❖ Circular saw or saber saw ❖ Paint scraper or pry bar ❖ Rubber mallet ❖ Safety goggles & work gloves

1 Turn off and disconnect the water to any fixture (toilets or pedestal sinks) that you will need to remove. Pick up a heavy toilet carefully, bending your legs to protect your back.

2 Use a circular saw, with the blade set to the thickness of the underlayment, to cut out any water-damaged areas that need replacing.

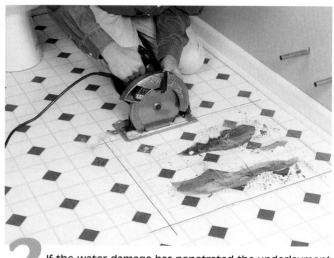

3 If the water damage has penetrated the underlayment and reached the subfloor, cut out those areas also, with either a circular saw or saber saw.

underlayment. After setting the depth of the saw blade to the thickness of the underlayment, cut out a large enough portion of it to determine whether damage is confined to the underlayment or whether it extends beneath to the subfloor. *(2)*

If the damage stops at the underlayment, pry it away from the subfloor using a paint scraper and rubber mallet. If the underlayment is glued to the subfloor with adhesive, you can try to remove the adhesive with a scraping or sanding tool, but you'll probably find it easier to remove the subfloor along with the underlayment. (See photo at right.)

If only portions of the subfloor are damaged, set your circular saw blade to a depth that will cut through the subfloor without cutting into the joists. Cut around the areas that you need to replace. *(3)* Be sure to extend the new patch so that both sides bear on one half of a joist, reserving the other half for the remaining subfloor. Separate the subfloor from the joists using a pry bar and mallet.

Underlayment

Joist

Closet Bend

If the subfloor has serious water damage or if removing the adhesive is difficult, you'll have to tear out the whole subfloor. Use a pry bar and a mallet to force up the nailheads; be sure to wear eye protection and work gloves.

8 Remodeling Floors

Keeping Out Moisture

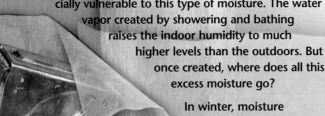

Most homeowners know that keeping surface water from penetrating floors and walls is essential if they want to prevent wood joists, studs, sheathing, and siding from deteriorating. But few realize that surface water is not the only menace. Airborne moisture can pose an even greater danger, and bathrooms are especially vulnerable to this type of moisture. The water vapor created by showering and bathing raises the indoor humidity to much higher levels than the outdoors. But once created, where does all this excess moisture go?

In winter, moisture migrates through walls, floors that are above crawl spaces, and roofs, condensing within the structural cavity. In time, it will cause insulation to lose its effectiveness, wood to rot, and paint to peel. An ideal time to address this type of problem is during a renovation when structural framing is exposed.

Here are some tips:

◯ Install a continuous vapor barrier over wall studs and floor and ceiling joists on the warm side of the insulation. A continuous sheet of 6-mil polyethylene (usually called poly) stapled to stud and joist faces forms an effective vapor barrier. Tape the overlapping seams. Seal the sheet to any electrical or plumbing fixtures that exit the wall with tape or caulk.

◯ Install 1 or more inches of approved foam insulation over the studs and joists if you are rebuilding outside walls and ceilings. Tape all joints, and seal around electrical outlets and pipe penetrations with caulk.

◯ Provide ventilating fans that exhaust to the outside, not into an attic or crawl space. (See "Installing an Exhaust Fan," page 170.) Ventilating fans are a must in high-moisture areas such as bathrooms and kitchens.

◯ Install double-glazed, low-e windows in your bathroom.

Insulating Crawl Spaces

If your bathroom sits above a crawl space, you can do away with a cold floor by adequately insulating the floor or the foundation walls. (To check how much insulation you'll need, see "Warming Up a Cold Bathroom," page 76.) If you insulate the floor, you'll need to insulate any water pipes on the cold side of the insulation to prevent it from freezing. For this reason, many builders believe it is better to insulate the foundation wall.

To prevent moisture from wicking up through the crawl-space floor and condensing on the wood structure above, it is absolutely essential to protect the space with a 6-mil polyethylene vapor barrier. Installing these items is relatively easy to do if you have easy access to your crawl space, or from above when the subfloor is removed, but more difficult when the finished floor is in place.

Working from below in a dark, cramped space, amidst spiderwebs and unknown hazards, can be neither safe nor enjoyable. Be sure you have a reliable source of light, and protect yourself with a good dust mask, safety goggles, a hard hat, full-length trousers, and a long-sleeved shirt.

Insulating the Floor Above

Cut lengths of insulation with long scissors or a sharp knife using a piece of 1×4 as a guide and a piece of scrap wood below as a cutting surface. Fit a piece of insulation between each pair of joists.

If you are insulating from above the floor, use kraft paper–faced insulation batts, and pull the paper tabs out and over the tops of the floor joists. Staple the tabs at 8-inch intervals. Cut the strips of insulation into pieces short enough to make them easily manageable (4 feet or so). Fit each strip into the space between two joists. Staple sheets of house wrap or vapor barrier to the bottom of the joists to keep the insulation from dropping down. *(1)* If working from below, use unfaced fiberglass batt insulation, friction-fitted into place.

Cover each heating duct and water pipe with fiberglass duct wrap or pipe insulation. Use duct tape to seal the insulation joints. *(2)* To keep down the moisture level, place strips of 6-mil polyethylene vapor barrier over the soil, overlapping the joints by at least 12 inches. Run the vapor barrier up to the top of the wall and staple it onto the sill plate. (See the illustration at right.)

Insulating the floor above a crawl space

Difficulty Level:

Tools & Materials: Long scissors or knife ❖ Staple gun & staples ❖ Fiberglass insulation batts ❖ Duct tape ❖ 4-mil or 6-mil polyethylene sheet ❖ Dust mask & work gloves

Insulating a Heated Crawl Space

Insulating between joists is often more difficult than insulating the sides of a foundation and keeping the crawl space heated. The latter approach eliminates the need to wrap pipes and ducts to keep them from freezing. If you choose this method, close off any foundation vents to the outside. The tools and materials you'll need are the same as for insulating a wood floor, except that you'll also need some 2×4s. And be sure to wear appropriate protective wear.

Staple sheets of 6-mil polyethylene to the sill plate. Run the sheets down the inside of the foundation wall and 12 inches over the soil, overlapping the joints by at least 12 inches. Measure the vertical distance between the top of the rim joist and the ground and add 36 inches.

Cut strips of batt insulation to this length. Place one end of each section of insulation between two floor joists, with the paper facing toward the crawl space, and staple the ends to the rim joist. Drape the strips of insulation down the inside face of the foundation wall and out over the ground.

Connect the strips of insulation by stapling the tabs of adjoining pieces together at 8-inch intervals. Insert strips of 6-mil poly beneath the insulation extending over the soil. The polyethylene should cover all exposed soil. Be sure to overlap the sheets by at least 12 inches. Place lengths of 2×4 lumber over the top of the insulation and a vapor barrier at the joint between the wall and the ground. This will hold the bottom edges of the insulation in place.

1 Install unfaced blanket insulation between the floor joists from below by fitting pieces into the spaces. Staple a sheet of vapor barrier or house wrap to hold it in place.

2 You should wrap all heating ducts and water pipes below an uninsulated floor. Seal the joints between batts of insulation with duct tape.

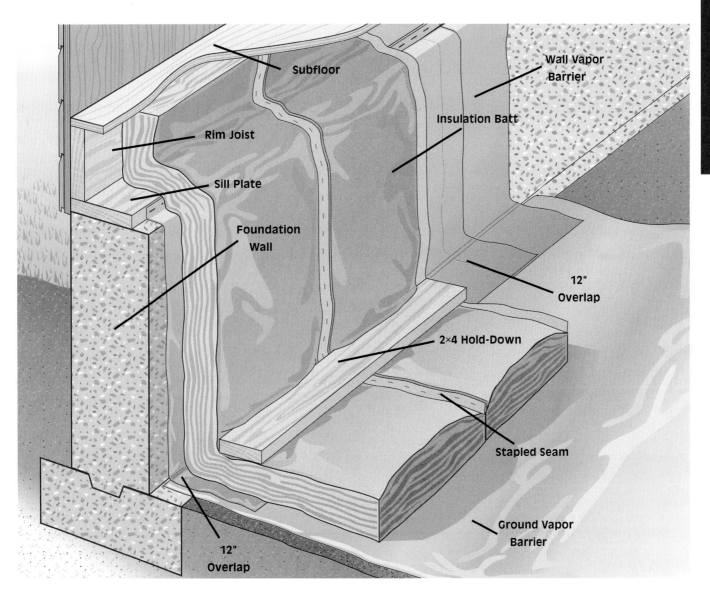

Subfloor

Wall Vapor Barrier

Insulation Batt

Rim Joist

Sill Plate

Foundation Wall

12" Overlap

2×4 Hold-Down

Stapled Seam

Ground Vapor Barrier

12" Overlap

Cover the inside face of the foundation and the surface of the soil using sheets of polyethylene as a vapor barrier, and short strips of batt insulation. Use lengths of 2x4 to hold the corners of the insulation batts in place.

Warming Up a Cold Bathroom

Maintaining a comfortable temperature in a bathroom is especially critical. No one leaving a bath or shower in the wintertime wants to step into a cold room. Poorly insulated ceilings, walls, or floors quickly lose heat to the outdoors, causing higher fuel bills and discomfort.

To keep a bathroom warm in January (and cool in July) requires the right amount of insulation. Insulation resists heat flow because of the many tiny air spaces within the material and the reflectivity of its foil vapor barrier, if it has one. The resistance of insulation to heat flow is measured in R-values—the higher the R-value, the better the insulating quality of the material. Adequate R-value depends on your climate. In regions where winters are cold, aim for levels of R-38 in the ceiling or roof, R-19 in outside walls, and R-22 in a floor above a crawl space (or around the perimeter of the crawl space).

When choosing insulation, consider the cost and type as well as the R-value. Listed below are the R-values per every inch of insulation and the relative cost per unit for some of the most widely used materials. Keep in mind that for finished walls and ceilings, the number of inches you can add is limited by the thickness of the studs or joists; in unfinished attics or basement floors, you can add more.

Insulation	R-Value per Inch	Relative Cost per Unit
Blanket and Batt		
Fiberglass	2.9–3.3	lowest
Mineral-wool batts	2.9–3.7	lowest
Rigid Sheets		
Phenolic foam	4.5–8.5	highest
Polyurethane/isocyanurate	5.6–8.0	medium
Polystyrene (extruded)	4.0–6.0	medium
Polystyrene (bead board)	3.8–4.4	medium
Fiberglass board	3.8–4.8	highest
Loose Fill*		
Cellulose (blown-in)	2.8–3.7	medium
Perlite (pellets)	2.6–2.7	medium
Fiberglass (blown-in)	2.2	medium
Mineral wool (blown-in)	2.9–3.7	medium
Vermiculite	2.0–2.1	medium

*If you install any of the loose fills yourself, the relative cost is lowest.

Blanket and batt insulation are well suited for friction-fitting between studs and joists. Nailing rigid insulation boards over studs or joists is a good way to increase R-value where wall and floor spaces already contain some insulation. Foil-faced rigid foam panels will also make a good vapor barrier if the joints are taped. Blown-in loose fill insulation provides an economical way to insulate an inaccessible ceiling space. Loose fill can also be blown into outside wall cavities, leaving the inside and outside finishes intact. Using a hole saw, the contractor drills access holes through the siding for filling each stud cavity with insulation. The circular cutouts are then repaired.

Upgrading the Floor Structure

Before you install new underlayment, check the old subfloor for loose spots. Drive in screws near any nails that may have worked themselves loose, trying to force the subfloor tight against the joists. *(1)*

You must replace rotten or damaged joists. The best way to assess the damage is to examine from below; if you can't get to the joists, remove some of the subfloor. Weak or sagging joists are a telltale sign of structural problems; check for them with a 4-foot spirit level. *(2)* If you don't feel able to judge the condition of the joists, solicit the opinion of a licensed architect or structural engineer. A licensed professional can determine whether the existing floor joists are safe and whether they will be able to support the additional load of a whirlpool tub or sauna.

If a joist is minimally damaged, you can reinforce it by adding a sister joist to its side. Install sister joists of the same depth and length as the originals, if possible. (Getting them into place may be difficult.) Fasten them to the sides of existing joists using 12d galvanized nails or 3-inch galvanized screws. *(3)* Follow the same procedure when doubling joists to support a new load, such as a new tub. If you can't extend the new joists over the supporting top plate, it may be acceptable to bolt each new joist to an original joist using 3½-inch-long hex-head bolts spaced no more than 12 inches apart and staggered between the top and bottom of the joist. However, unsupported double joists should be designed by a licensed architect or structural engineer.

Reinforcing old floors

Difficulty Level:

Tools & Materials: Power drill with screwdriver bit ✧ Galvanized screws ✧ 4' spirit level ✧ Extra joist (must match the existing joists) ✧ Construction adhesive & caulking gun

1 Before installing new underlayment or flooring, check the old subfloor for loose spots where nails may have popped, and drive them tight against the joist with screws.

2 Locate a weak or sagging joist by checking across several joists with a 4-ft. spirit level. It will rock over the lowest one where the floor dips.

3 Strengthen a weak joist (after propping it up if need be) by adding a second joist secured with construction adhesive and screws.

Selecting the Right Underlayment

The correct underlayment will ensure that your new floor covering lies flat and resists water for many years. Selecting the right thickness will help you match the new floor level to that of an adjacent floor, or at least minimize the difference between the two. It's important to match the floor covering with a compatible underlayment.

Types of Underlayment

Always avoid particleboard, especially in the bathroom, because it will swell when wet, causing the floor covering to separate or bubble. Underlayment-grade plywood made from fir or pine is available in 48 × 96-inch sheets in thicknesses of ¼, ⅜, ½, ⅝, and ¾ inch. If permitted by code, you can use oriented-strand board (OSB). Because it can expand when damp, plywood or OSB is not as good a choice for ceramic tile underlayment as cement-based backer board.

Lauan plywood, made from a species of mahogany, is often used under resilient flooring. It is available in 48 × 96-inch sheets. The usual thickness for lauan underlayment is ¼ inch.

Cement-based backer board, also called tile backer board, is made of a sand and cement matrix reinforced with fiberglass mesh. It is usually available in 36 × 60-inch sheets in a thickness of ½ inch. This is the preferred tile base for ceramic tile and stone floors.

When to Install Underlayment

Resilient floor coverings (vinyl, rubber, and linoleum sheet flooring and tiles) and wood parquet can be laid over an existing layer of similar material if the original is in good condition. The existing covering must be tightly adhered, have no cupped edges, and be free of any water damage. If the existing flooring is not in good condition, remove it and smooth out the existing underlayment before installing new floor covering. If you can't remove the old floor covering, fill in any uneven spots, and install a new underlayment over it.

Ceramic tile and stone can be set over existing ceramic tile if the original flooring is tightly adhered and in good condition. They can also be installed directly over a concrete slab floor. With the exception of shower stalls, tile and stone are usually set on an underlayment using a troweled-on adhesive called thinset. Showers require greater water resistance and sloped floors for drainage. The best way to achieve this is by setting the tiles on a mortar (thickset) base over a PVC or CPE membrane. Over wood bathroom floors, the ideal underlayment for ceramic tile and stone is cement-based backer board. Underlayment-grade plywood is a second choice.

New Construction

If you are working with new floor construction, plan the job to provide extra-strength framing and a subfloor for tiled areas. If a standard floor in the house has 2×8s covered with ½-inch plywood sheathing, there are two approaches you could take to build in extra strength: increase the joist size or decrease the joist spacing. You could switch to 2×10s or, if there is not enough room for the extra depth, decrease the spacing between joist centers from the standard 16 inches to 12 inches.

As for the subfloor, you could leave the existing ½-inch panels in place and cover them with another layer of ½- or ⅝-, or even ¾-inch-thick plywood. There also are special-order floor systems that provide exceptional strength. These include

Underlayment Options

Floor Covering	Acceptable Underlayments
Resilient floor coverings	Existing vinyl or linoleum in sound condition
	Underlayment-grade plywood
	Lauan plywood
Wood parquet flooring	Existing floor vinyl or linoleum in sound condition
	Underlayment-grade plywood
	Lauan plywood
	Hardboard
Ceramic tile and stone	Existing tiles, if sound
	Concrete slab
	Cement-based backer board
	Underlayment-grade plywood

I-beam wood joists, and 1-inch-thick plywood panels milled with overlapping edges. It generally pays to install the plywood with screws instead of nails: they provide more holding power.

If you install an extra layer of subfloor (most jobs require either extra plywood or cement-based backer board), avoid aligning seams with the existing material. Joints between panels on the different layers should bear on different floor joists.

Installing New Underlayment

To prevent nails from popping out, let the underlayment acclimate to room temperature and humidity for a few days before installing it. Measure and cut each section of underlayment to lengths that will accommodate staggered joints. Using a circular saw with a crosscut plywood blade, cut the underlayment. *(1)* Use a saber saw or keyhole saw to cut openings for the drainpipes.

Place the board sections over the subfloor so that the joints will be offset from those in the subfloor or existing underlayment. Leave a gap of 1/16 inch between sheets and 1/4 inch at the walls. Lay full sheets first; then cut the pieces to complete the floor. *(2)* Using 1-inch ring-shank nails or galvanized screws, begin at one corner of the room, and tightly fasten the underlayment to the subfloor. Space these fasteners in rows along the joists, no more than 4 inches apart along the joists and 1/2 inch from the edge. *(3)*

Installing plywood underlayment

Difficulty Level:

Tools & Materials: Circular saw ❖ Power drill with screwdriver bit ❖ Measuring tape ❖ Chalk-line box ❖ Plywood ❖ Galvanized screws

1 To install a half sheet and stagger joints to miss the seams in the existing floor, snap a chalk line as a guide, and cut the sheet in two with a circular saw.

2 Set a half sheet next to a full sheet to stagger the seams. Leave at least a 1/4-in. gap between the edges of the sheets and the walls.

3 Drive screws long enough to reach through the old and new floors. Snap a chalk line so that you drive them into supporting joists.

Remodeling Walls & Ceilings

CHAPTER 9

At its simplest, a bathroom remodeling might involve stripping off old wallpaper and replacing it with a fresh coat of paint. However, more extensive remodeling plans—anything involving moving fixtures, adding ceramic tile, or changing the way you use the space—is going to involve a lot of serious work on your home's walls. Stripping off old drywall or ceramic tile isn't skilled work, but it fills your house with dust and covers your curb with trash bags full of debris. Just be sure that there aren't live wires or water pipes behind those walls before you start bashing away with a crowbar.

Sometimes even when you don't plan to tear out your old walls, you may find conditions worse than you first thought. Damage to walls and ceilings may appear to be only skin deep, but a closer inspection may reveal a variety of more serious problems. Even if a wall or ceiling surface seems to be in sound condition, it may need to be demolished to provide access to the electrical and plumbing systems or to upgrade the insulation. Whatever work is required below the surface, be sure to do it with extreme care. You will be rewarded with a sound base for the final wall and ceiling finishes.

Wet-stripping wallcovering

Difficulty Level:

Tools & Materials: Scoring tool ❖ Rubber gloves ❖ Safety goggles ❖ Wallcovering remover ❖ Steamer (may be rented or purchased) ❖ Wallpaper scraper (for plaster walls) ❖ Sponges or rags ❖ Utility pail ❖ Phosphate-free trisodium

1 Score wallcovering by making circles with a scoring tool. The sharp teeth will penetrate the covering but not the wall underneath.

2 To make quick work of removing wallcovering, rent a wallpaper steamer. The steamer will saturate the scored wallcovering.

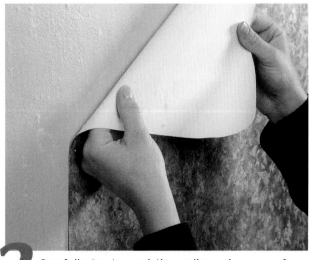

3 Carefully try to peel the wallcovering away from the wall, or for "strippable" papers, the top layer away from its backing.

4 If the steamed wallcovering won't peel away easily, use a paint scraper. Take care not to mar the wall underneath.

5 Finally, before painting or installing a new wall covering, wash the wall with a phosphate-free trisodium solution.

Removing Wallcovering

Deciding whether to remove an old wallcovering—and how to remove it— depends on the new finish. While existing wallcovering may serve as a base for some paints, the water in latex paint may cause it to bubble or stain through unless you first prime the surface with an oil-based stain-killing primer/sealer.

If you want to install new wallcovering, your best bet is to strip off the existing layer, using either the dry- or wet-stripping processes detailed below.

Dry-Stripping a Wall

Regardless of the material, always first try to dry-strip a wallcovering off the wall. Use a paint scraper or putty knife, and lift a small corner of the existing paper away from the wall. Pull the paper away at a shallow angle. If the wallcovering strips off without causing damage to the surface underneath, continue peeling. If not, move on to wet-stripping.

Some wallcoverings are made up of a vinyl facing backed by cloth or paper. When you strip away the surface layer, the backing remains on the wall, where it can serve as the base for a new application of vinyl wallcovering.

Wet-Stripping a Wall

Wallcoverings without vinyl facing, such as wallpaper, usually need to be removed by applying water or steam with a wallcovering remover added. To begin, score the wallcovering by making circular motions with a scoring tool. *(1)* This tool is shaped like a triangle with round disks at each point. Each scoring disk has two toothed wheels attached to its bottom surface, which perforate the wallcovering without damaging the the drywall or plaster underneath.

Hold the perforated plate of the steamer against portions of the wall until the steam permeates the covering and breaks the bond. *(2)* Wait no longer than 15 or 20 minutes; otherwise, you risk damaging the drywall underneath. Then you simply peel away the covering at a shallow angle to the wall. *(3)* Use a scraper when necessary to coax the wallcovering away from the wall, but be careful not to gouge the wall. *(4)*

When the walls are bare, mix phosphate-free trisodium in warm water, and wash the wall surfaces thoroughly with a wet sponge. *(5)* Allow the walls to dry for at least a week. Note that water or steam may also remove drywall facing paper. If this happens, you must seal the drywall with a primer/sealer.

Two Other Ways to Steam Off Wallcoverings

If you can't locate a steamer to rent, you can still wet-strip wallcovering by using a pail or garden sprayer. Here's how:

○ **With a pail:** Fill the pail with a mixture of hot tap water and wallcovering remover. (Follow the manufacturer's recommended proportions.) Cover the floor with a water-proof tarp sealed at the edges with tape. Protect your hands with latex gloves, and then dip a rag or sponge into the pail and rub the wallcovering with it. Be sure to soak the material well before scraping it off—the wetter, the better.

○ **With a garden sprayer:** First score the wall-covering as shown at left (Step 1). Then fill a sprayer (that has been thoroughly cleaned) with a mixture of hot tap water and wall-covering remover, following the manufacturer's instructions. Use the sprayer to saturate the wallcovering with the mixture. Then scrape off the wallcovering.

Stripping down to the Studs

Think twice before you tear into a wall or ceiling. The work almost always adds up to more than you bargained for, and the dust and debris somehow finds its way into all corners of the house—even if you take heroic measures to contain it.

Still, there are many unavoidable conditions that necessitate pulling off the tile, plaster, or drywall—if not over the entire wall—in at least one spot. New fixtures may require new pipes. Rewiring may be called for. You may want to insulate the wall and install a vapor barrier. Finally, the old substrate may be showing the effects of years of dampness.

Health Concerns

Before you begin, take measures to protect yourself and the house from the stuff that will come loose. Wear gloves, safety goggles, heavy shoes, and a hard hat. If you buy a hard hat, look for one with built-in eye and ear protectors. Ear protectors can prevent hearing loss caused by exposure to noisy power tools.

Keep the door closed to the work area. Line the path to the outdoors with tarps. If the room has an outside window, setting up a chute leading from the window into a dumpster or trash can will save you from carting the debris out through the house.

Caution

You risk damaging pipes and electrical wiring when you poke into walls and ceilings, so take extra care around areas where you suspect these items might be located. Also, cover openings in heating ducts and exposed drains to keep out falling chunks of debris.

Tearing Down the Wall

After you've shut off the power and water to the room in which you're going to work, remove any wall, door, and window trim you intend to save. *(1)* To tear out the drywall, you'll need to make a starter hole with a claw hammer—it creates a huge mess. *(2)* The neatest way to remove drywall is to cut along the stud right alongside the panel seams (which should be every 4 or 8 feet along the wall) with a reciprocating saw. *(3)* Once the panel has been cut, pry it off the nails. *(4)* Then pry off the remaining nails from the studs using a pry bar or claw hammer. *(5)*

Old plaster is an even bigger mess to tear out than drywall because it won't come free in large pieces. After whacking a hole in the plaster with a hammer, start pulling out the lath near the top with a pry bar.

Removing Ceramic Tile

You can remove small areas of ceramic tile with a cold chisel, prying tiles off one by one. (See photo at right.) But as the drywall underneath may have to be replaced anyway, it's far easier to cut away chunks with a reciprocating saw and remove the chunks whole. (See photo at left.) Always wear eye protection: flying pieces of tile can be dangerous.

Gutting a wall or ceiling

Difficulty Level: 🔧🔧 to 🔧🔧🔧

Tools & Materials: Pry bar ❖ Wood shims ❖ Hammer ❖ Cold chisel ❖ Mallet ❖ Reciprocating saw ❖ Safety goggles & gloves ❖ Blankets & tarps to protect floor & fixtures

1 Pry off all trim with a pry bar. If you want to salvage the trim, insert shims along the length of each piece, which keeps the trim from breaking.

2 To tear out drywall, first bang holes into the wall with a claw hammer near a few adjacent studs to find the panel seams.

3 Use a reciprocating saw to cut right next to the panel seams alongside the stud. The seams are 4 ft. apart either horizontally or vertically.

4 Once you have cut the panels, pry them off the nails or screws with a pry bar, in the largest chunks you can manage.

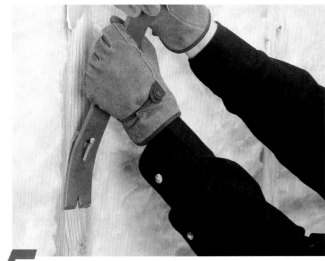

5 Once you have removed the drywall panels, pry off any remaining nailheads with a pry bar; pull out screws with a power drill.

9 Remodeling Walls & Ceilings

Adding Insulation

The usual way to install insulation in a stud wall is to fill the cavities between studs. This can be done from the inside, after the wall finish is stripped off, or from the outside by blowing loose-fill insulation through holes in the siding. (This method does nothing to improve the wall's resistance to moisture.) A third option allows you to add both insulation and a vapor barrier to the inside of the wall without having to first remove the wall finish. This may be your best solution if you can live with a fatter wall.

Choosing Insulation

Two main factors affect your choice of insulation: the configuration (such as loose fill or rigid foam board) and the R-value. Many types of insulation are available, so you can pick the most efficient product for the job. Some DIYers may also consider ease of application, how the material is packaged, and potential drawbacks such as possible skin irritation. Insulation is commonly available in batts to fit between 16- or 24-inch-wide framing, either paper- or foil-faced; loose fill to blow or pour into structural cavities; and foam boards, used mainly on roofs and on the outside of walls and foundations.

Insulating a Ceiling

Bathroom ceilings under attics or roofs should have adequate insulation just above the ceiling itself (with a cold attic space above) or between the rafters (warm attic or cathedral ceiling). The easiest way to add insulation to an attic is by pouring in loose-fill insulation or hiring an insulation contractor to blow-in fiberglass.

Before adding insulation, check to be sure that there is a vapor barrier. Go into the attic and remove a portion of the insulation (if any), and see whether a plastic sheet lies just above the plaster or drywall. If not, consider adding a vapor barrier. You can do this in one of two ways:

• Remove the ceiling finish, and staple a sheet of 4-mil polyethylene to the joists; then reinstall the drywall (or plaster). (See the illustration at right.)

• Staple a sheet of 4-mil polyethylene to the room side of the present ceiling finish; then apply a second layer of drywall.

You can add a vapor barrier to exterior walls in the same ways. If the walls need insulation as well, you can add it by one of the following methods.

Insulating an Open Wall

To install batt or blanket insulation in a wall cavity, begin after you've completed all framing alterations and roughed in the plumbing. You can install new wiring after insulating (but before installing the vapor barrier). When working with fiberglass insulation, wear goggles, gloves, and a long-sleeved shirt to protect as much of your skin as possible.

Cut lengths of insulation from rolls or batts using long scissors or a sharp knife. Use a 2x4 as a cutting guide and a scrap piece of plywood below against which to cut. *(1–2)* Fit each piece of insulation snugly into the stud cavity. If you are using unfaced insulation, the friction between the edges and the studs will keep it in place. For kraft paper-faced insulation, staple the tabs to either the sides of the studs or, better yet, to the stud faces. *(3)*

Tuck insulation around the outside of any water pipes, leaving the room side uninsulated (to keep the pipes from freezing). *(4)* After you've completed any plumbing rough-in and electrical wiring, staple a layer of polyethylene over the insulation. *(5)* Set each overlapping edge in a bead of polyurethane caulk before stapling. Wrap polyethylene around all penetrations, such as pipes and electrical boxes, then seal the patch to the face layer with caulk to prevent moisture from leaking into the wall.

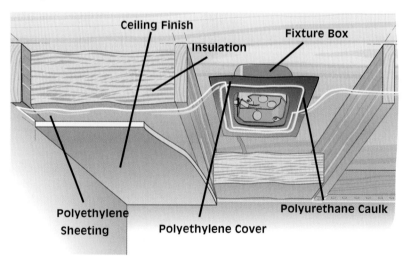

Install a vapor barrier between the ceiling insulation and the ceiling finish. To prevent moisture leaks around electrical boxes, wrap them with special polyethylene covers caulked to the main sheeting.

Adding insulation to an unfinished wall

Difficulty Level:

Tools & Materials: Fiberglass insulation blankets or batts ❖ Long scissors or knife ❖ Scrap wood for cutting guide ❖ Staple gun with ¼-inch staples ❖ 4-mil polyethylene sheet ❖ House-wrap tape or duct tape ❖ Polyurethane caulk & caulking gun ❖ Safety goggles, work gloves & face mask

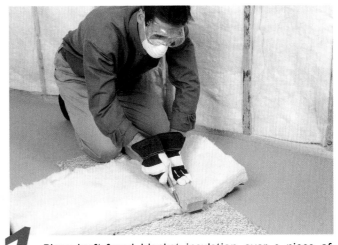

1 Place kraft-faced blanket insulation over a piece of scrap plywood or carpet to protect the floor, and hold the insulation down with a board.

2 Using the board as a guide, cut the insulation using a knife. You may have to score it a few times before cutting all the way through.

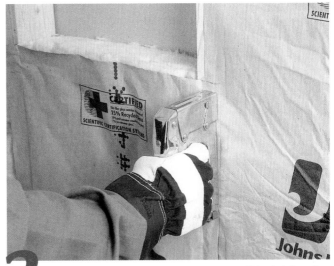

3 Attach kraft-faced insulation to the wall by folding the edge tabs over the face of the studs and stapling it to the studs with ¼-in. staples.

4 Wrap insulation around the outer side of water pipes and waste pipes to prevent freezing. Leave the room side of the pipe uninsulated.

5 After all insulation, wiring, and plumbing are in place, staple a vapor barrier to the stud faces. Use polyurethane caulk to seal it at all joints.

9 *Remodeling Walls & Ceilings*

Adding insulation to a finished wall

Difficulty Level:

Tools & Materials: Furring strips & cleats ❖ Measuring tape & straightedge ❖ Stud finder ❖ Hammer & 20d nails or power drill & 3" screws ❖ Rigid foam insulation ❖ Knife ❖ T-square ❖ House-wrap tape or duct tape ❖ Polyurethane caulk & caulking gun ❖ Safety goggles & work gloves

1 Secure furring strips to the wall surface with nails or screws. Drive one through each stud underneath the wall surface.

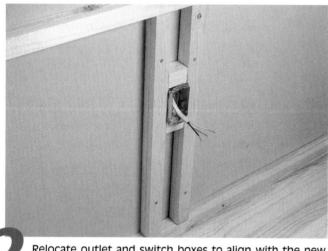

2 Relocate outlet and switch boxes to align with the new surface by pulling the box out and attaching it to vertical cleats between the furring strips.

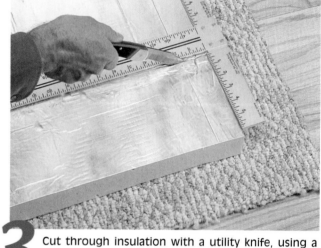

3 Cut through insulation with a utility knife, using a drywall T-square as a guide. Protect the floor with scrap wood or carpeting.

4 After installing rigid foam insulation panels between the furring strips, tape the joints with house-wrap tape or duct tape.

5 Seal all the holes around projecting pipes and the spaces around electrical boxes with polyurethane or silicone caulk.

Insulating a Closed Wall

If you can afford losing a few inches of floor space to a fatter wall and there are no windows, doors, or other obstacles on the wall you want to insulate, it may be more practical to add insulation and a vapor barrier over the top of the existing wall finish before installing a new wall finish over it.

Adding the Furring. The first step is to install furring strips over the existing wall. Measure lengths of furring (1×2s, ¾×3s, or even 2×4s) to extend across the face of the wall. The furring should be the same thickness as the insulation you'll be adding. Starting at the floor, mark horizontal lines on the wall at 24-inch intervals. Place each strip on the wall so that its bottom edge is on the line; then screw or nail the strips to the studs with 3-inch screws or 20d nails. **(1)**

If there are any switch or outlet boxes on the wall, you will have to pull them forward to align with the new wall finish. After shutting off the power to the circuits, detach the box from the stud it is nailed to, and pull it out of the wall a few inches. Add vertical cleats to support the box, making the cleats of the same stock as the furring strips. Attach the box to the cleats. **(2)**

If there isn't enough wire in the box, you may have to reposition the box slightly to gain some slack. Do not leave the old box in place and make a connection to a new box. Concealing electrical boxes is a fire hazard that violates the National Electrical Code.

Adding the Insulation. Lay a sheet of rigid foam insulation over a cutting surface, such as scrap plywood or carpet. Measure and mark the pieces to fit between the furring strips.

Cut through the foam using a straightedge or drywall T-square as a guide. Use a sharp utility knife and make two or three passes to cut cleanly through the foam and facing material. **(3)**

Fit each piece of rigid foam snugly between the furring strips. Cut smaller pieces, as necessary, to fit around pipe projections and electrical boxes. Then tape each joint with plastic house-wrap tape or aluminum-faced duct tape. **(4)** Caulk around all projections in the foam with polyurethane or silicone caulk, taking extra care to seal the sides of electrical boxes.
(5) You can now apply drywall over the insulation. Attach it to the furring strips.

Blowing-In Insulation through Exterior Walls

Blowing-in insulation makes the most sense when the framing cavity is empty. New material won't be blocked by old batts, and thermal improvement will be dramatic, even though the dead air trapped in an empty wall cavity does provide some insulation. A contractor can fill the empty space by cutting small holes through the drywall, inserting a hose, and pumping insulation into the bay between each pair of framing members. You do wind up with a row of little cutouts, but you can patch, sand, and paint them.

It may be easier for the contractor to gain access from the outside, by removing a course of clapboards and cutting a channel in the sheathing over the studs. It depends on which way into the wall cavity causes the least damage while providing the best access. In most cases, it's simpler to remove and replace exterior siding than it is to patch and repaint dozens of small holes in an interior wall. But even working blind with a hose through a hole, experienced contractors should be able to gauge how much insulation the cavity should take and know when the flow of loose fill has been blocked, say, by a construction brace or plumbing. In those cases, they may have to make a second hole to be sure that the bay is completely filled.

You might want to make a thermographic test before and after the insulation is blown in to confirm the results. This test is a temperature-sensitive photograph that can reveal where heat is escaping from your house; heat leaks are highlighted in bright colors.

Drywall

Drywall, also called wallboard, largely replaced plaster in houses built after World War II. It has a core of gypsum plaster sandwiched between two layers of paper. Drywall comes in sheets that are 48 inches wide and in lengths from 8 to 16 feet, in 2-foot increments. Sheets come in thicknesses of ¼, ⅜, ½, and ⅝ inch. For studs spaced 16 inches apart or less, use ½-inch drywall. Use a ⅝-inch thickness if the studs are spaced 24 inches. In some old houses, studs are spaced still wider or are irregular. In that case, support the drywall from 1×3 or 2×4 furring strips, nailed horizontally across the studs spaced at 16 or 24 inches on center.

Use standard-grade drywall in dry areas of the room and water-resistant drywall (greenboard or blueboard) or cement-based backer board in wet areas to be tiled. (Cement-based backer board is preferred.) Before you begin, make sure the framing is straight and rigid. Pull out and replace studs that are out of alignment. Mark stud locations on the floor so you will know where to sink nails or screws.

Planning a Drywall Installation

Measure the height of the wall and width of the stud bays you want to cover with a single sheet. You can install drywall vertically or horizontally—horizontal installations are easier to tape and sand, but it will be easier to install panels vertically if you're working alone. Before starting your installation, plan ahead to avoid awkward cuts near doors, windows, or other obstructions. To prevent cracks, avoid making joints directly next to doors and windows. If you are installing the panels vertically, cut lengths about ¾ inch shorter than the wall height.

Cutting Drywall

Mark the sheet with a straightedge. Draw the utility knife against the straightedge to score the paper facing. **(1)** Slip a length of lumber under the cut line, and gently push down on one side to snap the drywall panel apart, separating the cut through the thickness but not through the backing paper. **(2)** Turn the panel up on edge, fold the two cut pieces slightly together, and slice through the paper backing to complete the cut. **(3)** (This step is easier if someone else holds the drywall at the top.)

Cut openings for pipes and electrical devices

Installing drywall

Difficulty Level:

Tools & Materials: Drywall ❖ Drywall nails or screws ❖ Measuring tape ❖ 4' aluminum T-square ❖ Utility knife ❖ Chalk-line box ❖ Drywall saw or keyhole saw ❖ Drywall hammer or power drill with drywall screw clutch ❖ Panel lifter or homemade wood-scrap lever

3 After you've snapped the cut line, stand the panel on edge, and cut through the paper backing with a utility knife.

using a utility saw or keyhole saw. Start by drilling holes in the corners of the shapes or by making repeated passes with a utility knife. **(4)**

Installing Drywall

For a horizontal installation, install the top panel first, butting it against the ceiling. If you're working alone, a pair of nails can support the panel before you nail or screw it in place. Fasten the panels by hammering in nails with a drywall hammer, which leaves a small dimple around the nailhead, or with a power drill fitted with a special clutch that disengages as soon as the screw is driven through the surface.

The bottom panel (or, in vertical installation, each panel) can be butted upward with a panel lifter or a simple lever made from scraps of wood. **(5)** Don't worry about the gap at the floor—it will be covered by the base trim.

1 To cut a drywall panel, first score its front with a utility knife drawn against a long drywalling T-square or other straightedge.

2 You can snap the panel along the score line with your knee, or lay it down over a piece of scrap lumber and snap it with gentle pressure.

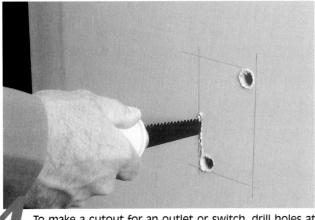

4 To make a cutout for an outlet or switch, drill holes at the opposite corners or each cutout, and cut the piece out using a utility saw or keyhole saw.

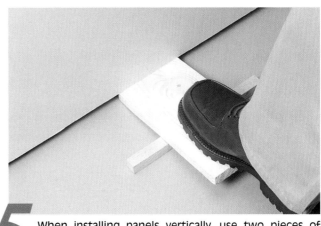

5 When installing panels vertically, use two pieces of wood (or a drywall panel lifter) to lever the bottom panel tight against the top one.

Nails or Screws?

For small jobs and patches, nails will suffice for drywall. Use 1⅝-inch ring-shank drywall nails for ½-inch drywall, and 1⅞-inch nails for ⅝-inch drywall. If you are doing an entire room, though, consider using drywall screws. Use galvanized screws that are at least 1 inch longer than the thickness of the drywall. You can drive them with a Phillips-head bit and your variable-speed electric drill. You can also fit your drill with a special drywalling clutch that releases the screws before they sink too far into the drywall. This makes for shallow indentations that are much easier to finish that the irregular dimples left by a hammer.

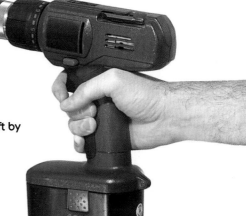

Finishing Drywall

You need to finish drywall intended as a base for paint or wallcovering with drywall tape and joint compound. Sand the compound smooth with the wall because even the smallest bumps show through paint. For a top-notch job, plan on applying joint compound in three stages, sanding the surface after each application. For drywall used as a tile under-layment, you just need one layer of joint compound.

Taping the Joints

Begin by applying compound to a joint with the 5- or 6-inch taping knife. Force it into the tapered drywall joints to fill them level with the wall. **(1)** At butt joints (where the nontapered ends of two panels join) fill the crack and create a slight hump. (This will be sanded nearly flat later on.)

Cut a length of drywall tape and, beginning at the top, place it over the compound-filled joint. Spread a thin layer (⅛ inch thick) of joint compound over the tape. **(2)** (If you use fiberglass mesh tape, apply the tape over the joint before you apply the first coat of compound—it is self-adhesive.) Go back over the joint with the drywall knife to scrape away any excess compound. **(3)**

Corners. If you are using paper tape, start by filling both sides of the inside corner joints. Fold a length of paper tape along its crease, and place it over the joint. To finish, spread a thin layer of compound over the tape. If you are using mesh tape, apply it first, and then fill the joint. Remove the excess compound. **(4)** If you have any outside corners, use tin snips to cut a length of metal corner bead to the wall height. Angle the cut ends inward a little to ensure a better fit. Nail the bead to the wall with drywall nails. Fill the edges with joint compound, using the bead to guide your knife. **(5)**

Finishing. Lastly, fill all nail or screw holes and dimples with joint compound. **(6)** After 24 hours, or when the compound is completely dry, sand smooth all joints and dimples. Fix a sheet of 100-grit sandpaper into your pole sander, if you have one. **(7)** If you are sanding by hand, use a sheet of sandpaper folded around a sanding block. Use a wide (10 or 12 inch) drywall knife to apply a second coat of compound to the joints and dimples. **(8)** Sand again, and repeat as necessary until you have a completely smooth surface.

Finishing drywall

Difficulty Level:

Tools & Materials: Small (5" or 6") & large (10" or 12") drywall taping knives ❖ Drywall tape (paper or fiberglass) ❖ Joint compound ❖ Sandpaper & sanding block ❖ Sanding pole (for ceilings) ❖ Corner bead (for outside corners) ❖ Hammer and drywall nails (for corner bead) ❖ Dust mask & safety goggles

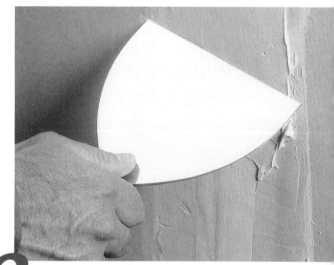

3 Working from the top down, scrape away any excess jo compound. When it dries, sand away the excess, and rep in a wider layer. (See Step 8.)

6 Use a 5- or 6-in. knife to fill all dimples around nails a screws and any other minor dents with a thin layer of jo compound.

1 Using a 5- or 6-in. drywall taping knife, fill the joint between the panel with compound. The thickness of the layer should be about ⅛ in.

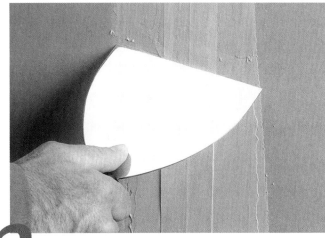

2 Embed paper drywall tape into the joint using the knife. (If you're using fiberglass tape, stick the tape over the joint before the joint compound.)

4 To finish inside corners, fold the paper tape along the prescored line, and press it into joint compound along both sides of the corner.

5 Outside corners are finished with metal or plastic corner bead. Nail it over the corner; then fill it with joint compound, using the bead as a guide.

7 Sand each layer of joint compound until it is nearly flat. A pole sander makes sanding ceilings and high walls much easier.

8 Taped joints are finished in three successive layers, feathered out at the edges. Use a 10- or 12-in. taping knife for the final layer.

9 *Remodeling Walls & Ceilings*

Estimating Quantities for Drywall

Quality drywalling requires accurate estimates of material quantities. Nothing breaks your stride like having to run out to the store for materials once you've started a job. Here are some tips on how to estimate materials.

○ **Joint Compound:** You'll need roughly a gallon for every 100 square feet of drywall.

○ **Joint Tape:** To finish 500 square feet of drywall, figure on using 400 feet of tape.

○ **Nails/Screws:** This figure can vary depending on stud spacing (walls framed 16 inches on center require more fasteners than those framed at 24 inches) and on your nail or screw schedule (panels attached with adhesive require fewer fasteners). Figure on one fastener for every square foot of drywall on your job. For example, an 18x18-foot ceiling (324 square feet) will require about 320 screws or nails. Because 1 pound of 1-inch drywall screws contains about 320 screws, you'll need a pound of screws for every 320 square feet of drywall.

○ **Drywall Panels:** Estimating how much drywall you'll need to cover a room is a matter of square footage. Calculate the wall surface of the room, and divide that figure by the square footage of the panels you intend to use. For instance, a 4x8-foot panel measures 32 square feet. If you have a 1,000-square-foot room, you'll need just over 31 panels. Because they come in units of two, order 32 panels.

○ **When estimating square footage,** don't subtract the door or window areas (except for bay windows or unusually large doors), because you'll need extra for mistakes.

Cement-Based Backer Board

Cement-based board is a better backing for ceramic tile than drywall in wet areas. Installation is more difficult, however, because of the greater weight and difficult cutting. This type of backer board is the same thickness as ½-inch-thick drywall, so you won't have to adjust the wall framing where the drywall leaves off and the backer board begins.

Cutting the Panels

Measure each panel so that its edge lands dead center over a stud. Mark the cut line. Using a straightedge as a guide, score a groove along the line using a utility knife or backer-board cutter. Insert a length of scrap wood under the groove, and press down over the panel to snap it in two. *(1)*

Lift up the panel and stand it on end, with the backside facing you, and cut through the mesh. *(2)* Measure the center of any holes for projecting pipes, and mark them on the panel. Start the hole by tapping a dent at the center point with an awl or center punch. Then drill through the dent with a carbide-tipped hole saw. *(3)*

Make the holes slightly bigger than necessary to make installation easier (the edges of the holes will be hidden from view by an escutcheon). Start the drill at slow speed, and gradually accelerate to prevent the bit from grabbing. If you don't have a hole saw large enough, make a starter hole with a small-diameter masonry bit, and use a saber saw to cut out the hole. Use this method for larger irregular cuts as well, but be prepared to go through several blades.

Installing the Panels

Unlike drywall, cement-based backer board is rigid; if you install it over uneven framing, you risk cracks. Use a straightedge vertically on each stud to check for any bows. Then run the straightedge across the studs in several places. Replace any deformed studs, or shim them out with wood shims.

Put the pieces of cement-based backer board into position, and screw them to the studs with cement-board screws set ½ inch in from the edges. Space the screws 4 inches apart around the edges and 12 inches apart along the studs in the center. *(4)* Cover each panel and corner joint with fiberglass mesh tape. Simply cut and press; the tape's adhesive backing holds it to the cement board. *(5)*

Putting up backer board

Difficulty Level:

Tools & Materials: Cement-based backer board ❖ 1½" galvanized cement-board screws ❖ Measuring tape ❖ T-square ❖ Utility knife or cement-board cutter ❖ Power drill with screwdriver bit & carbide-tipped hole saws ❖ Masonry drill bit & saber saw (optional) ❖ Fiberglass mesh tape ❖ Thinset adhesive

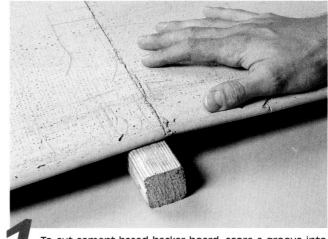

1 To cut cement-based backer board, score a groove into the cut line, using a T-square as a guide. Place the panel on a piece of scrap lumber, and snap the cut.

2 Stand the panel on edge and, using a utility knife or cement-board cutter, cut through the fiberglass mesh at the back to separate the pieces.

3 To make circular holes in the panel—such as for protruding pipes—use a power drill fitted with a carbide-tipped hole saw.

4 Screw the cement backer board to the framing with 1½-in. cement-board screws—every 4 in. around the edges and every 12 in. in the field.

5 Cover all edge and corner joints with fiberglass drywall tape. You do not need to use drywall joint compound, as the seams will be covered.

Installing Windows

CHAPTER 10

You probably know what's wrong with your existing bathroom windows, but when you finally get around to figuring out what to do about that leaky double-hung window above the bathtub, some difficult questions will arise. Should you trash the old window and replace it with a better window of the same type and size? Should you replace it with a different type of window? Would a new window in another location be better?

These days you can get inexpensive custom-made replacement windows with double glazing that drastically improves the unit's insulating value. You could also opt for low-emissivity glass or even triple glazing if you live in an area with very cold winters.

Unless you live on an estate, your bathrooms windows are probably quite small compared with other windows in your house. For most people, a bay window in the bath would let in a lot of light, but attract a lot of unwanted attention. A more discreet way to bring the day into your bathroom would be a skylight or roof window. If your bathroom is on an outside wall and there's nothing above it but empty attic, it's a difficult but not impossible homeowner project.

Improving Old Windows

After years of use and layer upon layer of paint, your windows may not be cracked, but they won't work as they did when they were new. In older homes, single-pane glass and worn jambs aren't doing much to keep the heat in during winter, and that old paint can make windows nearly impossible to open and close. You could spend hours scraping the windows down to bare wood and wind up with the same old energy-inefficient model. Replacing them makes better use of your time and money.

Choices for Improving Windows

You have three basic choices—sash kits, replacement windows that fit into existing frames, or entirely new windows that have their own frames and casing. With sash kits, you get new standard-sized sash—the window glass and the frame around it—plus new jamb liners (the tracks that hold the sash in place).

Sash are usually wood or vinyl. Your existing window frame, casing, and trim all stay in place, and all installation work is done from the inside. (For installation, see "Replacing the Sash," at right.)

Replacement windows are energy-efficient units custom-made to fit into an existing window frame. These windows have less glass area than the old ones, but if cost is a major consideration, vinyl replacement windows are the way to go. (For installation, see pages 106 to 107, "New Windows.")

New windows give you a wider range of options—larger sizes and different shapes—but the installation involves more work because you have to rip out the old window entirely. If the new one is only a little larger, you may be able to take advantage of extra space in the rough frame formerly occupied by the sash weights. For larger windows, it means cutting a bigger opening and adding new framing. (See page 103, "Enlarging a Rough Opening.")

Replacing Broken Panes

If you don't want to replace an entire window or even the sash—say you have an older house with unusual windows you wish to keep—the best thing to do is to take them apart for a thorough cleaning and repainting. Cracked panes are easily replaced.

The first step is to remove the old putty that holds the panes in place. The old putty may pop off with a putty knife, or you may need to scrape it away slowly bit by bit until the glass is free. *(1)* At this point, you should scrape away the old paint and reprime and paint the sash, if you wish. If you're not repainting, prime the area that will receive new putty to protect the wood. *(2)* Place a roll of fresh glazing compound in the sash. *(3)* Secure the glass into the sash with glazier's points. *(4)* Finally, spread an exterior layer of compound over the joint. *(5)*

Replacing the Sash

Visit your home center, window supplier, or building-products store to check out the various types of replacement sash available. Some, such as the one described below, require a precise fit into the existing frame. Others, such as all-vinyl (PVC) units, come with their own frames, which can be adjusted to fit into misaligned existing frames.

Here's how to replace an existing double-hung sash with new wood replacement-sash units that ride in vinyl guides (called jamb liners) instead of being suspended from ropes or chains concealed in the frame. Unlike the old window, this type of window not only slides up and down, but each sash tilts inward on a pivot for easier cleaning.

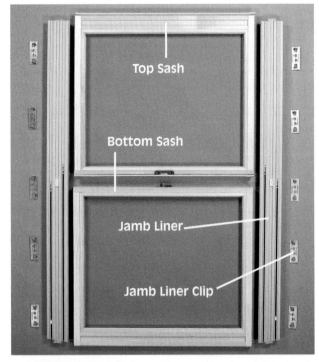

A replacement-window kit usually includes jamb liner clips (to attach the liners to the frame), vinyl jamb liners, and preglazed top and bottom sash.

Replacing glass panes

Difficulty Level:

Tools & Materials: Replacement panes ❖ Putty knife ❖ Paintbrush ❖ Primer ❖ Glass cutter ❖ Glazing compound ❖ Glazier's points ❖ Safety glasses & work gloves

1 On an old window, the exterior putty may pop off the glass and frame easily when you scrape it with a putty knife.

2 Prime raw wood where new glazing compound will rest. This keeps moisture from seeping into the wood and weakening the bond.

3 Roll out a rope of fresh glazing compound to back up the glass, set it against the sash, and press it in place with your fingers.

4 Lay the glass pane in place. To secure the glass, set small metal holders called glazier's points. Use a putty knife to force the points into the sash.

5 The exterior layer of glazing compound covers the points. Spread this layer with a putty knife, and use the edge of the knife to trim any excess.

Measuring the Sash

Measure the window's width (across the frame rather than the distance between stops). Take one measurement across the top and one across the bottom. If they differ by more than ⅛ inch, you will need a replacement kit that can accommodate variations in frame width. Next, measure the height from where the sash abuts the top frame to where it abuts the top of the sill. Use the width and height to order your replacement-sash unit. Measure for all sash you will replace—even if they look to be the same size, they may vary a bit, especially in older homes where windows were built on-site.

Removing the Stops & Sash

If you're lucky, the stops were secured with screws. However, you'll often find the stops painted and attached with small nails. Separate the paint between the sash stops and adjacent trim by scoring the joint with a utility knife. Pry off the stops from the sides and top of the sash. *(1)* Remove the bottom sash from the frame, and disconnect the weight cords from the sash. Lower the weights before letting go of the cords; then pry off the parting stop. Finally, take out the top sash, disconnecting the cords in the same manner. *(2)* Open the sash-weight cover in the lower part of one of the jambs. Pull out and discard the old ropes and weights, and then replace the cover. Next, remove the pulleys, and fill the voids with loose-fill insulation. *(3)*

Installing & Leveling

Measure and cut the jamb liners (guides) to the proper height using a hacksaw; then position them in place and attach them to the frame. *(4)* This is usually done with two preset nails at the top and bottom. Insert the top sash into the jamb liners, holding the sash at an angle. *(5)* Make sure the clutch pivot (the projecting hardware at the side of the sash) is above the clutch in the outside track on both sides. *(5–inset)* Turn the top sash to a horizontal position and tilt it up to vertical, pressing in the liners while pushing the sash to the outside track, one side at time. Slide the sash down to engage the clutches; then slide it back up. *(6)* Install the bottom sash using the same methods as explained in Steps 5 and 6, using the inside tracks of the jamb liners instead. *(7)* Replace the original stops, or install new ones if you cannot salvage the original ones. *(8)*

Installing new sash in an old frame

Difficulty Level:

Tools & Materials: Wood chisel or pry bar ❖ Utility knife ❖ Hacksaw ❖ Sash-replacement kit ❖ 8d finishing nails ❖ Loose-fill insulation (vermiculite) ❖ Cup and cardboard guide for insulation

3 Remove the sash weights, cords, and pulleys. Enlarge the pulley opening with a drill, if necessary, and pour loose-fill insulation inside the cavities at each side of the window.

6 Level the sash and tilt it vertical, pressing in the liners while pushing the sash to the outside track one side at a time. Slide the sash down to engage the clutches; then slide it back up.

1 Run a utility knife down the length of the sash stops to break the paint seal. Then pry the inner stops off with a pry bar or wood chisel.

2 Remove the bottom sash, and disconnect the cords from the sash weight. Pry off the parting stop (the vertical guide piece between the upper and lower sash).

4 Cut new jamb liners to the required length using a hacksaw or power miter saw. Then secure them to the sides of the opening.

5 Place the top sash into the jamb liners at an angle. Engage the clutch pivot above the clutch in the outermost track on both liners. (See inset.)

7 Insert the bottom sash the same way as the top sash, but use the inside tracks of the jamb liners instead. When the clutch engages, slide it down.

8 Replace the original stops. If they were damaged during removal, install new ones. They are available premilled at any lumberyard or home center.

Removing an old window

Difficulty Level:

Tools & Materials: Pry bar ❖ Wood chisel ❖ Hammer ❖ Wood shims (as needed) ❖ Reciprocating saw with metal-cutting blade ❖ Lumber (for packing out the rough opening, as needed) ❖ Work gloves & safety goggles

1 To remove an old single-glazed window for replacement, use a pry bar, hammer, and chisel to pry loose the surrounding trim.

2 Use the same techniques inside to remove interior trim. If you want to reuse it, pry gradually because the trim may be brittle.

3 To release the window, use a reciprocating saw to cut through the nails that extend from the frame into the house-wall studs.

4 Once you cut the nails, you can pry out the window. First you may need to release shims at the sides of the frame.

5 Pack-out the old opening as required, using 2x4s or other lumber to make a rough opening to match the new window.

Replacing Whole Frames

Installing a complete unit, including the sash and frame, begins with removing the old unit—trim, sash, and frame. You may then need to alter the framing of the rough opening to accommodate the new unit's size or shape. Here's how to install a new window in a wood-framed wall, which is clad with siding. Many of the same steps also apply to brick-veneer walls, but to avoid having to change the brick, choose a replacement window of the same size as the old one. Begin the job by removing the old sash as described in Steps 1 and 2 on page 102.

Remove the Old Window

Remove the old window unit entirely. First pry off the inside and outside trim and the stool using a pry bar, hammer, and chisel. *(1–2)* If you want to salvage the inside trim, pry each piece off bit by bit, inserting shims as you go. Insert blocks between the prying tool and the wall to prevent damage to the plaster or drywall. Cut through the nails that hold the window in place using a recip-rocating saw. *(3)* After removing the trim and any nails holding the window frame to the house framing, pull out the frame. *(4–5)*

Enlarging a Rough Opening

If you have to enlarge the opening to fit the new window unit, be sure you don't cut through the studs until you know you will not be damaging a bearing wall, or you have a plan for replacing the necessary supports. Get the opinion of a builder or architect to determine whether the wall is a bear-ing wall and if so, how to reframe the header above the window to maintain the wall's integrity.

In general, you can probably widen an exterior window opening to as much as 96 inches without temporary shoring in the following cases:

• The window is below a floor, rather than a roof. (The rim joist can likely carry the load of the floor joists.)

• The window is under a roof in the gable end.

If the window sits below the eave end of a roof, it carries the weight of the roof and ceiling. You must support these loads with temporary shoring while you replace the header above the window opening with a longer one.

Cutting the New Opening

After determining the required rough-opening size from the instructions or catalog description of your new window, mark the rough opening dimensions on the outside of the house. Use a cir-cular saw to cut through the siding and sheathing, and then remove them. (See the photo on page 104.) This will allow you to see what will have to be done to rework the framing for the new win-dow. Remove the wall surface from the studs above and below the existing window and at the side where it will be widened. (See page 85, "Gut-ting a Wall or Ceiling.")

Making a New Header

If you're putting in a larger window, you'll need to install a new header—the built-up framing member that spans the top of the rough open-ing. The header would be strong enough if you made it simply by doubling two pieces of two-by lumber of the appropriate width. However, because two-by lumber is actually 1½ inches thick, a doubled two-by would be only 3 inches thick. Because 2x4 studs are actually 3½ inches wide, you need another half-inch of thickness so that the header will be flush with the inside and outside of the stud wall.

The answer is a piece of ½-inch ply-wood cut to the width and height of the header and sandwiched between the two-bys, as shown in the photo. Assemble the header with 12d nails.

½" Plywood Spacer

Two-by Lumber
(Width per Local Code)

12d Nail

Providing Temporary Support

Place a 2×10 plank on the floor about 24 inches from the wall. The plank should be at least 24 inches longer than the new window opening. Place one adjustable jack post at each end of the plank to align with the sides of the window opening. Adjust the jack posts to the approximate height needed by setting the pins in the correct holes. Then place a second 2×10 plank above the jacks, under the ceiling. Screw the threaded rod at the top of each jack upward until the 2×10 is tight to the ceiling, but do not tighten beyond this point.

Plan the Reframing

Using the rough-opening dimensions specified with your replacement window, first determine the size of the new header. Use the size recommended by your builder or architect, or use the following rule of thumb to size the header:

Opening Width	Header Size
5 feet	doubled 2×6
5 to 7 feet	doubled 2×8
7 to 8 feet	doubled 2×10
8 to 9 feet	doubled 2×12

To cut an opening in the outside wall, first mark the dimensions on the siding. Then cut through the siding and the sheathing with a circular saw. Tack on a guide board to keep the saw level.

Make a sketch of the framing, showing the location of the new header and supporting members. Set the bottom of the new header at a height to match the old one. Cut through the studs at the side and bottom of the old window opening as required for the new opening. Remove the cut studs and existing header.

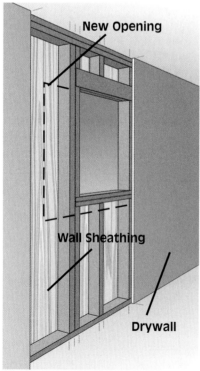

To enlarge a rough opening, first remove the interior wall surface that falls within the opening's area.

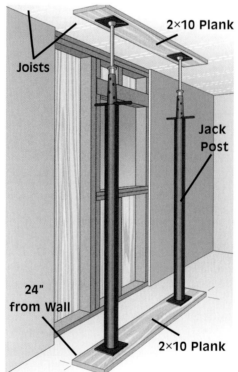

Place an adjustable jack post at each end of a 2x10. Top the jacks with another 2x10, and bring the jacks tight against the ceiling.

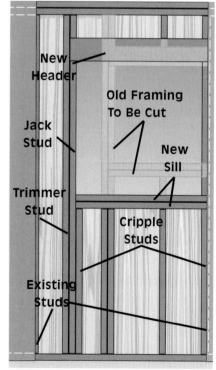

Cut and remove portions of the studs, and add in the new header and framing as required by local building codes.

Using the dimensions on your sketch, install the new framing, starting with an extra stud to support the new drywall, if needed. Then toenail in a full-length trimmer stud to the top and bottom plates with four 8d common nails.

Next, cut and install cripple studs below the windowsill; then cut and nail in a double sill plate across them. Install jack studs at the sides. Install the header above the jack studs and end-nail with 16d nails. If you can't end-nail (from the closed-in side), use L-shaped framing hardware to attach the sill to the studs. Finally, toenail additional cripple studs above the header and below the sill.

Making an Opening Smaller

Installing a smaller window calls for plugging the excess opening with a new wall. It's an approach you'll probably want to avoid if possible because it will require you to match existing house siding. The instructions below assume the top of the window will remain at the same height. In general, follow these steps after removing the old window.

Cut new studs as required to close in the side (or sides) of the opening. Toenail the new studs into the existing header and sill with 10d common nails. Then cut and install trimmer studs that will end at the top of the windowsill. Next install a double sill. Finally, add cripple studs below the sill. Use a framing square to make sure your new framing is true and plumb.

Cut pieces of plywood to cover all new framing. Match the thickness of the house's original sheathing. Nail it to the framing with 8d galvanized nails spaced 8 inches apart. Next, staple house wrap (plastic sheeting that keeps out the elements) or building paper to the sheathing. Tuck the edges under the uncut siding, if possible.

New Jack Stud

New Double Sill

New Cripple Studs

Plywood Sheathing

House Wrap or Building Paper

To make a rough opening smaller, cut new studs to fill the opening; then nail them to the existing header and sill. Add new double sill and supporting members as indicated.

Nail plywood sheathing over the new framing. Then staple house wrap or building paper to the sheathing, tucking the edges under the uncut siding if possible.

New Windows

Insert a new window unit into the opening from the outside. Have a helper hold the window against the outside wall. (The nailing flange or brickmold will keep it from falling through the opening.) *(1–2)* Meanwhile, go inside to shim and level the unit. Place wood shims under the sill and sides to level the window. Use a spirit level to check your work.

When the window is where you want it, drive ⅞-inch galvanized roofing nails through the predrilled holes in the window's nailing flange and into the sheathing; space the nails about 6 inches apart. *(3)* If the unit has a wood brickmold instead of a nailing flange, use 8d galvanized casing nails.

Installing the Trim

If your window design includes exterior window casing, it is often easier to install the drip cap before the head casing (especially when siding is already in place). Slip the drip cap under the siding so that the flange of the cap extends under the siding and the edge protrudes out over the window frame. The head casing should hold the drip cap snugly in place so that you will not need to nail the drip cap.

Reinstall exterior trim—or install new trim, if

Installing a new window & frame

Difficulty Level:

Tools & Materials: New frame & sash ❖ Interior & exterior window casing ❖ Spirit level ❖ Shims ❖ Hammer ❖ ⅞" galvanized roofing nails and 8d casing nails ❖ Exterior-grade caulk & caulking gun ❖ Fiberglass or foam-spray insulation ❖ 6-mil polyethylene vapor barrier ❖ Work gloves

1 Some new windows have the jambs as a separate unit. In this case, install this frame first, and nail it into the rough opening framing with 8d finishing nails.

4 Replace the exterior casing, nailing it in place with 8d casing nails. If needed, cut pieces of siding to match the existing material and nail it on with siding nails.

5 To seal the new window completely, run a bead of exterior-grade caulk between the siding and window or between the siding and the trim.

necessary. Use galvanized casing nails long enough to extend at least 1 inch into the house framing. *(4)* If you are installing a smaller window than the original, you may also need to replace a portion of the siding.

Insulating a New Window

Run a bead of exterior-grade caulk between the siding and the window (or siding and trim). *(5)* Exterior-grade siliconized acrylic latex caulk with a 15- or 20-year warranty is the easiest to apply, because you can clean it up with water. Silicone and polyurethane caulks also stay flexible but are messier to work with.

Stuff fiberglass insulation into the gap between the window and framing (or fill it with low-expanding foam insulation from a pressure can). *(6–7)* Patch the vapor barrier (if one exists) with 6-mil polyethylene sheet. Seal the polyethylene to the existing vapor barrier with polyurethane caulk. Then apply a bead of caulking around the inside edge of the window, and staple the polyethylene patch into the bead.

Nail casing around the inside of the window after the drywall is in place. Prime and paint the trim and any new siding on the outside. Paint all raw or primed wood parts; however, do not paint aluminum or vinyl parts.

2 Put in new window from the exterior—it's best to have a helper inside holding the window against the wall. Tap in a few temporary nails for security.

3 Once the window is plumbed and leveled, fasten it by nailing on all sides through the perforated flange with 7/8-in. roofing nails.

6 Insulate the gap between the window frame and the rough framing with fiberglass insulation. Then patch the vapor barrier with a 6-mil poly sheet.

7 You can also seal the gap with foam insulation sprayed from a can. After sealing, reinstall the interior trim or the base for ceramic tile.

Roof Windows & Skylights

Installing a roof window or skylight is possible for some do-it-yourselfers, but before deciding to go ahead, be sure you are up to the task.

You'll need to do some of the work inside a cramped attic and part of it crawling around on the roof. If you build a light shaft between the roof and ceiling, you're in for measuring and cutting framing and finishing materials that have tricky angles.

When you have selected your skylight or roof window, read and follow the manufacturer's instructions. The steps below cover some aspects of installation not always included in the instructions.

Planning the Location

First, use a keyhole saw or a saber saw to cut out a piece of the ceiling drywall about 2 feet square, somewhere near the center of where you want the shaft opening to be. Standing on a stepladder and armed with a flashlight, look through the test hole, and inspect the roof and ceiling framing to determine the final location for the opening. Although where you want the sunlight to fall is an important factor, you should also locate the ceiling opening to minimize rework of the framing.

Most skylights and roof windows are designed to fit between two rafters (or three rafters with the middle one cut out). You will need to orient the ceiling opening the same as the roof opening, ideally with joists for its sides. You can make the ceiling opening somewhat larger than the roof opening by adding a light shaft with angled walls. (The end of the skylight nearest the eaves is usually directly underneath the skylight, and the end nearest the roof's ridge is angled wider to allow in more light.)

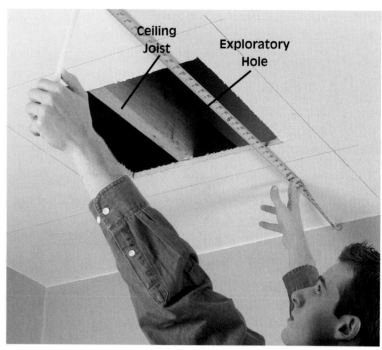

The ceiling opening for a skylight can be any size—the light shaft can be flared outward from the roof opening to flood a room with light. It will be easier to frame, however, if it has ceiling joists on two of its sides.

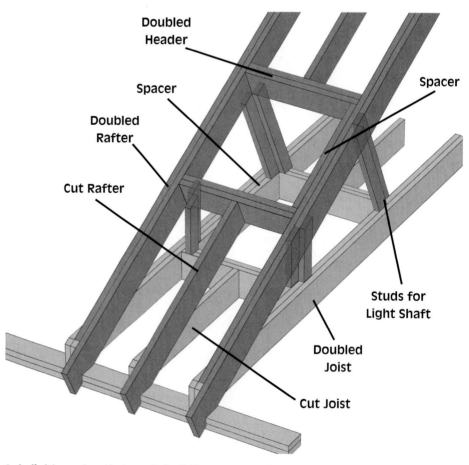

A skylight requires that you to build two new rough openings—one in your roof rafters and one in your ceiling joists—as well as a light shaft, which will run through the attic.

Cutting the Ceiling Opening

When you have decided where the skylight will go, remove the insulation at that spot in the attic, and mark the final opening of the bottom of your light shaft on the ceiling drywall. Cut along the outline with a keyhole saw or saber saw, and remove the ceiling drywall or plaster. (See the photo at left.) If there is a joist in the middle of the opening, don't cut it until you're ready to frame the new opening.

Marking the Roof Opening

Hang a plumb bob from the underside of the roof the corners of the ceiling opening that face the eaves, and mark the positions. *(1)* Use these marks to measure the rough opening for the skylight (provided by the manufacturer). Drive a pilot nail through the roof sheathing at each corner of the opening. If you'll be cutting out a rafter for the roof opening, you'll need to reinforce the roof framing before you cut. Reinforce the rafters at the top and bottom of the openings with 2×4s nailed across them. *(2)* Then, cut through the roof to make the new opening as described on page 111, "Cutting a Roof Opening," and remove the shingles and sheathing.

With a sliding T-bevel, mark where you'll install the new headers for the rough opening—they should be the same dimension lumber as the rafter you're removing. *(3)*

Framing & installing a skylight

Difficulty Level:

Tools & Materials: Skylight kit ❖ Keyhole saw ❖ Plumb bob ❖ Measuring tape ❖ Framing square ❖ Hammer ❖ Utility knife ❖ Circular saw or saber saw with carbide-tipped blade ❖ Reciprocating saw ❖ 12d and 16d nails ❖ Two-by lumber for framed opening ❖ Sliding T-bevel ❖ Power drill ❖ 6-mil polyethylene vapor barrier ❖ Drywall & drywalling tools ❖ Roofing compound ❖ Aluminum step flashing ❖ ⅞" roofing nails

1 Transfer the lower corners of the ceiling opening to the underside of the roof sheathing by holding a plumb bob over each corner.

2 Before cutting through the roof, reinforce the rafters with 2x4s nailed across the framing above and below the planned roof opening.

3 After you strip off the shingles and peel back the felt paper from the roof, use a circular saw to cut away the roof sheathing, making sure not to cut into the rafters.

Continued on next page

Framing & installing a skylight, cont'd

4 Cut the center rafter, and install new headers of the same dimension in order to pick up the roof load of the missing rafter.

5 Mount the skylight in the opening according to the instructions. (Some skylights need a curb, or a supporting frame of 2x4s, to be raised off the roof.)

6 Install aluminum step flashing under each shingle as you replace them. Apply a bed of roofing compound over each layer before moving on the next course.

7 Frame the light shaft with 2x4s running between the rafters and the joists. Use a 2x4 to mark the framing locations on the ceiling joists.

8 The rough opening in the ceiling requires headers and doubled-up joists on the sides to make up for where ceiling joists have been removed.

9 Finish framing the light shaft by adding studs to support the interior finish. Then finish the inside of the light shaft with drywall as you insulate.

Framing the Opening

For a skylight that spans more than two rafters, cut out the rafter in the center of the opening using a reciprocating saw. *(4)* Then end-nail the headers in place with 12d nails.

Installing the Unit

Follow the manufacturer's instructions for installing the window. *(5)* For some skylights you'll need to build a curb, a frame made from 2×4s placed on edge, then installed on top of the roof opening. This curb raises the skylight a few inches above the surface of the roof. Secure the skylight in only one place until you have made sure that the window is properly aligned. If it is not straight, you'll likely notice it when you trim out the inside.

Replace the shingles, installing aluminum step flashing as you go. *(6)* Aluminum step flashing comes in packages of precut pieces. Interweave one flashing piece to overlap and underlap each successive shingle, as shown. Apply roofing compound under each course of flashing and shingles.

Building the Light Shaft

Use a 2×4 to locate the opening on the ceiling joists, and at the same time mark the angle cuts on the bottom of the 2×4. *(7)* Cut the angles accurately: a circular saw or power miter saw makes this easier. Follow the same steps for building the rough opening in the ceiling as for the roof. If you remove joists, provide double joists at the sides to compensate. Install double header joists across the opening at both ends. Use two pieces of lumber of the same width as the ceiling framing. *(8)*

Next, install trimmer joists to close in the sides of the hole to the final dimensions of your ceiling opening; use 12d nails. To provide a better connection than toenailing, you can use L-shaped framing anchors. (Use 4-inch anchors for 2×4s, 6-inch anchors for 2×6s, and so on.)

Frame the sides of the shaft with 2×4s. Insulate between the framing, and staple a sheet of 6-mil polyethylene over the inside face of the studs for a vapor barrier. Use polyurethane caulk to seal the sheet to the existing ceiling barrier (or the back side of the ceiling drywall if there is no barrier). Finally, apply drywall as described in "Installing Drywall," pages 90–91. *(9)* Apply wood trim, if necessary, at the joint between the roof window and drywall.

Cutting a Roof Opening

If you've left the nails that you drove in at the corners of the roof opening, that makes it easier to snap a chalk line on the shingles to mark the opening. Cut asphalt shingles along this line using a utility knife to bare the roof sheathing below. Drill a test hole to gauge the depth of your roof sheathing; you want to set your circular saw blade at that depth so that you don't damage the rafters underneath.

Use the circular saw to cut the opening through the roof sheathing. If you need to cut through wood shingles, place a board below the saw. By doing this, you can ease the saw forward without bumping into the bottom of the shingles. When cutting through the roof sheathing, keep in mind that you will probably hit nails, so use a carbide-tipped blade.

Glass Block Walls

Installing glass block is simple enough for most DIYers, but it's also expensive. You must reinforce the subfloor to take the weight of an 8-foot-high masonry wall. This will mean doubling or tripling the joists in the vicinity of the new block wall. To be on the safe side, get the opinion of a builder or structural engineer. When you install glass block next to a wood-framed wall, you'll need to place the new construction near an existing stud or add a new stud inside the existing wall.

Setting the Blocks

Use white-colored mortar mix specifically made for glass block. Use as little water as possible to make a stiff mix. You can tell when you have it right if you can make a ball out of the mortar. *(1)*

Preparation. Joint anchors and expansion strips are used where the block meets walls and ceilings. If you are using 6-inch block, you'll need an anchor every third block; for 8-inch block, every other block. The anchors are 24 inches long. Cut each piece into two 12-inch anchors, and bend them so there is a 4-inch leg. Nail the leg along the walls and ceiling, positioned as needed for the block. Cut the expansion strip to a width that will fit between the ridges on the block. Staple the strip along the walls and the ceiling. When you come to a joint anchor, cut the strip to cover the 4-inch leg, then continue the strip along the wall or ceiling. Next, spread a bed of mortar ½ inch thick on the curb or floor. *(2)*

Making a glass block wall

Difficulty Level:

Tools & Materials: Lumber for sill curb forms, blocking, and sistering joists ❖ 10d nails ❖ Concrete mix for curb (optional) ❖ Glass block ❖ Glass block mortar mix ❖ Masonry trowel ❖ Plastic tub ❖ Foam expansion strips ❖ Metal wall anchors ❖ ¼" plastic joint spacers ❖ Wire joint reinforcement ❖ Jointing tool ❖ Silicone caulk & caulking gun ❖ Rubber gloves

1 Mix prepared glass-block mortar mix in a plastic tub or wheelbarrow, using as little water as possible. Make a mixture stiff enough to form a "baseball."

4 Complete the first course, mortaring a vertical edge of each block before setting that edge against the last block set. Add joint spacers as you go.

5 At the start of the second course, slip a block under the wall anchor, spread mortar atop the entire course, and then embed wire reinforcement in the mortar.

The First Course. Glass blocks are installed with spacers between them. Spacers are cross-shaped and are placed where four blocks come together; you can also cut them into an L for corners and a T where blocks meet walls, floors, and ceilings. For the first course, cut two L's for the corners and L's for between each block. Press the first block firmly in place with its L-shaped spacer against the expansion strip. Insert T's below and above the block. *(3)*

Put a ½-inch-thick layer of mortar on one edge of the second block, and place it next to the first block. Install spacers and complete the first course. *(4)* Check this course periodically with a spirit level to be sure it is level and plumb. When the first course is done, put a layer of mortar on top of it, and continue the wall.

Finishing the Wall. When you come to a course with wall anchors, slip the end blocks under the long arm of the anchor. Lay down mortar on top of the entire course. Then gently embed wire reinforcing in the mortar. *(5)* Because it meets an expansion strip, the top course gets no mortar on top. Apply mortar to one vertical edge of each block and install it with L and T spacers, as shown. *(6)*

When the mortar has set for about an hour, use a plastic jointing tool to smooth the joints into a concave profile. *(7)* Caulk the joint between the glass block wall and the original wall and top plate or ceiling with silicone caulk. Tool the joint to a smooth, concave shape with your finger. Then buff the dried mortar film with an old towel.

2 Install joint anchors as appropriate for the block you are using. Staple an expansion strip to the existing wall; then spread mortar ½ in. thick on the curb (or floor).

3 Use full spacers and spacers cut into L and T shapes to create the proper spaces for joints between blocks. The notch on the spacers fits into the block's seam.

6 Put mortar on one vertical edge of each new block and set it against the preceding block with T- and L-shaped spacers.

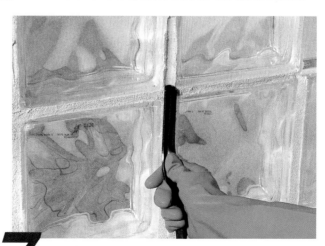

7 Smooth the mortar joints using a plastic jointing tool. When the mortar dries, seal the joints between blocks and walls or ceilings with caulking.

Working with Plumbing

CHAPTER 11

Bathroom plumbing improvements can be as simple as replacing an old leaky faucet or as complicated as rerouting pipe and installing a new whirlpool. If you have ventured beyond fixing a leaky tap, you have an idea of what you can do and when you'll need to call in a plumber. If you are new to plumbing, you should get a good idea of what is required from the step-by-step instructions in this section.

Because regulations differ from place to place, you should check with the plumbing inspector before beginning any plumbing project to see how local codes could affect your plans. Code specifies the design of pipe systems and the acceptable materials for a particular application.

Local regulations determine who may do certain kinds of work and how the work will be inspected. Plumbing work is unforgiving; even minor mistakes can result in leaks, which will have to be repaired at a greater cost in the long run. It pays to know what you're doing. It's also important to understand the hazards involved in plumbing work and to take appropriate measures to protect yourself and your home.

Bathroom Plumbing Basics

Bathroom plumbing has to do three things:
- Deliver hot and cold water to the fixtures
- Remove waste to the sewer or septic system
- Vent the waste pipes to the outside

Here's what's required to achieve each of these goals.

Getting Water to the Fixtures

Every fixture except the toilet requires separate hot- and cold-water supply pipes. (The toilet requires only a cold-water supply pipe.) Locate a shutoff valve in a convenient place below the fixture. This way, you can make repairs without shutting down the water to the entire house. By shutting off the main valve, not only will every fixture be out of commission for hours, or even days, but you'll have to run back and forth between the master shutoff valve in the basement and the bathroom.

Hot- and cold-water pipes were previously made of galvanized steel joined with threaded connectors. Cutting and threading pipes was difficult, and required specialized tools. Little wonder this work remained firmly in the domain of plumbers. Today, do-it-yourselfers can install their own hot- and cold-water pipes, thanks to rigid and flexible copper pipe alternatives, which are far simpler to work with and more economical to install and rework when mistakes are made. Polybutylene (PB) and chlorinated polyvinyl chloride (CPVC) plastic are also used for supply pipes, but these materials are not as widely accepted by building inspectors as is copper.

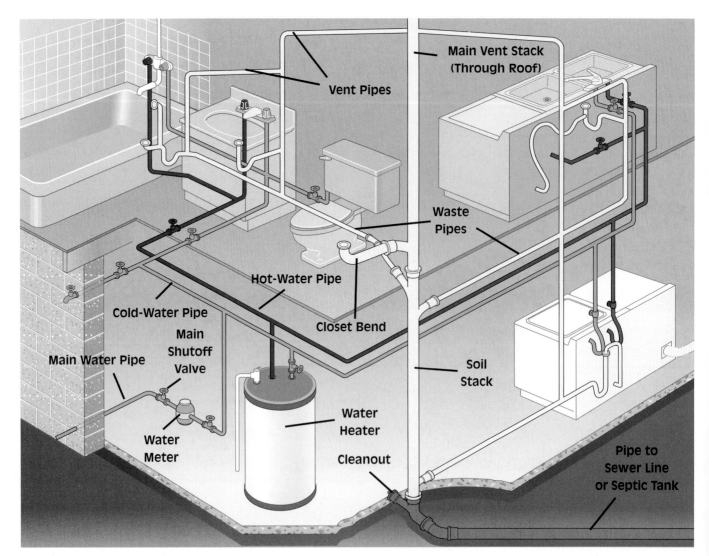

Here is a typical household plumbing system. Water arrives from the municipal system or a private well. The cold-water supply lines branch from this main line; hot-water lines are first routed through the water heater. All fixtures receiving water are also connected to drainpipes and vent pipes. All drain and vent lines converge on the soil stack, which extends through the roof.

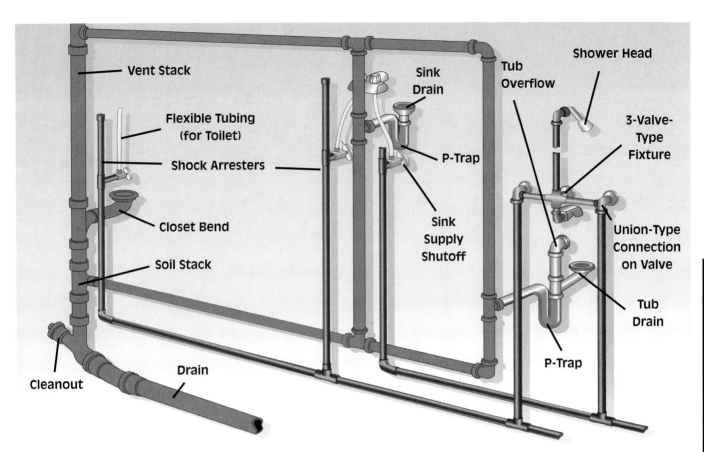

Above is a plumbing rough-in for a typical bathroom, with the toilet, sink, and bathtub along one wall. The sink faucets and shower head are shown for clarity; they are not included in the rough-in work.

Waste & Vent Pipes

The pipes that remove waste to the sewer and vent fixtures to the outside work together as a drain-waste-vent (DWV) system. Waste pipes carry off water, while vent pipes allow outside air into the system. The soil stack is a single large-diameter pipe that carries waste down to the sewer and vents air through the roof. Getting water to the fixtures requires pipe that is ½ or ¾ inch in diameter; home waste lines are 3 or 4 inches in diameter, depending on the number of fixtures served.

As with water-supply pipe, installing a DWV system was pretty much a plumber's realm in the past. Cutting heavy cast-iron sections and then uniting them by pouring melted lead into bell and spigot joints were beyond the capabilities of most homeowners. By contrast, plastic pipe can be installed by anyone with moderate skills and ability. What could be simpler than cutting pipes with a handsaw and joining them with solvent cement?

Waste Pipes. The waste lines in the DWV system consist of pipes that are sloped to drain to the sewer. Like branches of a tree, small-diameter pipes feed into a the soil stack, which usually sits in the wall just behind the toilet. Each of the branches contains a trap, a curved part near the fixture drain to trap water, preventing sewer gas from entering the room. To allow the trapped water to refill instead of being sucked into the sewer, a vent is located between the trap and the sewer.

Venting. In a simple arrangement with a sink, toilet, and tub on the same wall, the soil stack is simply extended through the roof to provide a vent. When plumbing fixtures are on more than one wall, set apart from each other, or more than a few feet away from the main vent, it is often more practical to provide a separate vent.

When planning to relocate fixtures or add new ones, try to use as much of the existing waste and vent pipes as possible. Snaking small-diameter water pipes through existing floors and walls is much easier than dealing with large DWV pipes. In this chapter, we'll begin with the simplest projects, which generally involve sinks, and then move on to more ambitious installations of toilets, bathtubs, showers, and whirlpool tubs.

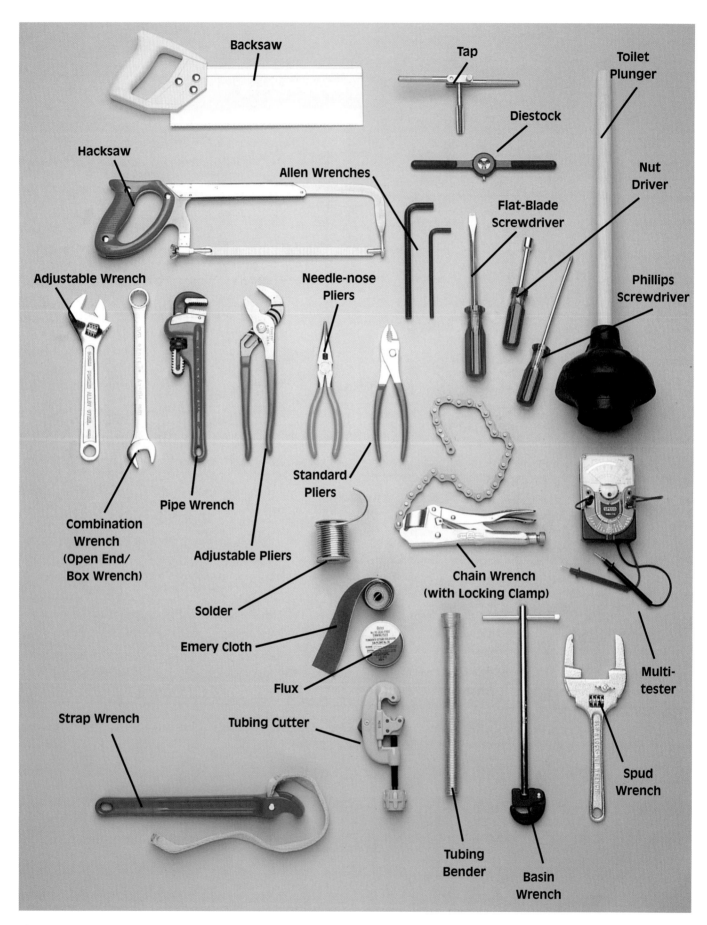

Backsaw

Tap

Toilet Plunger

Diestock

Hacksaw

Allen Wrenches

Flat-Blade Screwdriver

Nut Driver

Adjustable Wrench

Needle-nose Pliers

Phillips Screwdriver

Pipe Wrench

Standard Pliers

Combination Wrench (Open End/ Box Wrench)

Adjustable Pliers

Chain Wrench (with Locking Clamp)

Solder

Multi-tester

Emery Cloth

Flux

Strap Wrench

Tubing Cutter

Spud Wrench

Tubing Bender

Basin Wrench

The tools shown here will suffice for most of the plumbing tasks in this book.

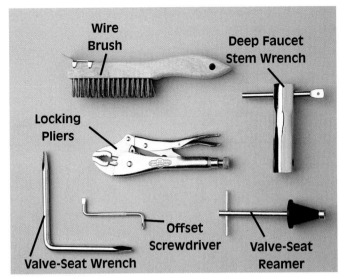

Wire Brush

Deep Faucet Stem Wrench

Locking Pliers

Offset Screwdriver

Valve-Seat Wrench

Valve-Seat Reamer

These less-often-used tools are very helpful for special tasks, such as tightening or loosening screws or nuts in hard-to-reach places.

Plumbing Tools

Most of the projects in this chapter will require basic plumbing tools, pictured at left. Tools used to cut and join copper, ABS, and CPVC plastic pipe are listed, but specialized tools that are used for cast-iron waste lines and galvanized steel pipes are not. Pictured above are more specialized tools that may come in handy for certain projects.

The Basic Kit

Every household should have these basic tools on hand: a toilet plunger for freeing clogs in toilets and sinks; a closet auger for clearing out more serious blocks in drains, waste pipes, and soil pipes; and a variety of wrenches for making simple repairs to fittings. More complex repair work and installation requires different, specialized tools—not just specific wrenches but valve-seat reamers, pipe cutters, and tube benders.

You should also include a round file and sandpaper in your basic tool kit. In place of a relatively expensive pipe reamer, you can use a file to remove burrs from the inner edge of freshly cut copper pipe. Use medium-grit sandpaper or emery cloth to clean the exterior surface of the end of copper pipes, which is important when soldering pipes together. You'll also need the propane torch, flux, and solder for that job. A Phillips and a flat-blade screwdriver for #8 and #6 screws are also important basic tools because machine screws in faucets and cutoff valves often need tightening or loosening during repairs.

Using a Propane Torch

If you're going to be working with metal pipe—whether copper, steel, or cast iron—you'll need to become familiar with the propane torch. Although it has the potential to be a dangerous tool, a few precautions and the proper safety gear will keep you safe from harm. Use a sparking tool to safely ignite the gas. Turn on a gentle supply of gas, and squeeze the sparker handle. Once you ignite the gas, increase the flow to enlarge the flame. It's wise to wear gloves when you handle heated pipes.

Before you try to heat up a pipe with a torch—to thaw a frozen section or to resolder a joint—first drain the line. You can't get copper hot enough to make solder flow when it is filled with water. Also, open a faucet just beyond the repair so that any steam that develops can escape. Be careful when using propane torches in tight spots where the flame may lick past the pipe and heat up building materials nearby. Use extra care working in framing cavities, particularly in older homes where the wood is very dry.

11 Working with Plumbing

Plastic Pipe

Lightweight plastic pipe ranges in diameter from 1½ to 6 inches. Most plastic DWV lines are installed with just a few simple tools. Making connections is easy and straightforward, but it requires a little practice to do with ease. After cutting the pipe with a handsaw, clean the ends to be joined, apply solvent cement, and join the pieces. Be sure to match the solvent cement to the type of plastic used in the pipe. You can even join a new section of plastic pipe to an existing cast-iron waste line with compression clamp fittings consisting of flexible gaskets and metal rings that screw-tighten.

Plastic waste pipes are made of ABS (black) or PVC (white) plastic. Check with the local plumbing inspector to find out which type is acceptable for your project.

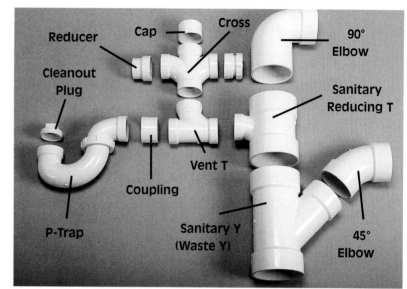

You'll need a number of different plumbing fittings—shapes that create bends, form branch lines, and connect different-sized pipe—to complete any rough-in.

Which Pipe?

Which type of pipe you can use for projects in this chapter depends on your local code. However, some typical uses are:

•PVC (polyvinyl chloride): drain and vent pipes, drain traps

•CPVC (chlorinated polyvinyl chloride): Hot- and cold-water supply pipes

•ABS (acrylonitrile butadiene styrene): drain and vent pipes, drain traps

•PB (polybutylene): Hot- and cold-water supply pipes

•Cast iron: Main supply and DWV pipes

•Galvanized steel: hot- and cold-water supply pipes; drainpipes

•Copper (rigid and flexible): Hot- and cold-water supply pipes

PVC

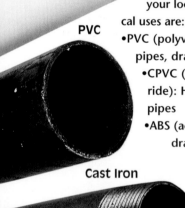

Cast Iron

Galvanized Steel

Rigid Copper

Working with Plastic Pipe

Measure the lengths required, allowing for the fittings. (Assume the pipe will fit all the way inside the sleeves of the fittings.) Unless you are cutting pipe already in place, put the lengths you're planning to cut in a miter box. Cut the pipe with a backsaw or hacksaw. *(1)* Use a utility knife or emery cloth (or both) to remove burrs from the cut ends and to dull the outer cut edge so that it will slide smoothly into the fitting.

After cutting the pipes, test-fit the parts that are to be joined. *(2)* If the new pipe is too long, simply trim to the correct size. If the pipe is too short to fit completely in the fittings, cut another piece of pipe, which you can add to the first piece, or start over with a new section of pipe. Use PVC primer to clean the ends of PVC pipe and fittings. *(3)*

Thoroughly coat the ends of each pipe and the inside of the fittings with the solvent cement. *(4)* Be sure to use the type of solvent cement intended for the type of plastic pipe you are using. Immediately after applying solvent cement, insert the pipe into the fitting, and twist the two parts against each other about one-quarter turn. *(5)* Hold the pieces together for about ten seconds. If you fit the joint properly, the solvent cement will form a continuous bead around the joint. Wipe off any excess cement around the pipe and fitting with a cloth.

Cutting & joining plastic pipe

Difficulty Level:

Tools & Materials: Plastic pipe ❖ Backsaw or hacksaw ❖ Miter box ❖ Work gloves & safety goggles ❖ Pipe primer ❖ Pipe solvent cement ❖ Compression clamp fittings (if joining to cast iron) ❖ Utility knife ❖ Emery cloth

1 Hold the plastic pipe in a miter box while cutting it to length. Remove the burrs from the cut ends with a utility knife or emery cloth.

2 Test-fit the parts you will join before assembly, and adjust to the correct size. If your pipe is too long, trim it; if it is too short, add another piece.

3 Clean the end of the pipes and fittings with pipe primer. Use a primer specifically made for the type of plastic pipe you're using.

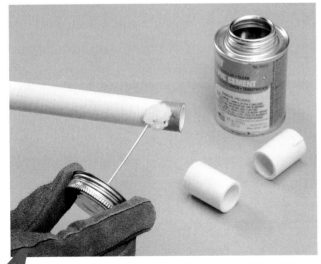

4 Coat the ends of pipes and the inside of the fittings with the appropriate solvent. Be sure to use the correct type of solvent for the pipe you're using.

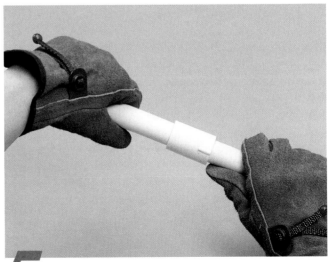

5 Insert the pipe into the fitting, and twist the parts against each other about one-quarter turn. Hold the pieces together for ten seconds.

Copper Couplings

You can join both rigid and flexible copper tubing with soldered joints and fittings, pictured on pages 124 and 125, or compression fittings. Soldered connections may be less prone to leakage over time, but they can't always be easily made.

Coupling

The fittings used to join sections of copper pipe include couplings, which join pipes in a straight line; reducers; 45- and 90-degree elbows to make bends; and reducer fittings, which join pipes of different diameters.

Compression & Flared Fittings

Compression fittings are often found on water-supply tubes and shutoff valves for fixtures. This is because, unlike soldered joints, compression fittings can be taken apart easily. They can also be used in spots where it's impractical or dangerous to solder, such as in an unventilated crawl space. These couplings become watertight when you tighten the threaded nut, drawing a flange against the end of the pipe. Couplings are available with threaded nuts on both ends or with one end threaded and the other straight, for soldering.

Female Adapter

Male Adapter

Reducer T Fitting

Flared fittings are usually only permitted for flexible copper pipe (Type L) used on gas lines, but some local codes may permit them in areas where soldering is not safe, as long as the pipes are not behind finished walls. Two tools are required for flared fittings: the flaring tools and the flaring set. The base part of the flaring tool clamps around the end of one of the pipes being joined, and the top of the flaring set forces the lip of the pipe against the clamp. This creates a bell-shaped flare. A flaring nut placed on one side of the joint threads into a flaring union on the other, much like compression fittings.

Reducer T Fitting

Coupling Nut

Compression Ring

Copper Tubing

Copper tubing is much easier to install than galvanized steel. You can choose between 20-foot-long lengths of rigid tubing or coils of flexible tubing. The advantage of flexible tubing is that you can bend it to snake through curves in existing walls and floors without making joints. The downside is that curves have to be gentle and without kinks: making the bends requires a little practice. By contrast, each turn in rigid tubing requires a joint with a soldered or threaded coupling, which can be easily made if you can get access to the joint but hard to make in places with cramped access.

Grades

Copper tubing is available in several different grades. Rigid tubing is sold in three grades: K (the thickest-walled), L, and M (the thinnest). Type K is most often found in underground lines. Type L is required by code for most commercial systems; type M, somewhat easier to work with, is usually acceptable for homes. Flexible tubing comes in two grades: K and L. Another grade, DWV, was once common in drain-waste-vent systems; it's been replaced by cheaper plastic pipe, for the most part. Always consult with the local building inspector to find out which types they accept before planning any additions to your plumbing system.

Cutting Copper Tubing

You can cut copper pipe with a tubing cutter or hacksaw. To use a tubing cutter, gradually tighten the cutting blade against the pipe as you rotate the tool several times until the pipe snaps apart. *(1)* Place the pipe in a grooved board or miter box for easier cutting. *(2)*

After cutting, you need to remove the burrs from inside the pipe. Some tubing cutters contain a burr remover. *(3)* Use a wire brush to clean the insides of the pipe and the fitting to which the pipe will be joined. *(4)* Before soldering, clean the ends of the pipe with emery cloth or a multipurpose plumber's tool, which contains an abrasive ring for cleaning the outside of the pipe and a brush for the inside. *(5)*

Cutting copper tubing

Difficulty Level: 🐟

Tools & Materials: Copper tubing ❖ Tubing cutter or hacksaw & miter box ❖ Multipurpose plumber's tool or wire brush

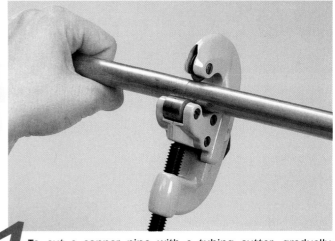

1 To cut a copper pipe with a tubing cutter, gradually tighten the cutting blade against the pipe, and rotate the tool several times.

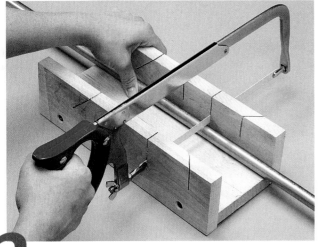

2 If you cut a copper pipe with a hacksaw, remember to place the pipe in a grooved board or miter box for easier cutting.

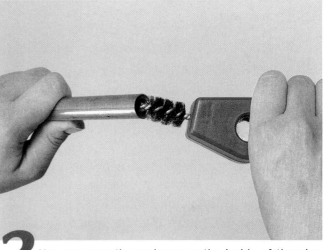

3 You can smooth any burrs on the inside of the pipe with a wire brush. The plumber's multipurpose tool has a rounded brush made for this.

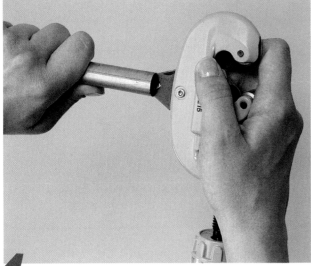

4 You can also smooth burrs on the inside of the pipe with the burr remover that is attached to the side of the tubing cutter.

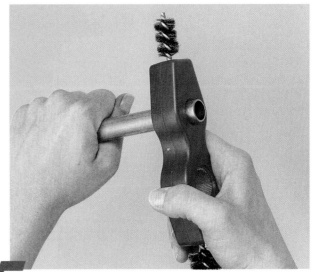

5 Clean the outside ends of the pipe with an emery cloth or, as shown here, a multipurpose tool before soldering.

Soldering Connections

From a home center or hardware store, buy a small torch that screws to a disposable propane canister. Also buy a good self-cleaning flux and solder. Use only lead-free solder (nickel or silver) for pipes that carry drinking water. When soldering with a torch, you can endanger both yourself and your house. Protect your eyes with safety goggles and your hands with work gloves. Get a 12 × 12-inch piece of sheet metal to insert between the joint to be soldered and any nearby wood to protect your house from catching on fire.

Use a small brush or toothbrush to coat the joint ends with flux. *(1)* Slide the fitting over the pipe ends so that half of the fitting is on each pipe. *(2)*

Light your torch, and heat the joint by running the flame over the pipe and fitting, taking care to avoid burning the flux. When the pipe is hot enough to melt the solder, take the torch away, and feed solder into the joint until it won't take any more. Heat the pipe for about five seconds. Then move the torch to the fitting as you feed more solder into the joint. *(3)* Continue until the joint stops drawing in the solder and there are no gaps in the solder.

If the solder around the rim of the joint stays puddled and does not draw in as it cools, reheat until the solder liquefies; then try again. Practice with some scrap pipes and connectors until you feel confident enough to solder your new supply lines. If soldering near wood or other combustible materials, place the piece of sheet metal between the soldering area and the material to prevent fire. *(4)*

Cool the pipe with a wet rag; then test the joint for leaks. *(5)* If more solder doesn't stop the leaks, melt the joint apart and start over.

CAUTION

It's easy to burn yourself when soldering pipe. Always make sure that you turn off your torch when it's not in use. Remember also that soldered joints are very hot; always let them cool before touching the pipes.

Soldering copper pipe

Difficulty Level:

Tools & Materials: Copper pipe ❖ Bristle brush ❖ Flux (soldering paste) ❖ Solder ❖ Propane torch ❖ Sparker ❖ Sheet metal ❖ Work gloves & face guard ❖ Clean rag ❖ Pipe fitting ❖ Coupling

Insulating Pipes

For pipes that will carry hot water, it's smart to save a little on your energy costs with pipe insulation. Fit preformed polystyrene insulation tubes around hot-water pipes, and tape in place. You can also wrap the pipes in strips from fiberglass batts. Either system will not only conserve heat loss but also prevent pipe sweating in the summertime. If you have pipes running through an unheated crawl space, both hot- and cold-water pipes should be insulated (or protected with heat cable) to keep them from freezing.

3 Heat the pipe for about five seconds. Then move the torch to the fitting as you feed solder into the joint. Continue until the joint stops drawing the solder.

Shutting Off the Water

Before you begin work on a section of pipe, you'll need to shut off the water supply to that part of your plumbing system. The main cutoff valve for your house's system (pictured at left) will be near the spot where the municipal pipe enters your home or, if you have well water, near the storage tank. Other cutoff valves farther along allow you to turn off just part of the water system, such as to one bathroom, while still allowing you to have water in the rest of the house. Most fixtures, such as sinks and toilet, should have their own cutoff valves (pictured at right), usually located right where the supply lines come through the wall or floor.

1 Coat the pipe ends with flux using a small brush or toothbrush. Make sure the ends of the pipe have been cleaned with an emery cloth.

2 Insert the fitting over one pipe end so that half of the fitting is on the pipe. Twist the fitting to spread the flux evenly. Then connect the second pipe to the fitting.

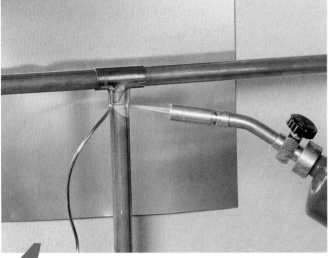

4 To prevent fire, place a small piece of sheet metal between the area you are soldering and any combustible material.

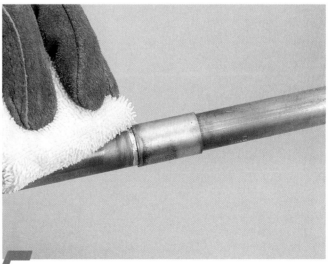

5 Wipe the pipe with a rag to clean the joint; then check it for leaks. Stop leaks with more solder. If that doesn't work, melt the joint apart and try again.

Faucets

A visit to a home center or plumbing-supply store will give you a good idea of the wide selection of faucets. In addition to the old tried-and-true dual-lever faucet with replaceable washers, you'll see single-lever types in a variety of styles. You can have handles that incorporate wood or ceramic. Spouts and bases come in polished or dull-finish chrome, brass, and nickel, as well as many colors of enameled metal. There are even some metal and ceramic faucets that look like miniature waterfalls.

Naturally, prices of these faucets range widely from style to style and material to material. To find your way through the options, it will help to have some idea of the basic faucet types.

Faucet Types

Your first decision is whether to select a dual- or single-lever faucet. Either is available with or without a drain-control lever. Faucets control water flow in various ways. Compression-type faucets depend on rubber washers or diaphragms to open or close the water flow. Newer types use other means than compression to control the water flow, such as cartridges, balls, or disks. Cartridge faucets regulate water flow with a movable cartridge and rubber O-rings. Ball faucets use a slotted plastic or brass ball atop a pair of spring-loaded rubber seats. The single lever rotates the ball to adjust the water temperature and flow. Disk faucets contain a pair of plastic or ceramic disks that move up and down to regulate the volume of the flow, and rotate to control the temperature.

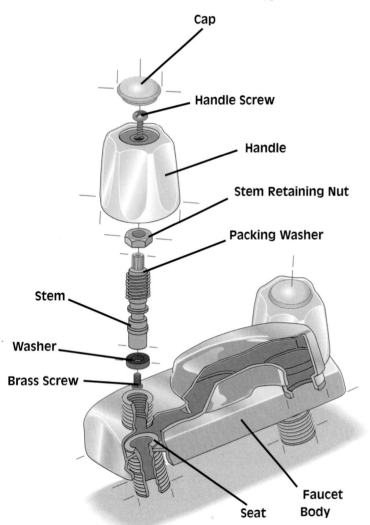

Compression faucets that use washers or diaphragms usually have two levers or handles. However, disk faucets can also have two levers.

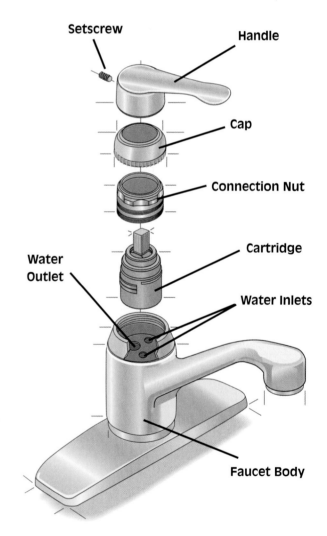

Disk faucets usually have a single handle. The cartridge contains a stem and washers similar to those found on compression faucets, as well as a temperature-control disk.

Replacing an Old Faucet

Before you buy a faucet set, be sure its offset (the distance, center to center, between the hot and cold taps) matches the spacing of the holes in the basin. Check this by measuring the center-to-center distance between the hot and cold supply risers under the basin.

Begin by shutting off the valves in the hot- and cold-supply pipes below the basin. If there are no valves, shut off the water supply at the main, which is probably in the basement. Set up a flashlight to shine on the pipes below the basin; then use a basin wrench to disconnect the faucet tailpieces from the supply risers. *(1)*

If the faucet contains a drain control, it must come out before you can remove the faucet. Loosen the clevis screw with a pair of pliers to free the lift rod from the clevis. Then use adjustable pliers to free the pivot rod from the drain. *(2)*

Last, disconnect the pivot rod from the pop-up plug, and remove both. Your new faucet set should come with replacement drain parts.

Remove the faucet mounting nuts and washers by turning them counterclockwise. *(3)* On single-lever faucets, the supply pipes converge at the center, and the unit is held in place by mounting nuts at the sides and a nut and retaining ring in the center. Use whichever tool fits: adjustable pliers, adjustable wrench, or basin wrench.

Removing the old faucet

Difficulty Level: 🐟 to 🐟🐟

Tools & Materials: Basin wrench ❖ Adjustable wrench ❖ Adjustable pliers ❖ Standard pliers ❖ Putty knife ❖ Penetrating oil (if needed)

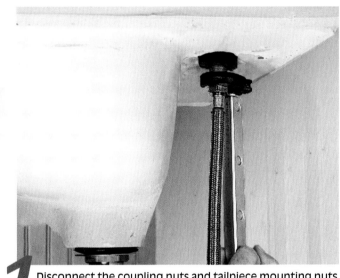

1 Disconnect the coupling nuts and tailpiece mounting nuts from the supply risers with a basin wrench or adjustable pliers. You may need to loosen them with penetrating oil.

2 Loosen the clevis screw, and then free the pivot rod from the drain. Separate the pivot rod from the pop-up plug; remove both pieces.

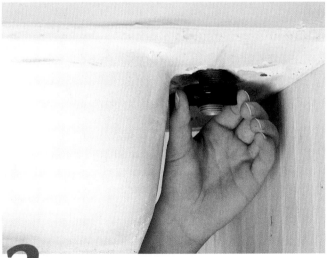

3 Turn the faucet mounting nuts and washers in a counterclockwise direction, and remove. Use whichever tool fits best.

Installing the New Faucet

If the faucet won't budge easily, coax it by inserting a putty knife under the baseplate. Then use the putty knife to remove any caulk or adhesive from the basin. *(1)* After cleaning the surface of the basin in the area in which the new faucet will sit, install the gasket. *(2)* If your faucet set came without a gasket, put down a bead of silicone sealant or plumber's putty around the lip of the faucet baseplate. *(3)* Insert the faucet tailpieces into the mounting holes of the basin, and press the faucet down into the sealant, if used. Wipe off any excess sealant with a rag.

Put the washers and mounting nuts if any, on the tailpieces, and tighten. *(4)* Do not overtighten. Attach braided stainless-steel risers to the faucet tailpieces and the water shutoff valves. This type is flexible, unlike chrome-plated copper, making it easier to adjust when connecting. Tighten the nuts, avoiding overtightening. *(5)*

Lastly, insert the lift-rod control through the top of the faucet. Next, link the lift rod and spring clip with the ball assembly inside the drain. Insert the pop-up stopper into the drain hole, and engage it with the pivot rod. Adjust the elevation of the stopper by selecting the appropriate hole in the clevis. When all the parts are assembled, turn the shutoff valves on, and check all the connections for leaks. If a connection is leaking, turn the nut a little at a time until the leak stops.

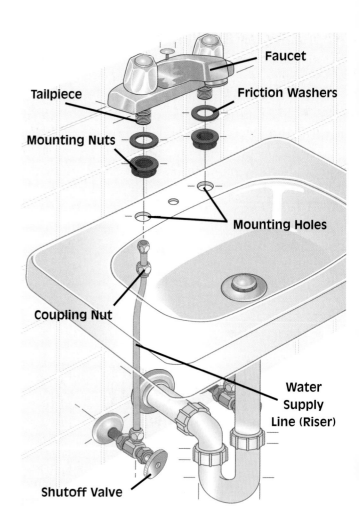

This is a typical setup for a dual-lever faucet set. To begin disassembly, close the water shutoff valves in the hot- and cold-supply risers below the basin.

Bending Tubing

If your faucet has flexible copper (or chromed copper) supply tubing pre-attached to it, you may need to bend the tubing slightly to reach from the tailpiece of the faucet to the shutoff valve on the floor. To accomplish this, you'll need to use a tubing bender, which looks like a pipe made from concentric rings. You just insert the flexible tubing into the sleeve, and bend it slowly into shape by hand. This tool will minimize the crushing or crimping that often occurs when you try to bend flexible tubing using only your bare hands.

Installing a new one-piece faucet

Difficulty Level:

Tools & Materials: New faucet ❖ Braided stainless-steel risers (if chromed copper supply tubing not included with faucet) ❖ Silicone caulk & caulking gun ❖ Adjustable wrench ❖ Tubing bender (optional) ❖ Clean rag

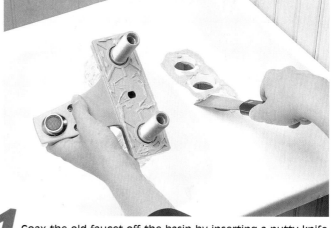

1 Coax the old faucet off the basin by inserting a putty knife under the baseplate, if necessary. Clean the basin of any remaining caulk or adhesive.

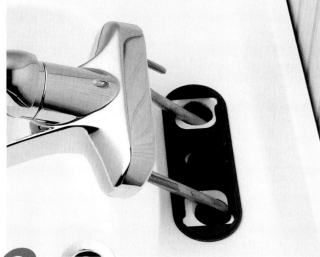

2 You must use either a gasket or caulk at the faucet's base to keep water from seeping beneath the faucet. Place the gasket where the faucet will be installed.

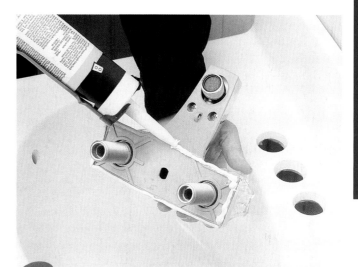

3 If there is no gasket, place a bead of silicone caulk or plumber's putty around the lip of the faucet baseplate. Press the faucet down to ensure a good seal.

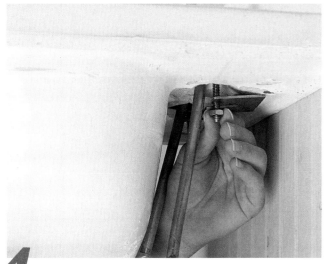

4 If the new faucet has pre-attached copper tubing, set the gasket, retainer ring, and locknut onto the tailpiece. Tighten with a basin wrench or adjustable pliers.

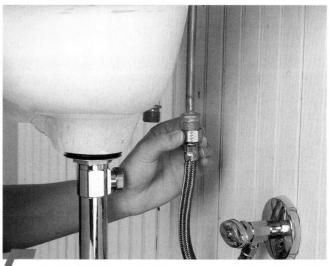

5 Braided stainless-steel risers are easy to bend from the shutoff valve to the faucet. Tighten the compression fittings first by hand, then with a wrench.

Showers

Replacing an existing shower won't require you to remodel the basic pipes, but installing a new one will mean baring the floor and wall that contain the water-supply and drainage pipes.

You can run hot- and cold-water lines through the floor, ceiling, or walls to reach the shower valve. Mount the valve about 48 inches above the floor. Use ½-inch rigid copper tubing if you can make straight runs and ½-inch flexible tubing if you need to snake the supply piping around difficult curves. Use 2-inch-diameter ABS plastic pipe from the shower drain to the soil stack. Join Ls and Ts, as needed, with solvent cement. (See "Cutting and Joining Plastic Pipe," page 121.)

Code Requirements

Building codes usually require the floor drain to be at least 12 inches away from a wall. Just below the drain, place a P-trap, then a drainpipe that slopes at least ¼ inch per foot into the soil stack. If you are using 1½-inch-diameter vent pipe, it should be within 42 inches of the P-trap. For 2-inch diameter pipe, the maximum distance is 60 inches. The vent must rise vertically until it reaches the overflow level of the fixture it serves, then it can run horizontally or vertically through the roof. Because the vent can be a smaller diameter than the drain line, the connecting T or Y needs to have a reduced opening on the vent side. After installing the drain, seal the joint between the lip and shower floor with plumber's putty.

Removing Old Shower Heads

Today's shower heads conserve water, which is good; but the resulting flow doesn't feel anywhere near as luxurious as the older, wasteful ones. Having a choice of spray patterns helps make up for the lack of water volume, and changing over from a water-hogging to water-conserving shower head is one of the simplest bathroom plumbing chores you can do. To remove an old shower head, first grasp the rear of the shower head with an adjustable wrench or adjustable pliers, and loosen it by turning the

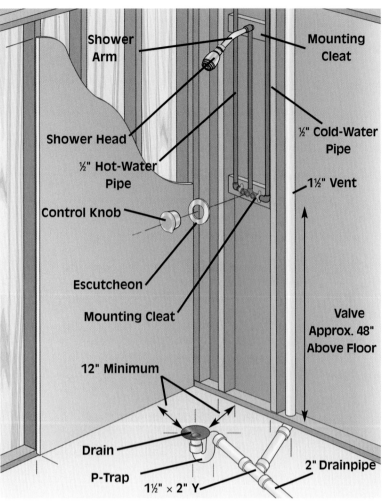

The rough-in plumbing for a shower stall includes hot- and cold-water supply and a drain connected to a P-trap. Codes typically require a separate vent (as shown) if the drain is more than 6 ft. from the soil stack.

wrench counterclockwise. *(1)* Don't use too much force, or you may twist the shower arm, and then it will need to be replaced. If the head assembly won't budge with mild pressure, wrap duct tape around the shower arm near the head, and use pliers (or a pipe wrench) to restrain the arm while you apply more pressure to the head. *(2)* As a last resort, you can remove the arm and the head and replace both.

Assemble the shower head according to the instructions. *(3)* If there is an O-ring, make sure it is in place. Then screw the shower head onto the shower arm by hand until you can no longer turn it. Give it another half-turn with adjustable pliers. Turn on the water to check for leakage. Tighten it little by little until there is no leak. If you must replace the shower arm as well, apply pipe joint compound or plumber's tape to the threaded end, wrap the wall end with duct tape to protect it, and screw it into the wall T with adjustable pliers.

Replacing a shower head

Difficulty Level:

Tools & Materials: Duct tape (if needed) ❖ Adjustable pliers ❖ Standard pliers ❖ New shower head ❖ New shower arm (if needed) ❖ Pipe joint compound or plumber's tape ❖ Adjustable wrench

1 Loosen the retainer or collar nut with adjustable pliers or standard pliers to free the shower head from the shower arm.

2 If needed, restrain the shower arm with pliers while you unscrew the shower-head retainer. Tape the arm first to prevent scratches.

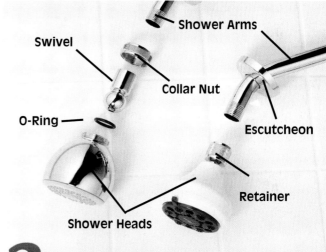

Swivel

Shower Arms

Collar Nut

O-Ring

Escutcheon

Retainer

Shower Heads

3 Be sure that you've assembled the new shower head correctly. Screw the collar nut or retainer of the new shower head onto the shower arm.

Conserving Water

Water-conserving shower heads—ones that deliver between 2½ and 3 gallons per minute—are usually required by local plumbing codes. They come in a variety of styles and spray patterns; some have adjustable heads that deliver more than one spray pattern. Choose the shower head that best fits your bathroom's design, with the type of spray pattern you prefer.

Handheld Showers

Standard shower heads fixed at 72 inches or so above the floor don't always get the water where it's needed and are inconvenient for people who can't stand while showering. A shower head mounted on a flexible hose allows the user to direct the spray to any part of the body. The trade-off is that it keeps one hand occupied. If you want to replace a fixed shower with a handheld shower you have two options:

• Replace the existing shower head with a handheld model (difficulty level 1).

• Replace the tub spout with a special spout containing a diverter, to which the handheld shower attaches —if your tub does not already have a shower (difficulty level 2).

Here are the pros and cons and installation instructions for each option:

Replacing the Existing Shower Head. The simplest way to install a handheld shower is to replace the existing shower head. *(1)* But because the new shower head mounts into a bracket built into the shower arm, it will be out of reach to a person who must sit while showering. To install the bracket of a handheld shower, follow the same steps under "Replacing a Shower Head" on page 131.

Installing a Diverter. Although it's a bit more involved than the first method, replacing the existing tub spout with one containing a special diverter puts the handheld shower low enough to be accessible while sitting in the tub or on a tub seat. *(2)*

If the existing spout has an Allen setscrew on the underside, remove it using an Allen wrench, and gently pull the spout off the pipe. If there is no screw, unscrew it with adjustable pliers. *(3)* (Alternatively, you can try inserting something into the spout hole to use as a lever to turn the spout loose.) Screw on the new spout, and then attach the shower hose. *(4)*

Mark the wall where you want to mount the bracket that holds the shower head. *(5)* For tile, drill holes with a carbide-tipped bit, and insert expansion anchors. Then screw on the bracket.

More Water, More Ways

Of course, you have a great many options for your shower besides different shower heads and a handheld massaging unit. Most major plumbing manufacturers have kits for home spas, which involve numerous shower heads along the front or sides of the enclosure. This array of shower heads delivers a powerful shower massage from a variety of angles—all you have to do is stand still.

Most of these kits require a great deal of plumbing rough-in before installation— each of those many shower heads still needs two water-supply lines going to it. For most DIYers, these home spas are best left to professional plumbers to install. Perhaps the ultimate in shower luxury is your own private waterfall. The item pictured here is designed to fit between a 16-inch stud opening. It requires not only new plumbing but also a special drain and a recirculating pump that shoots out 80 gallons of water per minute. This assumes you have enough room behind the wall to house the pump and the money to pay the water bill.

Installing a handheld shower

Difficulty Level:

Tools & Materials: Pipe wrench or adjustable pliers ❖ Power drill with carbide-tipped bit ❖ Allen wrench (if spout has Allen setscrew) ❖ Handheld shower head kit (with spout) ❖ Rubber mallet ❖ Expansion anchors

1 You can replace a handheld unit with a fixed shower head if you place its mounting bracket at the same height as the old shower head.

2 If you prefer, install a handheld shower head low on the wall by using a special attachment to the tub spout called a diverter.

3 Remove the spout with smooth-jaw adjustable pliers. If your existing spout has an Allen setscrew on the underside, use an Allen wrench to remove it.

4 The new spout comes with an adapter that directs water to either the shower head or the tub. Connect the new spout; then attach the shower hose.

5 Select the spot on the wall for mounting the shower head, and position the bracket to mark the holes. Then attach the bracket using expansion anchors.

Anti-Scald Shower Controls

Have you ever been jolted out of a peaceful shower by a sudden rush of scalding hot or icy cold water? This can happen when someone turns on a tap or flushes a toilet elsewhere in the house, causing the pressure in the hot- or cold-water supply line to drop. Standard shower fittings do nothing to control this, but anti-scald valves do. Also called pressure-balancing valves, these single-control fittings contain a piston that automatically responds to changes in line water pressure to maintain the same temperature, blocking abrupt drops or rises in temperature.

Installing an anti-scald valve requires tearing into the wall, separating the water-supply lines, removing the existing control valves, and soldering on the new anti-scald valves to the supply pipes. The steps here apply to copper water pipes. (See "Copper Tubing," pages 122 to 125.) If you must rework steel pipes, hire a plumber.

Taking Out the Old Valve. Shut off the water at the nearest valve below the faucets (usually in the basement). Open the bleed valves. *(1)* Then open the faucets to drain any trapped water. Protect the tub or shower floor with a drop cloth; then remove the wall surface that is covering the pipes. *(2)* (See "Gutting a Wall or Ceiling," pages 84 to 85.)

Separate all the pipes from the old valve assembly, and remove it. If possible, use a torch to melt the solder joints, holding a piece of sheet metal behind the pipe to protect the wall. *(3)* As you heat each joint, the solder will melt. Wearing gloves, pull the pipe out of the joint. If you can't separate the pipes from the valve by melting the solder, cut the pipes with a hacksaw or tubing cutter about 2 inches back from the joints.

Installing the New Valve. Before you solder in any new items, be sure the pipes are dry. Trapped water turns to steam and prevents the formation of a water-tight connection. One way to dry out the pipes is to stick a sponge into their ends to absorb as much water as possible, and then heat the ends by moving a torch over them (after removing the sponge). *(4)*

If you needed to cut pipes to remove the old valve, add extensions to restore the pipes to the original length. Cut pieces of copper tubing in the necessary lengths, and connect them by soldering copper sleeves to the pipe ends.

Place the new valve into position with the pipe ends inserted into the sockets, and solder each joint. *(5)* When the solder hardens, wipe the joint with a cold wet cloth to cool the pipe. Turn the water back on, and check each joint for leakage. If a joint is leaking, turn the water off again, open the shower valve to drain the water, and add more solder to the leaking joint. If you are not successful this time, disconnect all the leaking components, and start over.

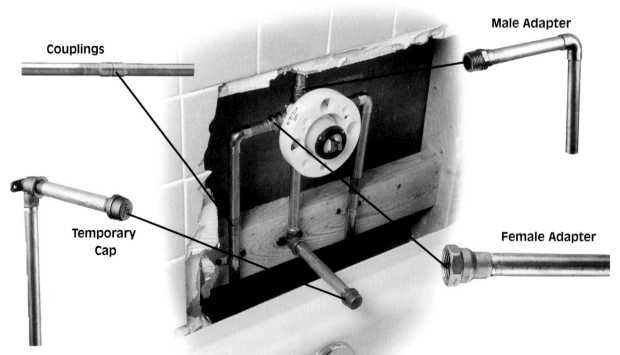

Couplings

Male Adapter

Temporary Cap

Female Adapter

To install an anti-scald shower control, join a piece of pipe to the new valve, and use couplings to make an arrangement similar to the one shown in this photograph.

Installing an anti-scald shower control

Difficulty Level: 🔧🔧🔧

Tools & Materials: Anti-scald valve ❖ Adjustable pliers ❖ Adjustable wrench ❖ Reciprocating saw or keyhole saw ❖ Pry bar ❖ Propane torch ❖ Hacksaw with metal-cutting blade or tubing cutter ❖ New tubing, pipe nipples & couplings as needed ❖ Tubing cutter ❖ Solder ❖ Flux ❖ Sponge & bucket ❖ Drop cloth ❖ Work gloves

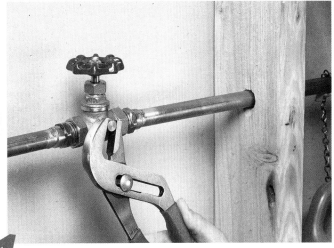

1 Shut off the water supply to the shower or tub. Open the bleed valves into a bucket underneath; then open the faucets to drain trapped water.

2 To replace a dual-lever control with a single-lever control, you need to remove part of the wall to gain access to the existing crossover.

3 Remove the crossover by melting the solder in the joints, if possible. If not, you'll have to cut the pipes with a hacksaw and install new ones.

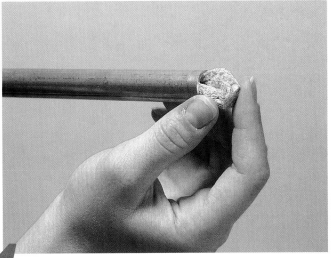

4 Remove trapped water by inserting a piece of sponge into the pipes. Remove the sponge, and then heat the pipe ends by moving a torch over them to vaporize drops of water.

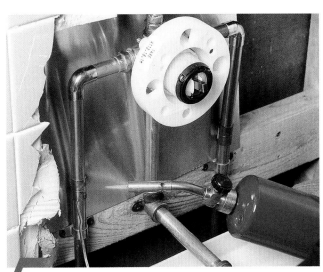

5 Solder all copper joints in place; use a piece of sheet metal to protect wood from igniting. Install the new valve. If a joint leaks, add additional solder.

Building a Separate Shower

If you have the space and budget for a separate shower, you can build the stall in several ways. Chapter 2, pages 22 to 32, showed the range of options, from prefab one-piece stall units to completely customized stalls with floors and walls built on-site. The instructions that come with prefab shower units will guide your installation work. The following section offers some useful advice to augment the manufacturer's instructions.

Here are the general steps for installing a one-piece or knock-down prefab shower stall. When considering a one-piece unit, be sure you can get it through existing doorways or an outside window, or be prepared to knock down part of the exterior wall. (See "Getting a Tub or Shower Inside or Outside the House," page 141.)

Prefab shower stalls come with their own watertight walls, so you won't need a special wall substrate such as cement-based backer board. You will need to check for any leaks in the plumbing before putting up wall panels or finishing the floor, though. Correcting problems afterward will be difficult.

Shower Pan. First, use the preformed shower base, pushed tightly against both walls, to mark the drain location on the floor. *(1)* Then cut the hole through the subfloor with a saber saw. *(2)* You can now install the shower-drain trap, cut into the existing hot- and cold-water supply lines, and solder in the connective fittings. If you're replacing an old shower, you may need to move the drain.

Wall Panels. Some kits have clips and screws

Installing a prefab shower stall

Difficulty Level: 🔧🔧🔧

Tools & Materials: Shower stall kit ❖ Marker ❖ Saber saw ❖ Hammer ❖ 12d common nails ❖ 1x3 furring strips ❖ 4' spirit level ❖ Power drill with screwdriver bit & hole saw ❖ Shower-pan liner ❖ Dry-set mortar ❖ Mason's trowel ❖ Mixing pan & bucket ❖ Silicone caulk & caulking gun ❖ Screwdriver

1 Use the preformed shower base, pushed tightly against both walls, to mark the drain location on the floor for a new shower.

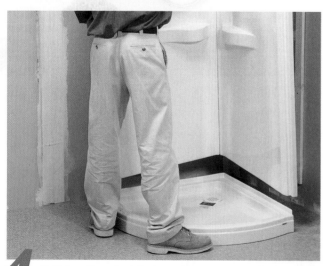

4 If the unit comes in two pieces, clip them together with the clips provided. Then, tip it temporarily in place on the furring and on top of the shower pan.

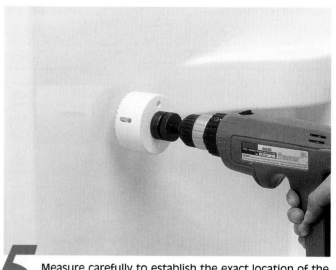

5 Measure carefully to establish the exact location of the faucet, and then drill an opening with a hole saw chucked into an power drill.

to join wall panels together and to the base. Do not drill too deeply, and be careful not to penetrate a surface that should not be drilled.

The way you install the shower side panels on your walls depends on your kit. The kit pictured below required furring strips nailed at the top and the sides to provide nailing surfaces for the flanges on the panels. **(3)** Before making the installation permanent, replace the shower pan, and set the side panels in position. **(4)** Measure carefully to establish the exact center of the faucet opening, and drill it through the shower panel with a hole saw chucked into a power drill. **(5)**

Next, install the shower pan. First you'll need to lay down a shower-pan liner. Sold from rolls at most home centers, you can have it cut to the size you need. Old-fashioned copper liners are no longer used, and may be prohibited by code.

Reinforcing the Pan. You should also consider installing a layer of lightweight masonry between the liner and the pan, even if your instructions don't call for it. Even well-made, reinforced fiberglass can flex under body weight. This may lead to cracks in the shower-floor finish, which may eventually lead to larger cracks that leak. So, to prevent flexing, mound a light masonry mix underneath the shower floor on top of the liner before installing the pan. **(6)**

Assembling the Unit. Once the masonry under the pan has set, you can place the assembled unit into position and check it for level. Insert shims where needed to adjust the unit. **(7)**

2 Using a saber saw, cut out the hole for the drain. Install the shower-drain trap, and connect it to your existing drain-waste-vent system.

3 Prefab units are installed in different ways. For this model, you need to nail 1x3 furring strips to the walls in order to provide a nailing surface for the flanges.

6 Cut and place the shower-pan liner. To prevent flexing, install the shower pan over a mound of dry-set mortar. Set the pan on top of the mortar.

7 Use the clips to attach the pan to the wall unit, and tip the entire unit into place over the pan liner and drain tailpiece, and over the furring strips. Check for level.

11 Working with Plumbing

Installing a prefab shower, cont'd

8 Screw the unit into place through the furring strips. Place the screws where indicated in the manufacturer's instructions.

9 Following the instructions, attach the side and top jambs and the bottom track for the shower door. Adjust them as needed so that the door slides smoothly on its tracks.

10 If there is a second door, snap it into place. Then attach door handles, if any, and waterproofing trim.

11 Install the escutcheons and then the shower head and controls as per the instructions. Also install the drain cap.

12 Once the hardware is in place, use a silicone caulk to seal the seam between the shower unit and the floor.

13 For additional protection, run a bead of caulk at the seams around the walls and along the top of the unit.

Securing the Unit to the Wall. If recommended by the manufacturer, remove the unit after shimming, spread adhesive on the wall substrates, and then put the unit back into place, making sure the drain opening goes squarely over the tailpiece of the drainpipe. While the adhesive sets, hold the floor and wall panels tight to the substrates by weighing the base down with bricks and propping 2×4s, wrapped in carpet scraps to protect the finish, against the walls. Following the manufacturer's instructions, allow the adhesive to fully cure before removing the weights.

The unit pictured here is screwed in place along the furring strips with galvanized screws. *(8)* Follow the manufacturer's instructions to place the screws in the proper places.

Installing the Door. If the unit comes with a door (instead of a rod for a curtain), follow the instructions to put the door parts together. Usually this will involve a metal jamb piece that snaps or clips into place around the opening. For a sliding door, the top jamb and the bottom threshold will include a track. Just slide the door or doors into the track, and adjust the jambs and threshold as needed for a smooth fit. A shower door that opens on a hinge will have a hinge pin on the bottom of the door, which slips into an opening in the threshold. *(9–10)*

Once the door is in place, install the door handles (if included). Some doors also have waterproofing trim or hardware.

Finishing Touches. To finish the installation, you need to attach the escutcheon plate over the faucet and the shower head, and set the drain cover in place. *(11)* As a final precaution against water damage, seal the base of the shower and the door jambs with silicone caulk. *(12–13)*

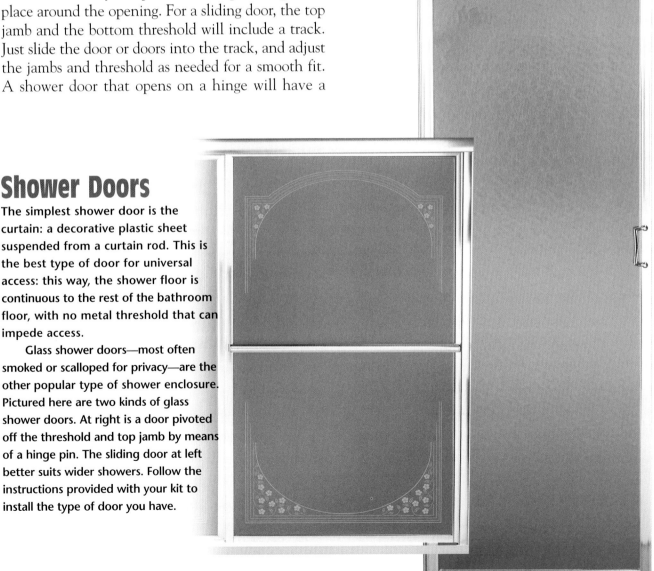

Shower Doors

The simplest shower door is the curtain: a decorative plastic sheet suspended from a curtain rod. This is the best type of door for universal access: this way, the shower floor is continuous to the rest of the bathroom floor, with no metal threshold that can impede access.

Glass shower doors—most often smoked or scalloped for privacy—are the other popular type of shower enclosure. Pictured here are two kinds of glass shower doors. At right is a door pivoted off the threshold and top jamb by means of a hinge pin. The sliding door at left better suits wider showers. Follow the instructions provided with your kit to install the type of door you have.

11 *Working with Plumbing*

Bathtubs

Hooking up your new tub may be the simplest part of the job—most of the hard work involves removing the old one. Here's how to replace a bathtub using the same supply and drain pipes.

Removing the Old Tub

Shut off the water supply to the tub. Open the taps to relieve any back pressure. Remove the overflow cover, and pull out the linkage-rod coil assembly. *(1)* To remove a plunger-type tripwaste, pull it out through the overflow hole. *(2)* Remove a pop-up-type tripwaste from the tub drain. *(3)*

Separating the old tub from the wall may be as simple as running a putty knife around the edge to break the bond between the tub and a caulked joint.

Or you may have to gut a portion of the wall and remove tiles. *(4)* Separate the tub from the floor, trying to protect the existing floor as much as possible, unless you intend to replace the flooring anyway. *(5)*

If the tub is steel, you'll have to remove it in one piece. *(6)* A standard-size tub (30 × 60 inches) will fit through doorways when turned on its side. Larger tubs may require you to remove them through windows or openings in walls.

Tubs that can't be removed in one piece may be cut up with a reciprocating saw if they are fiberglass or pressed steel. If they are cast iron (as are many old tubs), they may be broken up into shards. Use a mason's hammer or sledgehammer, applying only as much force as necessary. *(7)* Protect yourself with safety goggles, gloves, and earplugs.

Removing the old bathtub

Difficulty Level:

Tools & Materials: Screwdriver ❖ Sledgehammer or mason's hammer ❖ Safety goggles ❖ Putty knife ❖ Pliers

1 Shut off the water supply to the tub, and open the taps to relieve any back pressure. Then remove the overflow cover plate, and pull out the linkage-rod coil assembly.

4 Separating the old tub from the wall may require gutting a portion of the wall. With a pry bar, remove any fasteners that attach the tub to the studs.

5 To remove the tub, you may also have to take up a portion of the floor. For tips on removing flooring, see "Taking Up the Old Flooring," pages 70 to 71.

Getting a Tub or Shower Inside or Outside the House

When you are planning the space and selecting fixtures, you should also devise a plan for removing your old tub or shower and installing the new unit. If you simply can't get the old unit out without more expense and hassle than you want, you will probably choose to leave it in place. When selecting a new fixture, you may want to make sure that you can carry it through the house to the bathroom. But if you have your heart set on a unit that cannot be moved into the bathroom through existing hallways or doors, consider ways to move it through an outer wall. The process can be as easy as removing a first-floor window or as complex as removing an entire wall on the second or third floor.

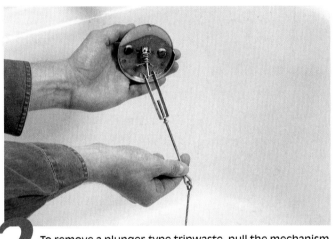

2 To remove a plunger-type tripwaste, pull the mechanism out through the overflow hole. Also remove any handles, spouts, and shower heads.

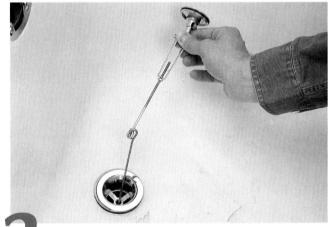

3 Remove the drain fittings. Then remove the pop-up tripwaste out of the tub drain. Disconnect the drain assembly from the drainpipe with pliers.

6 If you have to remove the tub in one piece, you will need assistance. Turn it sideways or on one end to move it through doorways and down any stairs.

7 Break up the tub if necessary. Use a mason's hammer or a sledgehammer for cast-iron tubs, or a reciprocating saw for pressed steel or fiberglass.

Installing a New Tub

Place the new tub into position, and use a spirit level to check that the unit is level in both directions. *(1)* Shim, as needed, between the base and the floor. Attach any retaining clips that come with the tub. After the finished wall and floor are installed, seal around the tub edges at the walls and floor with silicone caulk.

Place the large beveled washer between the back of the tub and the overflow pipe. Place the flat washer between the drainpipe and the bottom of the tub. Position the drain-waste-overflow assembly, and tighten the slip nuts to lock it into place. Press plumber's putty around the underside of the crosspiece, and then screw it into the tub drain hole. Tighten the crosspiece with pliers handles and a screwdriver. *(2)* Then screw down the strainer cap.

The linkage assembly allows you to open and close the drain using a lever in the tub wall. Loosen the locknut to turn the threaded rod, and adjust the linkage to the right length. *(3)* After adjusting, tighten the locknut, and slip the linkage into the overflow hole. Lastly, attach the overflow plate.

After restoring the wall finish, slide the escutcheons and sleeves onto the protruding faucet stems, and screw on the handles. *(4)* (For single-lever controls, follow the manufacturer's instructions.) Use a measuring tape to measure the distance from the pipe L to the face of the tile or other finish. To this measurement, add the depth of the spout from threaded end to wall end. Add another ¾ inch to get the length of the nipple you'll need. *(5)*

Get a brass nipple from a plumbing store, and coat the threaded ends with pipe joint compound; then screw it into the wall. Finally, screw on the spout.

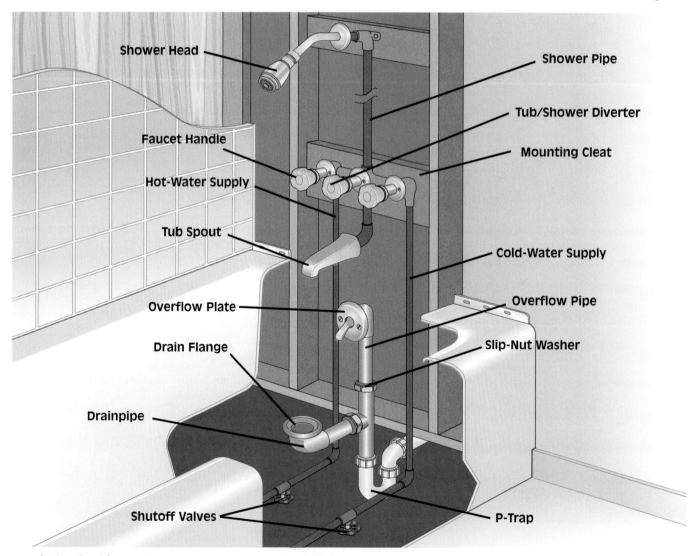

Here is the plumbing system for a typical tub-and-shower combination. You'll need to have all the plumbing roughed in before the tub is installed. The drain and overflow assembly are attached to the tub before it's set into position.

Installing a new bathtub

Difficulty Level:

Tools & Materials: New bathtub unit & drain-waste-overflow kit ❖ 4' spirit level ❖ Shims ❖ Silicone caulk & caulking gun ❖ Locking pliers ❖ Standard pliers ❖ Screwdriver ❖ Hacksaw ❖ Adjustable wrench ❖ Galvanized deck screws ❖ Measuring tape

1 Slide the tub into position. Use a spirit level to check its position, and shim as necessary. Screw or clip the tub to the wall framing.

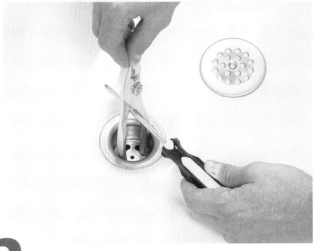

2 Attach the drain-waste-overflow assembly in the tub. Stuff plumber's putty around the drain flange; then install the drain piece with pliers and a screwdriver.

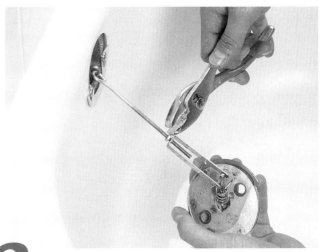

3 Adjust the linkage length by loosening the locknut and turning the threaded rod. Then slip the linkage into the overflow hole, and attach the overflow plate.

4 After the faucet stems are attached, slide on the escutcheons and sleeves; then screw on the handles. Follow the instructions for single-lever faucets.

5 Before screwing on the spout, measure its depth, and add ¾ in. to get the required length of the pipe nipple.

11 *Working with Plumbing*

Installing a Tub Door

Do you mind being caressed by shower curtains that somehow waft into the cramped compartment when you are showering? Are you tired of the water that always seems to spill out on the floor, even when you think you have closed the curtains tight? If so, it's time to consider replacing the curtain with a more substantial barrier, such as a bifold or sliding glass tub door. Do keep in mind, though, that it's easier to work around a curtain than a door when you're bathing a small child.

Below are some basic guidelines for installing a simple sliding door. Always carefully follow the manufacturer's instructions that come with your door, because some specifics may vary from kit to kit.

Measure the length of the tub to ensure that your door kit will fit. Cut the bottom channel from the kit to this measurement using a hacksaw or a saber saw fitted with a special metal-cutting blade.

Center the bottom channel along the front edge of the tub. When it is positioned, tape it to the tub with masking tape. Mark the inside edge along the tub with a pencil. *(1)*

Hold one of the side channels in place perpendicular to the bottom channel, and use a spirit level and framing square to make sure that it is plumb. *(2)* Mark the screw holes on the wall with

Mounting a door on a bathtub

Difficulty Level:

Tools & Materials: Door enclosure kit ❖ Marker ❖ Power drill with ³⁄₁₆" bit (carbide-tipped, if wall is tiled) ❖ Screwdriver ❖ Hacksaw & miter box ❖ Spirit level ❖ Framing square ❖ Silicone caulk & caulking gun ❖ Masking tape

1 Position the base of the door track in the center of the tub wall. Tape it to the front edge of the tub, and mark its position with a pencil.

3 Drill pilot holes for the screws that will hold in the side channels using a power drill equipped with a carbide-tipped drill bit.

4 Apply a bead of silicone caulk to the outside bottom edge of the bottom side channel; then position the channel on the line you drew.

a pencil, and then repeat for the other side. Remove all the channels, and drill the wall holes with a ³⁄₁₆-inch drill bit. **(3)** Use a carbide-tipped bit for drilling through tile. (Place an X of masking tape over the hole before you drill to keep the tile's glaze from cracking.)

Apply a thick bead of silicone caulk to the outside bottom edge of the bottom channel, and press the channel into place on the tub's rim, using the lines you drew as a guide. **(4)** The bottom channel of a tub door (or, for that matter, the threshold of a shower door) should never be screwed in place, because the resulting holes could cause leaks.

When the caulk has set firmly, install the door guides into the bottom channel. (In some kits, the bottom door guides are part of the bottom channel.) Put the side channels into place, and tighten the screws just enough to hold the channels but loose enough to allow you to adjust their position. **(5)**

Lay the top channel across the side channels. Hang the doors in the rails to test the fit. **(6)** If the side channels need to be cut, place them in a miter box and cut them with a hacksaw. When everything fits, remove the doors and the top and side channels. Apply silicone caulk to the side channels, and then screw them to the wall. Install the top channel and the door panels, as well as any additional hardware or trim.

2 Hold one of the side channels plumb against the wall; then mark the position of the screw holes on the tile. Repeat this process on the other side.

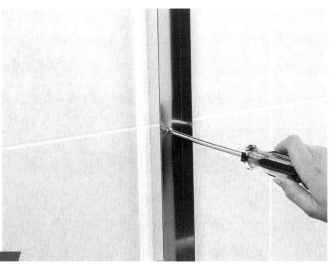

5 Put the side channels into place, and tighten the screws just enough to hold the channels in place but leaving ample room for adjustment.

6 Lay the top channel in place; then test-fit the doors. Adjust the fit as needed. Caulk the channels before screwing them to the wall. Install top and door panels.

11 Working with Plumbing

Whirlpools & Spas

The simplest way to replace a tub with a whirlpool or spa is to select a whirlpool of the same size as the tub. That way, you can reuse much of the supply lines, venting, and drainpipes. The problem is that you are probably attracted to a whirlpool for the luxury, and small units don't provide much.

Choosing a Location

Before settling on a particular model, carefully plan where it will go and how you will get it into position. You can mount whirlpools into various kinds of surrounds built on top of the floor, or you can recess them into the floor. Recessing isn't usually possible, though, unless the whirlpool will sit over a crawl space or basement. Recessing also means that you have to build the floor structure to provide adequate support. Although whirlpools are available with one or two finished sides, most are designed to be set into a base, at floor level or raised. You can make the platform as high as you like, but you will have to provide steps for any rim height above 16 inches, and steps can be hazardous when wet.

If the whirlpool will rest on an upper floor, ask the supplier how much it weighs when full and what is the best way to support the load. If the unit is larger than your present tub, you will probably have to reinforce the existing joists to support the additional weight. (See "Reinforcing Old Floors," page 77.)

Installing a Whirlpool

If you are retrofitting the whirlpool into an existing bathroom, you will need to remove enough subfloor to allow for roughing-in the hot- and cold-water pipes and the drain and vent system. You can use ½-inch copper pipe for the water supply, but with ¾-inch pipes you will get speedier filling. Use ABS or PVC plastic pipe (as required by your local code) for drain and vent pipes. If you need to cut joists for pipe runs, cut the holes in the center portion of the joist. Notching the top or bottom of a joist will weaken it. (See the drawing below.)

Preparing the Base. Mark the cutouts for the drain and water-supply stubs on the subfloor. Cut and drill these holes; then secure the replacement subfloor or new subfloor with 8d nails or screws. Lay a piece of ¾-inch plywood over the floor to serve as a support platform. After cutting out holes for pipes to pass through, secure the platform piece to the subfloor with 8d nails or screws. *(1)*

Lift the whirlpool onto the platform, and check for level. If necessary, lever up the base with a crowbar, and insert pieces of sheet metal for shims. *(2)* If you will be tiling around the whirlpool, attach the backer board now. *(3)* (See "Putting Up Backer Board," page 95.)

Building the Enclosure. Frame up the base enclosure with 2×4s. Starting at a corner, draw the outlines of the base enclosure on the subfloor, using a level from the top edge. *(4)* Then cut the headers (top horizontal pieces) and sills (floor horizontal pieces). Cut enough studs for a 16-inch spacing. Nail the headers and sills to the studs with the assembly laid flat; then tip it up into place. Put a piece of backer board and a piece of tile on the frame to be sure it fits. If it does, nail the sills to the subfloor. *(5)*

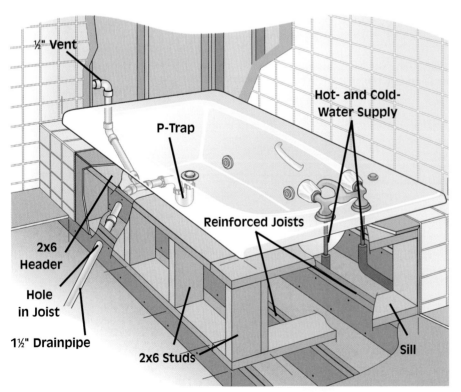

½" Vent

P-Trap

Hot- and Cold-Water Supply

Reinforced Joists

2x6 Header

Hole in Joist

1½" Drainpipe

2x6 Studs

Sill

Drainage rough-in for a whirlpool consists of a P-trap and vented drain. Use 1½-in. plastic waste and vent pipe, and ½- or ¾-in. copper for the supply lines.

Installing a whirlpool

Difficulty Level:

Tools & Materials: Whirlpool ❖ Pry bar ❖ ¾" subfloor-grade plywood ❖ ¼" x ½" panel edge trim ❖ Bolts & washers ❖ Waste & drain pipes ❖ 8d nails or 3" drywall screws ❖ Power cable ❖ Wire connectors ❖ 2x4s or 2x6s for framing ❖ Junction box ❖ Receptacle box ❖ GFCI receptacle ❖ Sheet-metal shims ❖ Cement-based backer board ❖ 10d galvanized nails or 2" cement-board screws ❖ 2 hinges or 6 1" flathead wood screws with washers ❖ ½" or ¾" AC plywood (for access panel)

1 After precutting holes for pipes and reinforcing the floor joists, install the subfloor and a platform for the whirlpool.

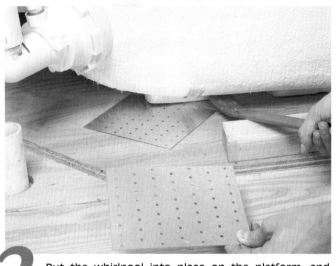

2 Put the whirlpool into place on the platform, and check to see whether it is level. If it needs adjustment, lever-up the unit, and insert metal shims.

3 Close the walls around the sides of the tub enclosure with cement-based backer board before you install the whirlpool.

4 Mark the outline of the base enclosure on the floor by using a spirit level held perfectly plumb from the top edge.

5 Put the enclosure framing into position to test the fit of the backer board and tile to the fixture rim. If the enclosure fits, nail it to the floor.

Installing a whirlpool, cont'd

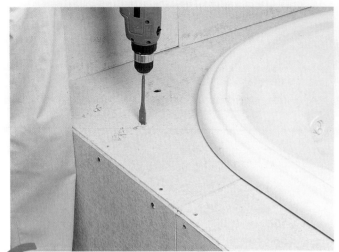

6 Attach the backer board to the frame with cement-board screws. Then drill holes for the water faucet supply lines.

7 Make an access panel the size recommended by the manufacturer. Read the instructions to determine the best location for this panel.

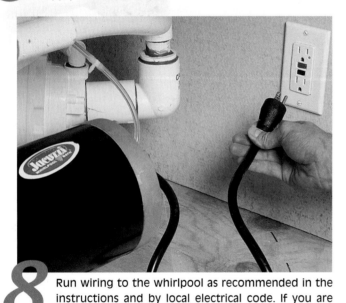

8 Run wiring to the whirlpool as recommended in the instructions and by local electrical code. If you are not confident working with wiring, hire a pro.

9 Tile is one of the best surfaces for installing around a whirlpool. It's best to install it at the same time that you tile the walls.

Wiring & Plumbing. Using an ordinary trap, connect the waste outlet to the drain and overflow. When all pipe is installed below the unit, attach backer board to the sides of the enclosure frame. Measure the supply lines, and drill the holes through the cement board. **(6)** Bring the lines to the faucet, but don't install the faucet until you've done the finish work on the wall.

Whirlpools require a removable panel to provide access to the electrical and mechanical equipment. The instructions will specify the size and location of this panel. To make a panel, frame the entire opening with 2×4s or 2×6s. **(7)** Then attach a panel, sized to overlap the rough framing by at least

1 inch. Make the access panel of AC plywood, edged with a solid-trim strip, ¼ × ½ inch. Attach the panel to the frame with two hinges or six 1-inch wood screws with washers. Later, you can paint the panel to match the surrounding wall.

Install a junction box to run a cable from the house's main service panel. You'll need to install a GFCI receptacle for the whirlpool's motor. **(8)** (See "Installing a GFCI Receptacle," page 167.)

Tile or solid-surface plastic makes a good finish for the surfaces around a whirlpool. You can even use wood if you seal it adequately. If you want to tile the base, install it at the same time as the walls. **(9)**

Toilets

Installing a new toilet in the same location requires careful removal of the old unit and mounting and connecting the new one. If you are installing the toilet in a new location, you will need to modify the existing pipe system.

Removing the Old Toilet

Shut off the water supply at the home's main valve even if the toilet has a separate shutoff valve. This is necessary because you'll be removing the old valve. Disconnect the riser, shutoff valve, and escutcheon with an adjustable wrench. *(1)* Remove the protective caps, if any, from the bolts that hold the toilet to the floor; then unscrew the nuts with a wrench. If the bolts are too corroded to come loose, soak them with penetrating oil, or just cut them with a hacksaw. *(2)*

Rock the bowl back and forth to free it from the floor; then lift it straight up off the drain. *(3)* Next, stuff a rag into the drain hole to keep sewer gas from escaping into the house. If any residue from the wax ring that seals the toilet to the drain remains behind, scrape it off the drain.

CAUTION Lifting the toilet can put stress on your back, so keep your knees bent while maneuvering the bowl. Always lift heavy objects with your legs rather than your back, and wear a lower-back support.

Removing an old toilet

Difficulty Level:

Tools & Materials: Adjustable wrench ❖ Open-end or combination wrench ❖ Hacksaw with metal-cutting blade (if needed) ❖ Penetrating oil (if needed) ❖ Lower-back support

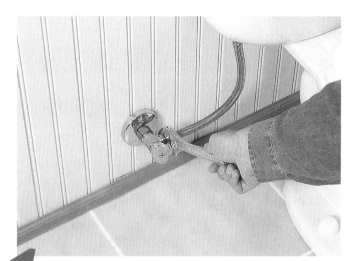

1 Before starting work, be sure the water supply is turned off. Then remove the riser, shutoff valve, and escutcheon, leaving only the stub-out protruding through the wall.

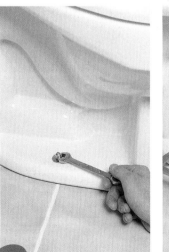

2 First, try to remove the bolt nuts with a wrench. (Nuts rusted shut can be soaked in penetrating oil first.) If this does not work, cut them off with a hacksaw.

3 After all disconnecting parts have been removed, rock the bowl from side to side to remove it from the drain. Be sure to bend your knees to avoid harming your back.

Installing a Toilet in a New Location

Begin by checking out your municipal plumbing code. The code might specify the allowable maximum distance between the toilet's drain and soil stack and vent. A separate vent is usually required when the toilet is more than 6 feet away from the existing vent. Getting a new vent through the roof might be more than you want to undertake, so be sure to think through your proposed layout.

Cutting the Existing Plumbing. Cut the pipe that supplied the previous toilet, and extend it with straight pipes and elbows that terminate in a hole in the floor or wall to the rear of the new toilet. If the existing supply line is copper tubing, extend the line by tapping into it at a convenient place with a T-fitting and copper pipes of the same size. *(1)* If the existing pipe is steel, use a threaded compression union at the old pipe's threaded end, and add a new section of copper tubing to other side of the union.

Select a shutoff valve with a compression-ring connection that matches the diameter of the pipe stub-out. Insert the nut over the end of the pipe stub-out, then the compression ring, then the valve. Tighten the nut, taking care not to overtighten it. *(2)*

Locating the New Plumbing. Remove the closet drain flange from the floor. *(3)* If necessary, cut the drain at the elbow, and stuff a rag inside it to temporarily cap it until you finish the piping and install the toilet. Place a board over the hole until you finish the floor. Extend the drainpipe to the new location with plastic pipe of the same type and diameter as the existing pipe.

Use a framing square to draw a centerline on the floor perpendicular to the wall. From the instructions, determine the required distance from the wall to the center of the drain hole, and mark it on the floor. *(4)* Turn the toilet upside down, and measure the distance from its drain hole to the sides and front of the base. *(5)* Mark these dimensions and the outline of the base on the floor.

Measure the outside diameter of the pipe of the closet bend flange, and scribe a circle of this diameter on the floor. *(6)* Drill a pilot hole at a point on the circle, and use a saber saw to cut out a hole in the subfloor. *(7)* Insert the closet-bend flange in the hole, and screw it to the floor. Use both an elbow and a straight piece of pipe of the proper diameter and length to join the tailpiece of the closet bend flange to the main drain. *(8)*

Adapting plumbing to move a toilet

Difficulty Level: 🐟🐟🐟

Tools & Materials: Measuring tape ❖ Hacksaw with carbide-tipped blade ❖ New water-supply pipes, pipe nipples & couplings as needed ❖ Threaded compression unit ❖ Closet bend flange ❖ Coupling nut & compression ring (for chromed copper pipes) ❖ Shutoff valve ❖ Framing square

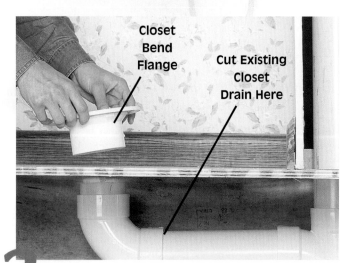

Closet Bend Flange

Cut Existing Closet Drain Here

3 If you don't have enough clearance to tie a new closet-drain extension to the existing drain, cut the existing pipe and add a new section of the needed length.

6 Measure the outside diameter of the closet bend flange pipe, and draw its outline on the floor, centered over the drain opening.

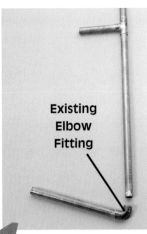
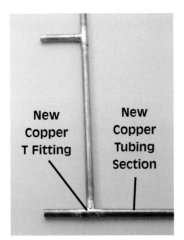

Existing Elbow Fitting

New Copper T Fitting　　**New Copper Tubing Section**

1 If you need to tap into an existing copper pipe to extend a supply line, melt the solder at an elbow. Break the elbow free, install a new connection, and solder all joints.

2 Slide the escutcheon over the pipe stub, and press it to the wall. Then slip on the nut and compression ring. Slide on the shutoff valve and tighten the nut.

4 Use a framing square to locate the center of the toilet drain on the floor. (If you can't get to the plumbing underneath, remove this section of subfloor.)

5 Measure the distance from the center of the toilet's drain hole to the outside edge of its base. Then mark the position of the toilet on the floor.

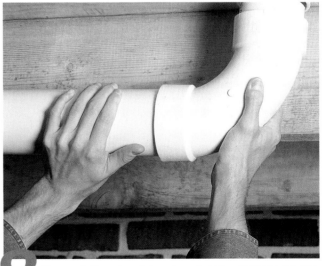

7 Cut the hole with a saber saw or a keyhole saw. Insert the closet-bend flange in the hole, and screw it to the floor.

8 Connect the closet bend and drain sections to the closet-bend flange and the soil stack. Also, connect the new toilet to the vent stack with a branch line.

Mounting the New Toilet

Slip the heads of the mounting bolts into the slots of the closet bend flange. *(1)* With the toilet turned on its side or upside down, press the wax seal ring over the horn at the base of the bowl. The horn is the protruding lip around the drain hole in the base of the toilet. *(2)* Then apply plumber's putty around the edge of the base.

Remove the rags from the drain hole; then turn the toilet right side up, and carefully lift it into position, aligning the bolt holes in the base with the bolts in the flange. Lift the bowl slightly, and slowly coax it to the floor, twisting it somewhat to seal the wax ring. *(3)* Then press down to tighten the seal on the wax ring and the putty.

Place a spirit level over the rim, side to side. Pour some water into the bowl to check for leaks. Re-mold the wax ring if leaks occur. When set, install the washers and nuts on the bolts. Do not overtighten the nuts, or they may crack the bowl.

If the tank is separate from the bowl, place the spud washer (a large rubber ring) over the tailpiece of the flush valve in the lower section. Then set the tank on the bowl, aligning the spud washer over the water inlet opening. *(4)* Attach the tank to the bowl rim with washers and nuts from below.

Installing the Risers

It is best to use a braided stainless-steel riser for the cold-water supply to the toilet, but you can also use chromed copper. Use pipe the diameter that's recommended by the toilet manufacturer.

To install a braided riser, fit one end into the shutoff valve and the other into the tank's threaded inlet, hand-tighten the nuts, and then tighten with an adjustable wrench.

To install chromed copper pipes, measure the distance from the toilet connection to the shutoff valve, and allow enough extra length for the fittings; then cut the pipe with a tubing cutter. Slip a coupling nut and compression ring over both ends of the pipe before inserting it into the shutoff valve and toilet inlet; then tighten the nuts. Take care not to make a sharp bend or kink in a copper tube.

Finishing the Job

Turn on the water supply, and check for leaks. If you can't stop a leak by a bit more tightening, disconnect the riser, and apply plumber's putty or Plumber's tape to the threads. Use a caulking gun to place a bead of silicone caulk around the base of the toilet. *(5)*

Toilets under Pressure

In 1992, the Department of Energy mandated low-volume, 1.6-gallon toilets as a water-conservation measure. But a nationwide survey conducted by the National Association of Home Builders found that roughly four out of five builders and homeowners experienced problems with low-flush units. Most builders surveyed said that they receive more callbacks on low-flush toilets than on anything else. Here are three common complaints: multiple flushes are needed to clear the bowl, residue remains even after multiple flushes, and they clog easily. New low-flush units work better than the first models, but many builders and owners still have to call in plumbers. To deal with the problems, most people revert to double flushing, which defeats much of the water-conservation potential of the system.

If you have a choice, there's a better way. Pressure-tank toilets (pictured at right) have a secondary container inside. It uses the pressure of water coming into the main tank to compress air and give each flush a pressure assist to push out wastes. This hybrid design is roughly twice the cost of gravity units.

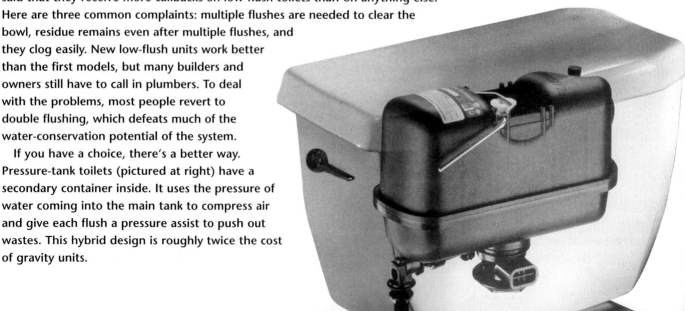

Mounting the new toilet

Difficulty Level:

Tools & Materials: New toilet ❖ Wax ring seal ❖ Plumber's putty ❖ Spud washer ❖ Adjustable wrench ❖ Braided stainless-steel riser or chromed copper riser ❖ Spirit level ❖ Silicone caulk & caulking gun ❖ Spirit level ❖ Washers & nuts

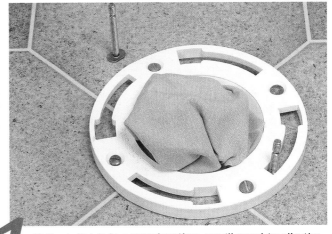

1 If the toilet is in a new location, you'll need to slip the flange bolts through the slots in the top of the new closet-bend flange.

11 *Working with Plumbing*

2 Press the wax ring seal over the horn of the toilet drain hole. The horn is the protruding lip around the drain hole in the base of the toilet.

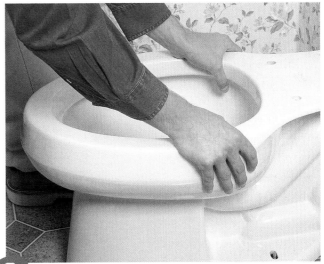

3 Lift the toilet into position, aligning the holes in the base with the bolts in the flange. Press down to make a good seal, and tighten the nuts onto the bolts.

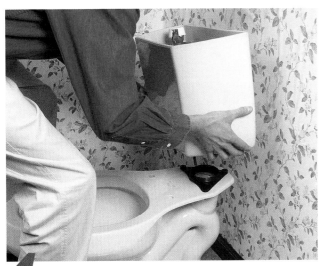

4 If the tank is a separate unit from the bowl, sandwich a spud washer between the drain hole and the tank. Fasten the tank to the bowl's rim.

5 After the toilet has been connected and you've checked that it is working properly, lay a bead of silicone caulk around the base.

Working with Wiring

*B*ringing a bathroom's electrical system up to current standards will make it both safer and more convenient. When planning new wiring, safety should be your first consideration. Protect outlets with ground-fault circuit-interrupter (GFCI) devices, which reduce the hazards of shock. Next, consider convenience. You may need to add additional circuits for special equipment like a whirlpool tub. If you want to add an exhaust fan, you will need both a power source and a switch.

Rewiring can be done without tearing up walls and ceilings, but it's easiest when the framing is exposed. Walls stripped to the studs give you the opportunity to replace outdated wiring, outlets, and switches, as well as to make any adjustments for your new scheme.

Working with wiring isn't difficult if you take the time and effort to understand what's required—but it is extremely unforgiving. A bad connection means all or part of a circuit won't work. More importantly, if you get caught between a live circuit and a grounding source, your body will take the brunt of the energy passing through the circuit, resulting in injury or death.

Wiring Basics

If your house is more than 50 years old, its electrical system is very likely outdated. Chances are that successive owners added bits and pieces over the years in no coherent fashion. Knowing this, you can choose to rewire the whole house at once or update it as you remodel the rooms. If you go room by room, at least be sure that the main electrical service is up-to-date and capable of carrying the additional loads required by many modern fixtures and appliances.

Getting a Power Source

Electricity enters your home through overhead or underground wires, where it passes through a meter before entering the main service panel (also called a fuse box or circuit-breaker panel). The meter measures the amount of electricity you use. At the main service panel, the electricity is divided into branch circuits, each of which is protected by a fuse or circuit breaker. Power travels in a closed loop through the circuit's hot wires to outlets or fixtures and returns to the service panel via neutral wires, unless it is interrupted by an open switch or short circuit. The fuses or breakers protect these circuits from overloading—that is, from drawing more power than the wires can handle.

Your bathroom lights and power outlets may be wired to a single circuit protected by a 15- or 20-amp breaker in the panel. If you rewire or change a few light fixtures or outlets, you won't need to change the power source. If you add new devices, you may overload the circuit, so get the advice of an electrician before proceeding.

CAUTION

Electricity can be dangerous, but if you use common sense, you can work with it quite safely. It's most important to remember always, without fail, to turn off the power at the main service panel before working on a circuit. Use one hand to disconnect or reactivate a fuse or circuit breaker, and keep the other hand in your pocket or behind your back. Before starting work, check the circuit with a neon circuit tester to be sure that it is shut off. If you always follow this rule, you will never suffer an electrical shock.

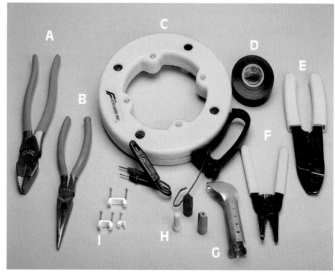

Basic tools for wiring include (A) lineman's pliers, (B) needle-nose pliers, (C) fish tape, (D) electrical tape, (E) multipurpose tool, (F) wire stripper, (G) cable ripper, (H) wire connectors, and (I) cable staples.

Basic Electrical Terms

○ **Amperes, or amps,** measure current flow. An amp rating is marked on many appliances. Electrical suppliers have charts showing the amp rating for various American wire gauge (AWG) sizes. The rating for your house's circuits is marked on the circuit breaker or fuse—generally 15 or 20 amps for most room circuits and 30 or 50 amps for heavy-duty circuits, such as those serving a kitchen range, a clothes dryer, or a water heater.

○ **Volts** measure the force of electrical pressure that keeps the current flowing through the wires. Products are marked with a voltage capacity, usually 120 or 240 volts. You can't hook up a product designed to operate at 120 volts to a 240-volt electrical outlet—it will burn out. The shape of the receptacle will prevent you from inserting the wrong type of plug.

○ **Watts = volts × amps.** The wattage rating of a circuit is the amount of power the circuit can deliver safely, determined by the current-carrying capacity of the wires. Wattage also indicates the amount of power that a fixture or appliance needs to work properly. Appliances with large motors, such as air conditioners, should not exceed 50 percent of a circuit's capacity because of start-up overcurrent—motors need more current to start than they do to run. Large appliances often need dedicated, or separate, circuits.

Assuming the wiring is sound and you want to leave the wall finishes intact, you can replace a light fixture, switch, or outlet in the same location by simply removing the existing device and installing the new one. If you want to add an outlet or light, you can tap into the box of a fixture you've removed or come off of a box containing an outlet. If you tap off an outlet box, replace the box with a larger one to contain the additional wiring.

Grounding

Electricity always seeks to return to a point of zero voltage (the ground) along the easiest path open to it. If you touch an electric fence, electricity will flow from the fence through your body to the ground—the electrical path is then "grounded" through you. A short circuit in wiring is a similar situation. Electrical current exits the closed loop of the circuit—because, for example, a hot wire is off its terminal and touches the metal box of a light fixture, which is now charged—and returns to the source by some other means. If the system is properly grounded, this short would be a fault to ground and pose no hazard. If it's improperly grounded and you touch the wiring path—and it could be something as innocuous as the metal pull cord on that light fixture—the electricity will seek to ground itself through your body.

To guard against this, your house's electrical system has grounding wires, which give the electricity a permanent alternative path for its return to the source. Each outlet and fixture has its own grounding wires that return electricity to the main panel—the third, grounding plug of most appliances extends this protection to them. The entire system is also grounded to your cold-water pipes or, if you have plastic plumbing, to a grounding rod buried underground next to your foundation—or to both.

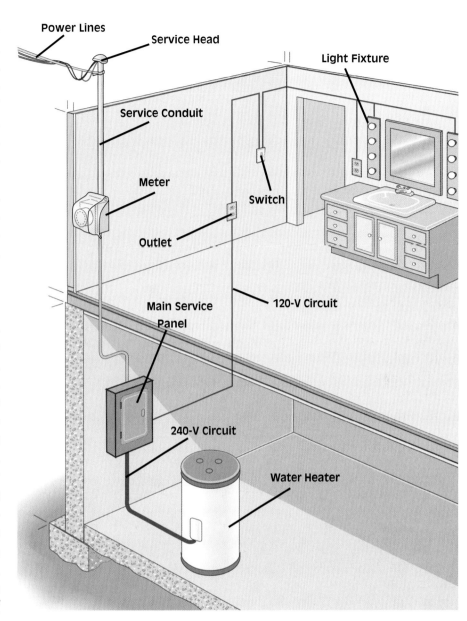

Electrical circuits are run from the main panel; they may contain outlets, fixtures, and switches. Large fixtures, like water heaters, require dedicated circuits of higher voltage.

Codes & Permits

All electrical procedures and materials are governed by local building or electrical codes. Some municipalities won't let anyone but a licensed electrician do any wiring work. Some will allow DIYers to rough-in their wiring as long as an electrician inspects it and makes the final hookup to the service panel. Local code may also prohibit the use of a certain type of cable or require a particular size wiring or minimum number of circuits, for example. The electrical code is for your protection. You may need to obtain a permit before beginning some projects. Always consult with a municipal building inspector.

12 Working with Wiring

Working with Wire & Conduit

Single wires are insulated to carry electricity or are bare (sometimes insulated green) for grounding. Most household wiring is contained in cable, inside flexible metal (as in AC or BX) or plastic insulation (as in NM). Wires have size numbers that express wire diameter as a whole number. For example, 14-gauge wire is 0.064 inches in diameter; 12-gauge is 0.081 inches. Smaller numbers indicate larger diameters that carry more power. The National Electrical Code requires a minimum of 14-gauge wire for most house wiring.

Wires have color-coded plastic insulation to indicate their function. Hot wires carrying current at full voltage are usually black, red, or white with black marks (marker or bands of electrical tape), but can be other colors. Neutral wires carrying zero voltage are white or gray. Grounding wires are bare copper or clad in green plastic insulation. A small piece of wire, called a pigtail, connects two or more wires to the same terminal.

Conduit

Insulated wires are sometimes run through metal or plastic pipe called conduit. Metal conduit comes in three types: rigid (preferred for outdoor applications), intermediate, and EMT (electrical metal tubing). Standard conduit diameters are ½, ¾, 1, and 1¼ inches. There are fittings to join conduit for straight runs and at 45-degree angles, and a special tool, called a hickey, for making more gradual bends in metal tubing. You may be required by codes to use conduit for wires run underground or in open, unfinished walls, such as a garage or basement.

You can cut both metal and plastic conduit with either a pipe cutter or a hacksaw. A pipe cutter is the best tool—the shoulders of the cutter keep the pipe square in the device and ensure an even cut. When cutting with a hacksaw, wrap the cutline with masking tape first to reduce burring, which can damage wires' insulation when it is pulled through. For more information, see "Plastic Pipe," pages 120 to 121, and "Copper Tubing," pages 122 to 123.

Bare Wire

Insulated Solid Wire

Insulated Stranded Wire

Nonmetallic Cable (NM)

Armored Cable (AC)

Splicing & Capping Wires

When you run cable and hook up outlets, fixtures, and switches, the individual wires inside each cable may need to be spliced together with the wires from other lengths of cable using wire connectors. To join wires, strip ½ inch of insulation, hold the wires parallel, and twist them together clockwise with a pair of lineman's pliers. The twisted part should be long enough to engage the wire connector without exposing any bare wire when you attach it. Screw down on a wire connector so that the exposed wires are covered. Tighten the connector by hand; don't use pliers.

Boxes

Each switch, outlet, and light fixture must be installed into a metal or plastic electrical box that is attached to the structure. Ask your building inspector which types of boxes are acceptable. Round or octagonal boxes are generally used for ceiling fixtures or junction boxes (boxes used to contain only wiring). Rectangular boxes usually contain switches or outlets. You can choose among boxes that come with various types of fasteners, screws, nails, brackets, and clips suited for new construction or for retrofitting into walls.

The main types of electrical boxes include (A) standard plastic receptacle and switch box, (B) standard metal receptacle and switch box, (C) metal octagonal box, (D) MP bracket switch box, (E) plastic ceiling fixture box, and (F) metal "pancake" fixture box.

Wiring Boxes

The National Electrical Code limits the number of wires you can install in any one box. Wire connections outside a box are not permitted at all. A single switch or duplex (two-plug) outlet and all the necessary wiring will fit into a 2½-inch-wide plastic or metal box. More than one device in a box—or more wiring than needed just to serve the device—calls for a wider or deeper box. Use the table at right to determine the required box size.

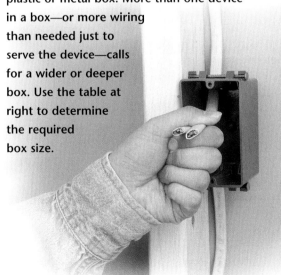

Maximum Number of Wires Permitted per Box

Type of Box	Wires Allowed (by Gauge)		
(Size in Inches)	14	12	10
Round or Octagonal Boxes			
4" x 1½"	7	6	6
4" x 2⅛"	10	9	8
Square Boxes			
4" x 1½"	10	9	8
4" x 2⅛"	15	13	12
Rectangular Boxes			
3" x 2" x 2¼"	5	4	4
3" x 2" x 2½"	6	5	5
3" x 2" x 2¾"	7	6	5
3" x 2" x 3½"	9	8	7

New Wiring in Open Walls

Gutting floors, walls, or ceilings down to the framing gives you the opportunity to replace outdated wiring and to locate electrical fixtures just where you want them. The easiest kind of wiring to install directly onto exposed framing is plastic-sheathed, nonmetallic cable, called NM cable or sometimes by the brand name Romex. NM cable contains a black-sheathed hot wire, a white neutral wire, and a bare grounding wire.

Always check with the electrical inspector to see which type and gauge of cable is acceptable for your project and by your local code. As a rule of thumb, you will probably get by with 14-gauge cable for bathroom lights and outlets. Special equipment such as whirlpools, heaters, and appliances will require 12-gauge wire or larger. (Use the product literature as a guide.) Appliances such as these usually require their own dedicated circuits.

Running Cable

Before reworking any branch circuit, shut off the power to the circuit at the main panel or fuse box. Begin your wiring by figuring out where you want to locate the boxes and nailing them to the studs. Plastic boxes come with their own nails; use 6d nails for the flanges of metal boxes. Mount them so that the face of the box will be even with the finished wall surface. Switch boxes are usually mounted 48 inches above the floor, while outlets are mounted 12 to 18 inches above the floor. Mount boxes at any convenient height above a counter. Check the local codes for any clearance requirements for the location of receptacles and switches.

Drill holes for the cable through the studs; set them at least 1¼ inches back from the facing edge so that the cable won't be pierced by nails or screws. *(1)* If you don't have a power drill that fits between the studs, you can cut out notches of the same depth. Starting from the junction box, run the cable through the holes in the studs from outlet box to outlet box. Run branches to the light-fixture boxes by stapling the cable to the studs or by using cable stackers. *(2)* Leave 6 inches or so of cable ends poking out the of each box to give you enough wire to connect the devices later. *(3)* Where cable runs up studs, and just above or below each box, use a hammer to attach cable staples or clips to the studs. *(4)*

Protecting the Cable

Code requires that the cable be protected from punctures; that's why the holes must be 1¼ inches from the face of the stud. If any cable ends up closer to the stud face, attach a wire shield over the stud at this location. *(5)* You can get metal plates made for this purpose at your electrical supplier.

Plastic Outlet Box

Mounting Bracket

6d Nails

16D Nails

Metal Outlet Boxes

Boxes for switches and outlets are made of plastic or galvanized steel. Many boxes are fastened to the studs with two 16d nails through slots and the top and bottom (left). Some are nailed through a tab to the face of the stud (right).

Running new wiring in open walls

Difficulty Level:

Tools & Materials: Power drill with ¾" bit ❖ Cable ❖ Cable staples or cable stackers ❖ Junction boxes ❖ Switch boxes ❖ Outlet boxes ❖ Metal stud plates or wire shields ❖ Saw (if cutting notches) ❖ 6d common nails ❖ Insulated hammer ❖ Cable clamps

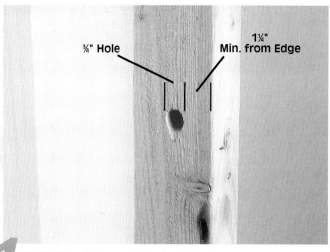

1 Drill ¾-in. holes at least 1¼ in. from the stud face. Special right-angle drills are available for drilling holes in tight spaces.

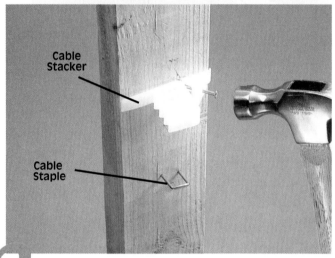

2 Attach plastic-sheathed cable to studs using metal cable staples or cable stackers. Stackers have channels that hold several cables.

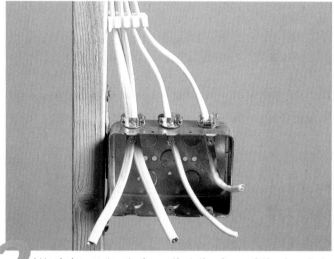

3 Attach boxes to studs so that the face of the box is in line with the proposed wall finish—½ in. or more proud of the stud.

4 Run cables through the framing in a straight line, if possible, and secure the cable to the framing with a staple every 48 in. and within 8 in. of a box.

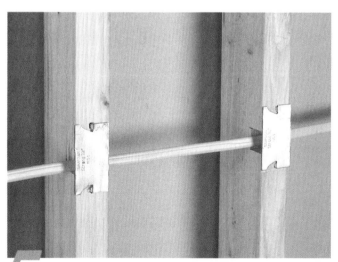

5 Nail a wire shield over notches (or holes placed closer than 1¼ in. from the stud face) to protect the cable against punctures by screws or nails.

12 *Working with Wiring*

New Wiring in Finished Walls

Snaking new wiring through floors, walls, and ceilings while leaving the surface finishes intact can be difficult, but it's possible to do. You'll still need to remove the drywall or plaster at key spots.

NM cable wound in spools is required for this job. You bend fish tape over the end of the cable and fish the other end through enclosed walls and floors. The cable emerges some distance away through a hole you've opened up in the wall or ceiling. Simply pull the cable through the hole. Be sure to turn off the power at the service panel before beginning.

Cutting a Hole

If the first box you want to wire is on the first floor, begin by cutting a hole in the wall to fit the box. If you are bringing the wire to the second floor, start by making an access hole in the first-floor wall. Make the access hole near the floor and directly below where the receptacle will be.

Drive a long nail through the floor close to the wall and directly below the first-floor receptacle or access hole. From the basement, drill a ¾-inch-diameter hole up through the subfloor and bottom plate into the wall above, using the pilot nail as your guide. *(1)*

Fishing a Wire

Take the roll of cable to the basement, and bend the ends of the wires over to make a U-shape. Feed the cable up through the hole in the floor. Have a helper stand upstairs, and feed fish tape into the wall through the hole you drilled. Once it's out of the opening, tape the cable end to the fish tape to prevent them from coming apart. *(2)*

Working together, move the cable and tape end around until they hook together; then have your helper pull on the tape to draw the cable up through the wall and out the opening. *(3)*

Running Cable Vertically

To pull the cable from somewhere inside the wall up to the ceiling, first remove part of the corner at the wall-ceiling joint above the wall hole. Cut a notch in the top plates to make a space for the cable run. Thread fish tape from the ceiling opening to the wall/ceiling joint opening and then down the wall. Attach the cable to the tape, and pull it back up through the structure and out the ceiling opening. (See the illustration below.) Nail a metal protective plate over the cable in the corner notch before patching the opening. The procedure is similar if you are running cable to a second-floor receptacle. Use the notch to get into the second-floor wall; then use the cable to snag the tape through the receptacle hole upstairs. Leave at least 6 inches of cable protruding out of the box to allow for your connections.

Running Cable Horizontally

If you want to run cable to another point on the wall—say you're adding a few outlets to an existing circuit—try to make the horizontal run in the open basement ceiling. If you can't run cable horizontally below the bathroom floor (such as

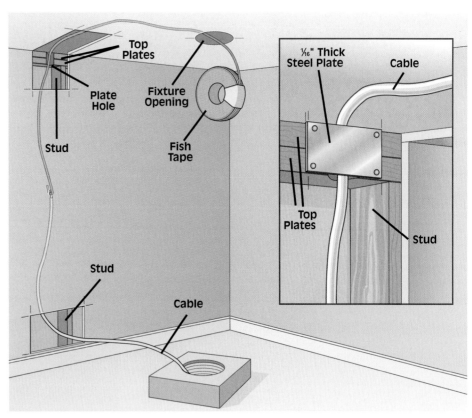

To run cable vertically behind a wall, cut holes in the wall-ceiling joint, and feed fish tape from the ceiling box to the opening and down the wall. Use the tape to snag the cable, and pull it through. Attach metal plates over the cable where shown before patching.

when you're wiring a second-story bath-room), you can run it through the bathroom's walls.

First, cut out temporary access holes into the drywall along the run, one for each stud. With a right-angle drill, cut a hole into each stud at the level of the box. If you don't have a right-angle drill, cut notches with a saw. For short runs, just pull the cable from one hole to the next by hand, feeding it through the holes in the studs. For long runs, feed the fish tape through the holes, and pull the cable through. (See the illustration at right.)

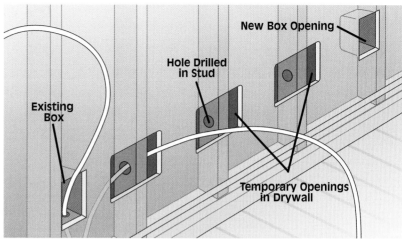

To run cable horizontally behind a finished wall, cut an opening for each stud, and drill holes or cut notches in the studs. Use fish tape to pull the new cable through the wall to the new location.

Running new cable from the floor below

Difficulty Level:

Tools & Materials: Power drill with ¾" bit ❖ Fish tape ❖ Electrical tape ❖ Keyhole saw or dry-wall saw ❖ Electrical boxes ❖ NM cable ❖ Metal plates for studs

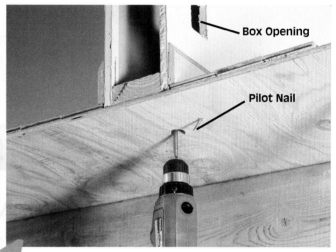

1 Drive a pilot nail through the floor to mark the position of the new box. Then drill an access hole through the sub-floor and the bottom plate of the wall.

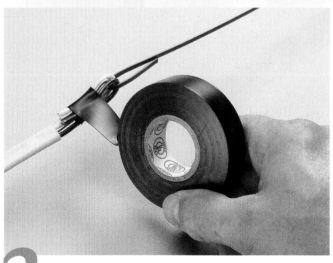

2 Make a hook in the end of the cable, and feed it through the hole. Attach cable to the hook at the end of the fish tape, and secure it with tape.

3 Once the cable is secured to the fish tape, you can pull the cable through the opening in the wall. Then pull it through the studs or up through the ceiling.

12 *Working with Wiring*

New Circuits

To add another circuit, you will need to tap into the main panel. Begin by determining how many new circuits you need and the voltage each must carry. A 120-volt circuit usually requires a single breaker of 15- or 20-amp capacity. A 220- or 240-volt circuit is wired to a special type of breaker. Do the rough wiring of the bathroom first, and extend the cables to the panel box.

Turn off the power to the house with the main breaker switch, which is mounted at the top of the service panel. *(1)* With the power off, remove the cover plate and note the breaker arrangement. *(2)* Each breaker in use is connected to a circuit cable; a label on the cover should identify each. Check whether there are any breakers not in use, or spare slots for additional breakers. *(3)* If you find no spare breakers, just empty slots, you can add a new circuit. If all slots are in use, you may be able to add a double breaker, which puts two breakers in the space of one. Otherwise, you may have to add a sub-panel. In any case, if you don't see a spare breaker or slot, it's a good idea to get an electrician's advice.

Bringing the Cable to the Panel

Use a screwdriver and hammer to pry out a knockout from the side or top of the panel box. Attach a cable clamp, and thread 12 inches of the cable through the connector, the hole in the box, and a locknut. *(4)* Tighten the screws against the cable, and tighten the locknut. *(5)* Remove about 8 inches of the outer sleeve of the end of the cable, and strip the wire ends. Insert the ends of the white neutral wire and the bare copper grounding wire into holes along the bus bars intended for these wires at the side or bottom of the panel (noting how the other circuits are connected), and tighten the setscrews. *(6)*

Adding the Circuit Breaker

If a spare breaker is not already in place, snap one into its slot on the panel board. Loosen the screw of the breaker, and insert the black wire of the cable into the hole below. Then retighten the screw to secure the wire end. *(7)* Screw the cover back on the panel, and record the new circuit on the panel door. *(8)* To prevent a power surge, turn off all the individual breakers; then turn on the main breaker. Turn the individual breakers back on one by one.

Difficulty Level:

Tools & Materials: Cable ❖ Insulated screwdriver ❖ Hammer ❖ Cable ripper ❖ Cable clamps ❖ Needle-nose pliers ❖ Circuit tester ❖ Multipurpose tool ❖ New single- or double-pole circuit breakers ❖ Flashlight ❖ Insulated hammer

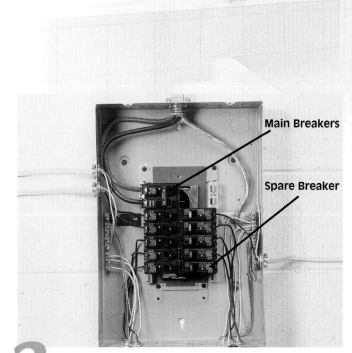

Main Breakers

Spare Breaker

3 Check to see whether there are any breakers that are not in use or any spare slots for more breakers. A breaker not in use won't have a cable attached to it.

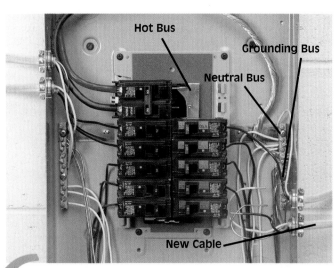

Hot Bus

Grounding Bus

Neutral Bus

New Cable

6 Connect the end of the white wire to the neutral bus bar, where the other white wires are connected. Then connect the grounding wire to the grounding bus.

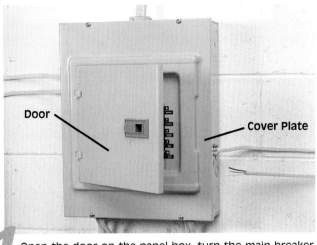

1 Open the door on the panel box, turn the main breaker to the off position, and unscrew the screws at the corners to remove the cover plate.

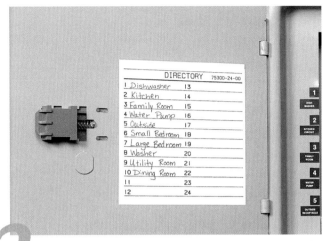

2 With the power off, remove the cover plate and note the breaker arrangement. Each breaker in use is connected to a cable. A label on the cover should identify each circuit.

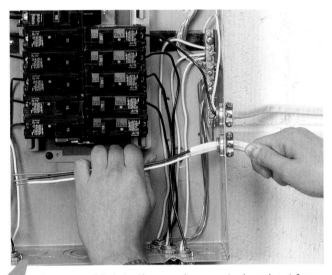

4 To run a cable into the panel, pry out a knockout from the side or top of the panel box. Thread the cable through a cable clamp and then through a locknut.

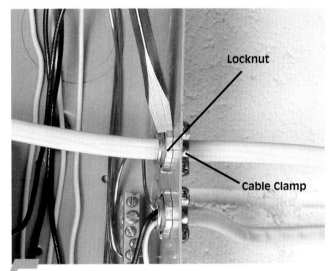

5 When you have enough cable inside the panel, tighten the cable-clamp screws and the locknut with an insulated screwdriver.

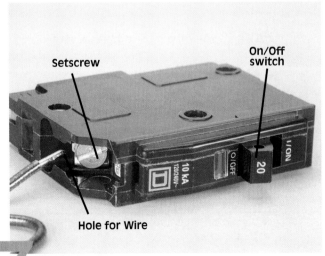

7 A typical 120-volt circuit breaker has a clip in the rear that plugs into the hot bus of the panel and a hole in the side for inserting the black wire of the cable.

8 Screw the cover plate back onto the panel housing, and record the new circuit on the panel door. Turn the main breaker back on.

12 Working with Wiring

Ground-Fault Circuit Interrupters (GFCIs)

Bathrooms pose hazards not found in most other parts of the house because of the presence of two good conductors of electricity: water and metal pipes. If a person is in contact with the pipe system while handling appliances or switches, the electrical current may pass through his or her body on its way to the ground. Ordinary power outlets, even when containing a grounding wire, don't completely protect you against the full brunt of an electrical shock. Ground-fault circuit interrupters (GFCIs) do. A GFCI senses an overload and cuts off the current in ⅟25 to ⅟30 of a second—25 to 30 times faster than a heartbeat.

Code requires that GFCIs be used in fans and lights above tubs or showers, in whirlpool and spa wiring, and in all bathroom outlets. You are required to install a GFCI in an older home whenever you're replacing an outlet in an area that is specified for a GFCI. (In old circuits without a grounding wire, this requires running a new three-wire cable from the panel.) But beyond the code, GFCIs just make good safety sense in the bathroom.

Installing a GFCI Receptacle

Go to the main panel box, and trip the circuit breaker that controls the receptacle. Make sure you have tripped the right breaker by plugging a neon circuit tester into the outlet. *(1)* Remove the cover plate and the screws that hold the receptacle in the box. Unscrew the hot (black) wires from the brass terminals and the neutral (white) wires from the silver terminals. Disconnect the bare or green grounding wire, and discard the receptacle. *(2)*

If there were two cables connected to the old receptacle, you need to use a neon circuit tester to determine which is feeding power into the box and which is taking power out. Make sure all bare ends of wires are safely away from the walls, well separated from each other. Turn the power back on. Touch one probe of the tester to a black wire, the other probe to a grounding wire. (All of the grounding wires should still be connected together.) When the tester lights, that black wire is the feed. Turn off the power. Label the feed black and white wires. *(3)*

Connect the GFCI black and white leads labeled LINE to the feed wires of the same color. Connect the GFCI leads labeled LOAD to the out-going wires in the box. If there are no outgoing wires, attach a wire connector to each LOAD lead. Connect the green GFCI grounding wire to the other grounding wires in the box. Fold the wires neatly into the box, insert the new receptacle, and secure it with the screws that came with it. Put on the wall plate, and restore the power. *(4)*

Make sure the button marked "reset" is pressed all the way in. Then press the button marked "test." The reset button should pop out. If it does, push it back into position. *(5)* You are all set. But if the device does not work, turn off the power, open up the box, and check the connections.

Three Ways to Protect with GFCIs

The cheapest and easiest way to use a GFCI is a portable device (top) that you simply plug into the outlet of the receptacle you want to protect. It protects only that outlet. At slightly more expense and effort, you can replace the receptacle with a GFCI receptacle (center), which offers the opportunity to protect receptacles "downstream" from the one you are replacing. Another way to protect all receptacles and devices connected to the bathroom is to wire them to a single circuit, and install a GFCI breaker (bottom) in the panel box. (See "Running New Circuits from the Panel," pages 164 and 165.) This is also the most expensive way to achieve protection, as GFCI breakers cost about four times as much as an ordinary 120-volt breaker. The steps at right describe how to install a GFCI receptacle.

When you buy your GFCI receptacle, it may have four screws at the sides and one below attached to it. One pair of black and white lugs is marked "line," while the other pair is marked "load." The fifth—green—lug is the ground connection. Another type of GFCI receptacle has five color-coded wires instead of lugs.

Installing a GFCI receptacle

Difficulty Level:

Tools & Materials: GFCI receptacle ❖ Neon circuit tester ❖ Insulated screwdriver ❖ Wire connectors ❖ Green wire for two pigtails & grounding screw

1 Insert a neon circuit tester to be sure that the circuit has been shut down. If the indicator light comes on, the circuit is live.

2 Use an insulated screwdriver to disconnect and remove the standard outlet from the box. Be sure to leave all wires and wire connectors in place.

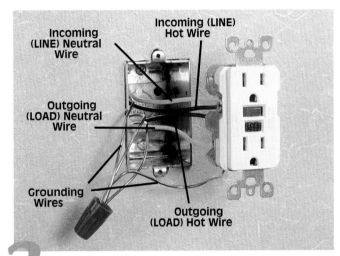

Incoming (LINE) Neutral Wire

Incoming (LINE) Hot Wire

Outgoing (LOAD) Neutral Wire

Grounding Wires

Outgoing (LOAD) Hot Wire

3 Incoming hot and neutral wires are connected to their respective terminals marked LINE. Outgoing wires, if any, are connected to the LOAD terminals.

4 After securing the new GFCI receptacle into the box, replace the wall plate using an insulated screwdriver and restore the power.

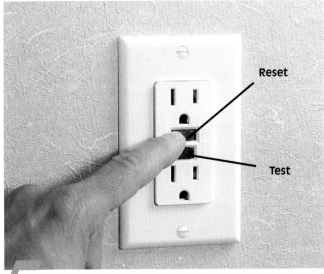

Reset

Test

5 To test the installation, press the reset button and then the test button. If the GFCI is working, the reset button should pop out.

12 Working with Wiring

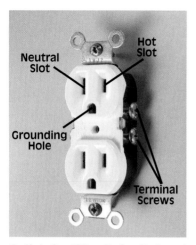
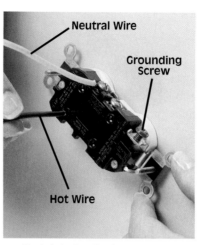

Outlets for 120-volt circuits have two vertical slots for the hot and neutral wires and a U-shaped slot for the ground. Outlets will also have terminals and holes for hot and neutral wires and a screw for grounding wires.

Outlets

If you protect all outlets in the bathroom with a single GFCI circuit breaker, you can install standard outlets intended for 120-volt circuits throughout the room. Outlets accepted by the National Electrical Code contain three slots: two vertical slots of slightly different length for the hot and neutral wires and a U-shaped slot for the ground wire. You can wire the outlets using the screws on the sides or, more simply, by inserting the stripped end of a wire directly into the proper hole in the back of the outlet. (Some electricians don't consider the holes to be

as reliable as screw attachment.) Outlets are installed in the wall according to where they fall in the circuit, as described below.

Wiring Mid-Run Outlets

Bring the incoming and outgoing cables into the box through the top or bottom holes. Connect the two hot (black) wires to the two brass-colored screws or insert the wires into the holes marked "black" on the back. Attach the two neutral white wires to the silver-colored screws or insert the wires into the holes marked "white." Connect the grounding wires together and to the grounding screw in the box, if metal. Wrap electrical tape around the sides of the receptacle to protect the terminal screws from contact with grounding wires.

Wiring End-of-the-Run Outlets

Bring the incoming cable into the box through the top or bottom hole. Connect the hot black wire to a brass-colored screw or insert the wire into the hole marked "black" on the backside. Attach the neutral white wire to the silver-colored terminal, or insert it into the hole marked "white." Connect the grounding wire to the grounding screw in the box, if metal. Wrap the sides of the outlet with electrical tape.

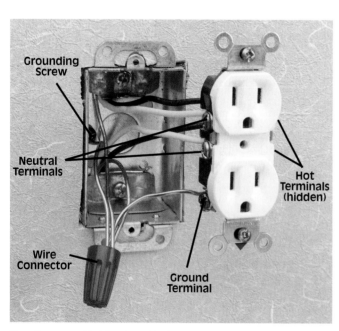

To wire an outlet in the middle of the run, connect the two black wires to the two brass-colored screws and the two white wires to the silver-colored terminals.

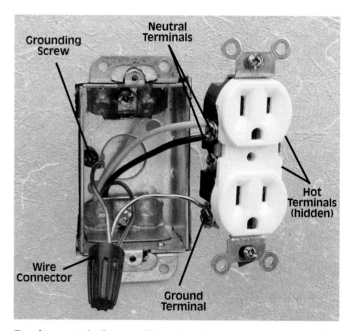

To wire an end-of-run outlet, bring the incoming cable into the box through the hole. Connect the black wire to the brass-colored screw and the white wire to the silver-colored screw.

Switches

A switch controls the flow of power in a circuit. Most residential switches are toggle types, also called snap switches. Older houses might have dial or even push-button switches. Other switch options can add convenience and save electricity. Timer switches, for example, are used to control fans in kitchens and baths so that you can turn them on and leave without turning them off.

Illuminated switches are handy if a switch controlling an overhead light isn't at the entry to a room. Instead of groping for a lamp, change the nearest standard switch to an illuminated one. Some have a small pilot light under the toggle; others have a toggle that emits a glow so that you can't miss it. You can exchange standard toggles that click on and off for more modern units such as paddle switches or silent switches that don't click.

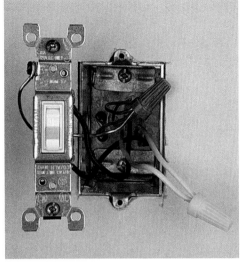

A single-pole switch in the middle of a circuit has two cables entering its box, each with hot, neutral, and grounding wires.

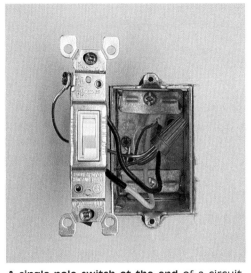

A single-pole switch at the end of a circuit has cable coming into the box but not going out. The cable clamps at the back of the box.

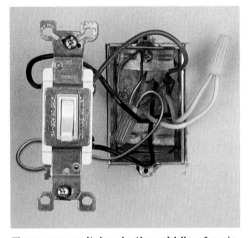

Three-way switches in the middle of a circuit have a red traveler wire. These switches control one light from two locations.

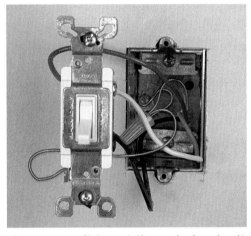

Three-way switches at the end of a circuit run still have a red traveler wire to connect switches—for example, at each end of stairs.

Typical Switch Wiring

A switch with two terminals (plus a grounding terminal) is called a single-pole switch; it alone controls a particular circuit. The incoming hot wire is hooked to one terminal screw and the outgoing hot wire to the other. A switch with three terminal screws (plus ground) is called a three-way switch; these control one fixture from two places and will not have ON/OFF on the toggle. There are also four-way switches, which control lights from three locations; and double switches, which serve more than one circuit in the same switch box.

Switch Stamps

Switches are stamped with code letters and numbers detailing operating specifications and safety information. Learn how to read these so that you buy the right switch. The switch at right is rated for 15-amp and 120-volt circuits on alternating current (AC) only; CU/ALR (or CU/AL) shows that it can be used with copper or aluminum wire; CU WIRE ONLY switches can be used with only copper wire. UL or UND. LAB. means that the switch has been tested by Underwriters Laboratories. (CSA is the equivalent Canadian organization.)

Amp/Volt Rating

UL Label

Wire Types

12 *Working with Wiring*

Exhaust Fans

To remove moist air and odors effectively from a bathroom, you need to match the fan capacity to the room's volume. Exhaust fans are sized by the number of cubic feet of air they move each minute (cfm). A fan should change all of the room's air at least eight times each hour. For 8-foot ceilings, the following formula can help determine what you need:

Fan capacity (cfm) =
Room Width (feet) × Room Length (feet) × 1.1

Fans are also rated in "sones" for the amount of noise they produce, from 1 to 4 sones. A fan rated at 1 sone, the quietest, is about as loud as a refrigerator.

Installing the Fan & Ductwork

Drill a hole through the ceiling in the place that you would like to install the fan. Push a length of wire through the hole to mark the spot. *(1)* If possible, take the fan housing into the attic. Find the wire that you pushed through. *(2)* Place the cutout hole near a ceiling joist to anchor the fan, and drill holes at the corner to the ceiling below. Trace the fan housing on the ceiling to mark the cutout, and cut the opening with a keyhole saw. *(3–4)*

You can vent a ceiling fan through the roof, as described here, or horizontally through an outer wall or the eaves. Except for wall-mounted fans, you'll need to connect the fan to a duct that terminates in the roof or eaves. (See the drawing on page 172.)

Nail the support brackets on the fan housing to the joists, or cut 2×4s to span between two joists as a support. Measure the distance between the fan and the opening where you want the vent. This distance plus 36 inches is the amount of flexible duct you need. Match the diameter of the duct to the fan. *(5)*

Clamp the sleeve of the flexible duct to the discharge opening of the fan housing. Wrap duct tape tightly around the clamp to make the joint airtight. Then pull the insulation over the sleeve, and wrap that tightly with duct tape. Attach a 10-inch length of rigid aluminum duct to the discharge end of the flexible duct with duct tape. *(6)*

Drill holes through the roof sheathing to mark the vent's corners. From the roof, use a saber saw to cut an opening for the duct. *(7)* Pull the duct extension through and connect it to the vent cap. Coat the underside of the flashing with roofing cement, and press it into place. Nail the flange to the roof. *(8)*

Installing an exhaust fan

Difficulty Level:

Tools & Materials: Exhaust fan ❖ Power drill ❖ Reciprocating saw, keyhole saw, or saber saw ❖ Hammer ❖ Flexible aluminum duct & vent-cap kit ❖ 10" long rigid aluminum duct ❖ Duct tape ❖ Screwdriver ❖ Screw clamp ❖ Silicone caulk & caulking gun ❖ 8d common nails ❖ Drywall screws ❖ Roofing cement ❖ Work gloves ❖ Safety goggles ❖ Face mask

3 When you've located the housing in the framing, drill holes at the four corners to the ceiling below. Then use the fan housing to accurately mark the cutout on the ceiling.

6 After attaching the flexible duct to the fan housing with a clamp and duct tape, attach a piece of rigid aluminum duct to the end of the flexible duct using duct tape.

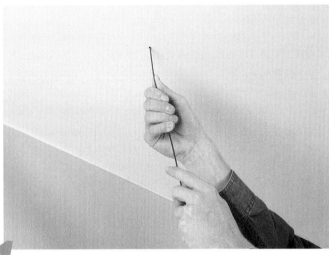

1 Drill a hole through the ceiling in the approximate location you want the fan, and feed a wire up through the drywall to mark the spot.

2 Pull back the insulation, and check where the wire has come through. You'll want to place the fan opening close to a structural member to provide support.

4 Cut the opening in the ceiling with a keyhole saw, reciprocating saw, or saber saw. Be sure to protect your eyes and mouth from falling dust.

5 Secure the fan housing to the ceiling framing. Once you decide where you are going to vent the fan, measure, cut, and attach the ductwork. (See the drawing on page 172.)

7 Use a saber saw to cut an opening through the roof for the vent. If you don't have a saber saw, you can drill a starter hole and cut with a keyhole saw.

8 After you pull the duct extension through the roof, connect it to the vent hood. Seal each shingle and the flange of the hood with roofing cement.

12 *Working with Wiring*

Wiring an Exhaust Fan

The electrical part of this project consists of bringing a power cable to the fan motor and hooking it to a switch. If the power source is closer to the fan than it is to the switch, a switch loop is used. If not, the switch can be wired in-line.

Wiring a Switch Loop. Run two cables into the fan housing, one from the power source and one for the switch loop. Coming from the fan housing will be a white wire, a black wire, and a green grounding screw. Wrap a piece of electrical tape around the white wire that goes to the switch to code this wire as hot. Attach the black wire from the power source to this recoded white wire. Attach the white wire coming from the fan to the white wire from the power source, and the black wire coming from the fan to the black wire going to the switch.

Connect a short piece of green or bare wire, called a pigtail, to the grounding screw in the fan housing. Connect this wire to the grounding wires from the power source and from the switch. *(1)*

Install a switch box in the wall near the door. Use a standard single-pole switch. Wrap black tape around the white wire coming into the box to recode to hot. Attach this wire to one of the switch terminals and the other black wire to the other terminal. If the box is plastic, connect the grounding wire to the green grounding screw on the switch.

If the box is metal, connect a short piece of green pigtail wire to the grounding screw on the switch. Connect another piece of grounding wire to the grounding screw in the box. Connect the two short wires to the incoming bare wire with a green wire connector. *(2)* Wrap the sides of the switch with tape to protect the terminal screws from contact with the grounding wires. Screw the switch into the box, and install the cover plate.

Plug the fan into the motor receptacle, secure the fan into the housing, and install the grille.

Wiring the Fan In-Line. If the power source is closer to the switch than the fan, run the power cable from the source into the switch. Then run another cable from the switch to the fan. Use cable of the same gauge as the cable that supplies power. Run a length of cable from the power source into a 3½-inch switch box in the wall near the door. Run a cable out of the switch box to the fan housing.

For a standard single-pole switch, connect one black wire to one switch terminal and the other black wire to the other switch terminal. Connect the white wires together. Connect a short piece of green wire to the green grounding screw on the switch. If the box is plastic, connect this wire to the two green wires coming into the box. If the box is metal, connect another short green wire to the grounding screw in the box, and use a wire connector to connect the two short grounding wires to the two bare wires from the cable. Wrap the sides of the switch with tape to protect the terminal screws from contact with the grounding wires. See the top left photo on page 169 for in-line wiring of a single-pole switch.

When the fan is wired in-line, only one cable comes into the fan housing. Connect the black wire from the cable to the black wire from the fan housing. Connect the white wire from the cable to the white wire in the fan housing. Connect the incoming green wire to the grounding screw in the fan housing. *(3)*

Plug the fan into the motor receptacle, secure the fan into the housing, and install the grille. *(4)*

Exhaust fans can be vented straight up through the roof or (if there isn't unused space above the bathroom) laterally into a soffit.

Vent
Vent Collar
Rafter
Optional Route for Ductwork
Fan Housing
Boxed Soffit
Flexible Duct
Joist
Vent

Wiring an exhaust fan

Difficulty Level:

Tools & Materials: Cable ripper ❖ Multipurpose tool ❖ Insulated screwdriver ❖ 14/2 NM cable with ground switch ❖ Pigtails ❖ Switch box ❖ Wire connectors

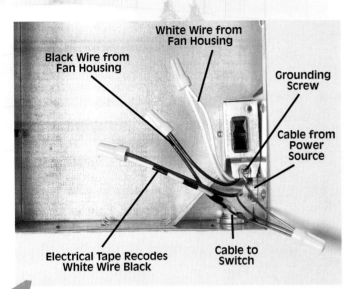

Black Wire from Fan Housing

White Wire from Fan Housing

Grounding Screw

Cable from Power Source

Cable to Switch

Electrical Tape Recodes White Wire Black

1 A switch loop brings power into the fan housing, then takes it out to a switch and back to the housing. Wire the switch loop as shown here.

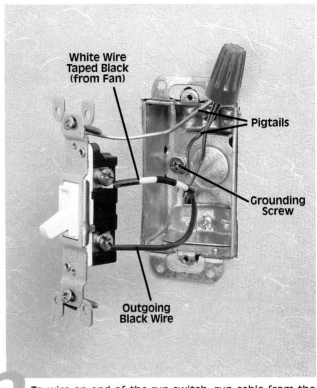

White Wire Taped Black (from Fan)

Pigtails

Grounding Screw

Outgoing Black Wire

2 To wire an end-of-the-run switch, run cable from the fan into the switch box. Mark the incoming white wire black, and connect it and the black wire to the switch.

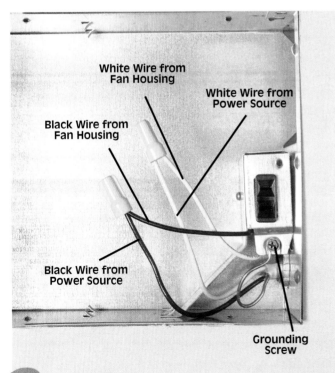

White Wire from Fan Housing

White Wire from Power Source

Black Wire from Fan Housing

Black Wire from Power Source

Grounding Screw

3 For in-line wiring, connect the white cable wire to the white fan wire and the black cable wire to the black fan wire. Connect the bare cable wire to the grounding screw.

4 Plug the fan motor into the receptacle, and secure the fan to the housing with the screws provided. Then attach the grille.

12 Working with Wiring

Light Fixtures

Lightbulbs are rated by lumens, which measure the amount of light the bulb produces, and watts, which measure the rate at which electrical energy is used. The ratio of lumens per watt is an indicator of a bulb's energy-efficiency. Watts don't measure brightness: though a 100-watt incandescent bulb is brighter than a 40-watt one, a 13-watt fluorescent may be brighter than the 40-watt incandescent.

Types of Bulbs

Compared with an energy-guzzling 100-watt incandescent, compact fluorescents use 75 percent less electricity and last longer. But the harsh, bluish light of a fluorescent is also not necessarily what you want over the bathroom mirror. If you are stuck with fluorescent fixtures, a lighting expert can help by choosing warmer bulbs or cooler tubes to suit the situation. Halogen bulbs have a kind of clear-white quality, and are about 25 percent brighter than standard incandescent bulbs of the same wattage, but they require special fixtures. They are also extremely hot and should be treated with caution. High-intensity-discharge (HID) bulbs, such as halide and high-pressure sodium, are also bright and efficacious, but require special fixtures.

Wiring Fixtures

Wiring lighting fixtures (or any electrical appliance in a permanent location) requires bringing a power supply cable to the fixture, wiring in a switch, and attaching the fixture to the wall or ceiling. You can wire a remote switch by running the power cable through the switch and into the fixture (in-line wiring) or by running the power cable to the fixture first, then taking a "leg" off the hot wire to the switch. Here's how to install a ceiling-mounted and a recessed light fixture (pages 176 to 177), using in-line wiring. (See page 172 for wiring a switch loop.) Always shut off power to the circuit at the main panel before beginning any wiring job.

Installing a Light in the Ceiling

After turning off the power, use a neon circuit tester to confirm that there is no power at the light circuit. Pull the cable from the switch into the electrical box, secure it in place, rip the cable sheathing, and strip the wires in the cable. *(1)* If the box does not have a built-in hanger stud, attach a mounting strap to the box tabs. *(2)* Screw a threaded nipple into the collar of the crossbar to support the weight of the light fixture. *(3)* Be certain that it will extend through the suspended fixture to engage the mounting nut.

Using wire connectors, splice the hot black wire from the switch to the hot black lead wire from the fixture. Next, connect the neutral white wire from the switch to the neutral white wire from the fixture. Then, splice together the grounding wires, and pigtail them to the green grounding screw in the electrical box or on the mounting strap. *(4)* Push the completed wiring neatly into the box, and install the fixture cover over the threaded nipple. Lastly, tighten the mounting nut. *(5)*

Lighting Capacity

Before deciding on a fixture, be sure to have enough lighting capacity. Determine how much you need by matching the power consumption in watts to the floor area to be lighted: for fluorescent lighting, 1.2 to 1.6 watts per square foot; for incandescent lighting, 3.5 to 4 watts per square foot.

Unfortunately, there is no simple rule of thumb for task lighting. Because task lighting must focus on a specific target to be effective, the location of the lamp is as important as the amount of light it yields. The size of the mirror at the main task area can clue you as to the number of lamps you'll need.

To light a mirror with incandescent lamps, figure on at least three bulbs of 15- to 25-watt capacity at each side or a series of strip lights (pictured at right) around the sides and top of the mirror. Ask your lighting supplier to show you strip-lighting fixtures from a catalog. They are generally available in 18-, 24-, 36-, and 48-inch lengths.

An enclosed tub or shower is another task area that requires lighting. Choose a recessed vapor-proof fixture with a 60- or 75-watt bulb. For safety, position the switch so that it is out of reach from inside the compartment.

Installing a ceiling-mounted fixture

Difficulty Level:

Tools & Materials: Surface-mounted light fixture ❖ Electrical box to match fixture ❖ Wire stripper ❖ Insulated screwdriver ❖ Mounting strap ❖ Threaded nipple ❖ Cable ripper ❖ Needle-nose pliers ❖ Cable clamps (for metal boxes) ❖ Wire connectors

1 After turning off the power, use a circuit tester to make sure the power is off. Then pull the cable into the box, and strip the insulated wires.

2 If the fixture box does not have a hanger to mount the light fixture, attach a mounting strap to the box. Most mounting straps have a grounding screw.

3 Screw a threaded nipple (usually included with the fixture) into the collar of the support. A retaining nut will hold the fixture to the threaded nipple.

4 Splice the fixture wires to the power wires, pigtailing the grounding wires to the grounding screw on the mounting bracket.

5 Place the fixture cover over the nipple, and tighten the retaining nut. Install a bulb of the recommended wattage, attach the cover, and turn on the power.

12 Working with Wiring

Recessed Light Fixtures

Recessed lighting fixtures for damp areas such as bathrooms must be clearly marked "Suitable for Wet Locations" or at least "Suitable for Damp Locations." These fixtures must be installed so that water cannot enter the wiring compartments. Recessed lights that are designed for wet locations can even be used inside a shower or over a tub or whirlpool. Make sure you use shielded fixtures so that reclining bathers aren't bothered by glare. Shatter-resistant white acrylic lenses that eliminate the danger of glass breakage are best. Always put the switch out of reach of those in the tub or shower to reduce the risk of electrocution.

Some recessed systems must be installed before the ceiling is closed. If that is not possible, be sure to buy a system that you can install from below in a finished ceiling. Also check to make sure that the housing you are considering is compatible with the clearances you have for both depth and proximity to insulation. Low-profile downlights and rectangular fluorescent fixtures called "troffers" can be used in spaces as shallow as 4 inches.

Insulation batts should be cut back so that they are at least 3 inches away from the fixture's housing. If the ceiling has loose-fill insulation, you'll need to install baffles to keep the insulation away from the fixture. Cut two pieces of lumber (the same size as the ceiling joists) to fit between the joists around each fixture, and toe-nail them into place.

Installing the Lamp Housing

Once you have determined where you'll mount the housing, pull out the extension bars on the lamp housing to reach the adjoining ceiling joist. *(1)* Make final adjustments to the housing position by sliding the fixture along the bars. Be sure that the face of the unit extends below the framing in it's final position so that it will be flush with the finished ceiling. Then, using nails or screws, fasten the extension bars to the joists.

Preparing the Electrical Box

Take the cover off the electrical box that is attached to the lamp housing. Using an insulated screwdriver and hammer, remove a knockout for the switch-leg cable. *(2)* Pull the cable into the box, and secure it into place using a cable clamp. *(3)* Leave about 10 inches of cable in the box. Rip the cable sheathing to within ¾ inch of the cable clamp, and remove the ripped-back sheathing. Then, using a multi-purpose tool, strip the wires in the cable, and cut away any excess wire. Repeat this procedure for each cable entering the box.

Wiring the Box

Using wire connectors, splice the white switch-leg wire to the white wire coming from the fixture. Next, connect the black switch-leg wire to the black wire coming from the fixture. *(4)* Pigtail the two bare or green grounding wires (one from the switch-leg cable and one from the fixture cable) to the green grounding screw terminal in the electrical box, and re-attach the box cover. *(5)*

When the ceiling is finished and painted, install a lightbulb with the recommended wattage into the fixture's socket. Attach the waterproof gasket, the lens, and the trim over the opening in the fixture housing.

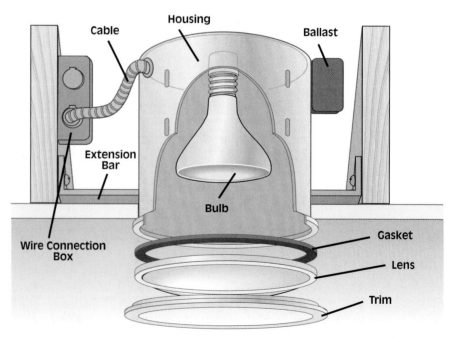

Cable Housing Ballast

Extension Bar

Bulb

Wire Connection Box

Gasket

Lens

Trim

A recessed lighting fixture in a bathroom should be clearly marked as suitable for wet or damp locations. It must have a watertight cover with a gasket.

Installing a recessed light fixture

Difficulty Level:

Tools & Materials: Recessed lamp housing & light fixture ❖ Insulated screwdriver ❖ Insulated hammer ❖ Nails or screws ❖ Power drill ❖ Cable ripper ❖ Needle-nose pliers ❖ Multipurpose tool ❖ Cable and locknut clamp ❖ Wire connectors

1 Install the bracket for the lamp housing, positioning it between two ceiling joists. Adjust the housing, and fasten the extension bars to the joists.

2 Use a screwdriver and hammer to remove one of the knockouts on the fixture box to accommodate the incoming power cable.

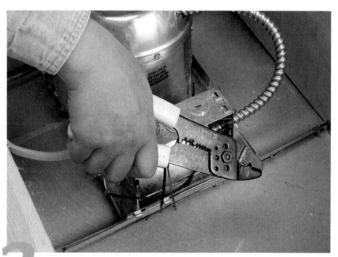

3 Pull the power cable coming from the switch into the junction box, and clamp it securely in place. Unwrap the cut end of the cable, and strip the insulation off the wires.

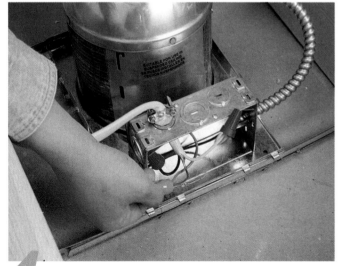

4 Splice the black hot wires, white neutral wires, and grounding wires from the switch-leg cable and fixture with wire connectors.

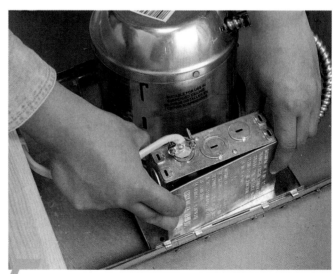

5 Attach the grounding wires to the green grounding screw in the electrical box with a short piece of green wire. Then reattach the cover of the fixture box.

12 *Working with Wiring*

Installing Cabinets

CHAPTER 13

Cabinetry projects tend to be both more complicated and more exacting than other home-improvement jobs. It takes a fair amount of skill and the right tools to make drawers that slide easily, doors that close smoothly, and joints that are strong, straight, and tight. Well-crafted cabinets and vanities can make a room, and new bathroom cabinets, countertops, and other accessories, such as mirrors, will increase the value of a home.

You can avoid a lot of work by buying factory-made cabinets and counters—you just attach the units to the walls and hook up the plumbing and wiring. The first step is selecting the materials. On cabinet faces, you have a basic choice between solid wood and composites such as particleboard covered in plastic laminate. For countertops and vanity tops, modern plastics—both thin laminates and thicker solid forms—are affordable choices and are by far the most commonly used.

Another useful means of storage is the medicine cabinet. This can be either installed on the finished wall surface or recessed into the wall cavity. Recessing the cabinet is a more difficult project, but it is still within the scope of a one-day DIY project.

Removing an Old Vanity

Don't install new cabinetry or mount accessories until the plumbing is roughed in and the walls are faced with drywall or cement-based backer board. Bars, hooks, and minor accessories go in after you complete the wall finish.

Removing the Sink

Turn off the water supply at the shutoff valves under the sink. If there are no shutoff valves, close the main valve near the water meter or well pump. Then open the faucets to let any trapped water escape. The handles of dual-lever faucets sit above threaded tailpieces that connect the faucets to the water-supply risers. Single-lever faucets have two pre-attached copper tubes that converge under the faucet. Compression fittings attach the copper tubes to the shutoff valves.

For a single-lever faucet, use an adjustable wrench to disconnect the copper tubing from the shutoff valve. *(1)* For a dual-lever faucet, you may need a basin wrench to disconnect the risers from the coupling nuts. *(2)* Basin wrenches let you get at hard-to-reach places. Spray the nuts with penetrating oil if they are hard to turn, and then allow the oil to sit for a few minutes. When the coupling nuts are free, disconnect the nuts holding the lower ends of the risers to the shutoff valves; then remove the risers.

Place a pail under the trap. Next, loosen the locknuts holding the trap by turning them counterclockwise with adjustable pliers or an adjustable wrench. *(3)* Turn the locknuts by hand until you

Removing an old sink & vanity

Difficulty Level:

Tools & Materials: Open-end wrench ❖ Adjustable pliers ❖ Basin wrench ❖ Pipe wrenches ❖ Pail ❖ Flashlight ❖ Penetrating oil (if needed) ❖ Putty knife or utility knife ❖ Power drill with screwdriver bit ❖ Keyhole saw or utility saw ❖ Wood chisel

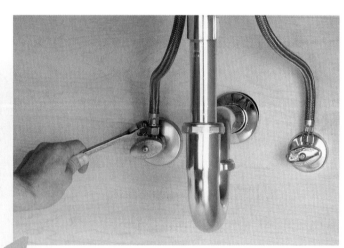

1 Single-lever faucets come with copper tubes that converge into the faucet valve. Disconnect the coupling nuts with an open-end wrench.

4 Free the pop-up drain linkage by unscrewing the retaining nut, and then disconnecting the lift rod, pivot rod, and clevis strap.

5 Disconnect any retaining clips, and separate the sink from the countertop with a putty knife or utility knife. Then carefully lift the sink off the countertop.

can pull the trap free. Pour out any water retained inside the curved section of the trap.

If you want to use the same sink, you'll need to disconnect the lift rod that controls the stopper to get the sink out of the vanity. Pull off the clip that holds the pivot rod to the clevis strap, and then loosen the setscrew that holds the clevis strap to the lift rod. Pull out the lift rod, and remove the pivot rod and clevis strap. *(4)*

The sink may be held to the vanity by caulk, clips, or both. After unscrewing any clips or restraints, use a putty knife to separate the sink from the countertop. *(5)* If you can't slice through the caulk, chip it away with a hammer and chisel, taking care not to break or chip the sink. Then pull the sink out of the countertop.

Removing the Vanity

Vanities are usually attached to the wall with screws or nails. Begin by enlarging the openings around the water shutoff valves in the back panel so that you can pull the vanity free. Drill a pilot hole, and then use a keyhole saw to enlarge the holes. Take care not to damage any parts to be salvaged. *(6)* Remove any nails or screws holding the vanity in place, and pull the cabinet away from the wall. *(7)*

Caution

Use a flashlight or a battery-powered work light with a clip to light the area below the vanity. If water drips down onto an electrical light and causes a short, you could get hurt.

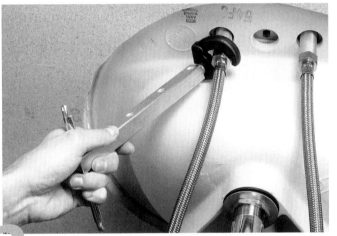

2 Use a basin wrench to access hard-to-reach coupling nuts on dual-lever faucets. If the connections are soldered, you'll need to cut them above the valves.

3 With a pail under the trap, turn the locknuts counter-clockwise to loosen. If the nuts won't turn, cut out the trap with a hacksaw. Pour out any water left in the trap.

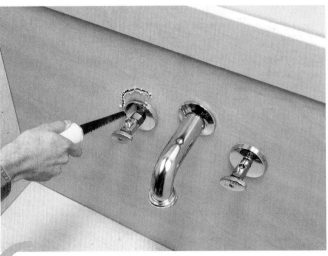

6 After you detach the mounting hardware and remove the top of the vanity, enlarge the openings around the shutoff valves in the back panel with a utility saw.

7 Take out the fasteners that are holding the back panel to the wall, cut through any caulk or adhesive along the wall and floor, and pull the cabinet free.

A New Vanity

If you want a truly custom vanity cabinet and have experience in cabinetmaking, consider designing and making your own (which is beyond the scope of this chapter). If you'd prefer to keep it simple, however, check out the selection of prefabricated units available from your building-supply or kitchen-and-bath store. Prefab units usually have post-form tops: particleboard that's been factory-laminated, often with a built-in backsplash. All vanities come as base-only units, a base with an integral sink-countertop, or a base with a countertop for a separate sink. The steps below describe how to install a pre-fab vanity cabinet that comes with a post-form countertop, complete with backsplash. (See page 191 for instructions to install a new sink into a laminated or post-form countertop.)

Installing the New Vanity

To minimize plumbing work, try to place the vanity so that the new sink will align with the existing plumbing. Outline the opening for the shutoff valves and drainpipe on the back panel of the cabinet. Then, using a saber saw, cut the opening, and set the vanity in place against the wall. *(1)*

Place a spirit level on top of the cabinet to see whether it is level front to back and side to side. If not, put wood shims under the base, tapping them in gently a little at a time until the cabinet is level in both directions. *(2)* For a tight fit without shims,

How to install a post-form vanity

Difficulty Level: 🔧🔧

Tools & Materials: Vanity unit ❖ Saber saw ❖ Straightedge ❖ Wood plane ❖ Power drill ❖ Adjustable wrenches ❖ Silicone caulk & caulking gun ❖ 2½" wood screws ❖ Shims ❖ 1¼" wood screws ❖ Masking tape ❖ Paint or sealer ❖ Wood glue or construction adhesive ❖ Clamps

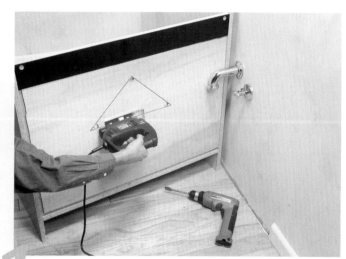

1 Cut a large triangular opening in the back of the new vanity through which the faucet valves and sink drain will be able to fit.

4 Use a saber saw to cut the countertop to length; a framing square or other straightedge clamped to the counter can act as a guide.

5 Once cut, the exposed ends of the countertop are covered with end-cap pieces. If they don't come with adhesive, attach them using wood glue.

mark the high spots of the vanity with a pencil, and plane them down so that the bottom of the vanity hugs the floor.

Locate the studs in the wall behind the cabinet. Drive two 2½-inch wood screws, one near the top and one near the bottom, through the back panel or mounting rail and into the two studs closest to the ends of the cabinet. *(3)* Caulk the seam between the back of the vanity and the wall.

Installing the Countertop

Use a saber saw to cut the countertop to length; a framing square clamped to the counter can act as a guide. *(4)* The cut ends are covered with end-cap pieces. If they don't have adhesive backing, attach them with wood glue on contact cement. *(5)*

Have a helper hold the counter firmly down and against the wall while you drill pilot holes up through the corner braces and into the particleboard of the countertop. Then drive 1¼-inch wood screws through the braces. *(6)* After the top is secured, attach a strip of masking tape along the wall ¼ inch above the backsplash and another strip on the top of the backsplash, ¼ inch away from the wall. Run a bead of silicone caulk colored to complement the countertop along the joint between the backsplash and the wall inside the two strips of tape. *(7)* Tool into a smooth, concave profile with a wet finger. Then carefully strip off the masking tape.

Check that the vanity is level front to back and side to side. Use shims to level it out. You can also use a plane to shave the bottom of the vanity to match an uneven floor.

Secure the vanity to the wall by screwing through the back and into the studs behind the wall using 2½-in. drywall screws.

Position the counter tightly against the wall, and attach it to the cabinet corner blocks from underneath using long drywall screws.

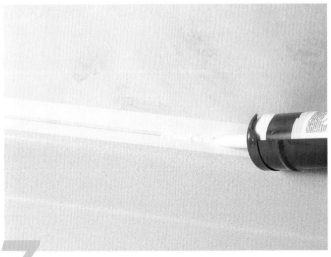

Apply a bead of silicone caulk in the joint between the wall and backsplash and in any other joints between the countertop and a wall.

Laminate Countertops

Plastic laminates are a popular choice for countertops and vanities because they are durable, fairly stain resistant, and quite inexpensive when compared with stone, tile, or solid-surfacing. Laminates are also available in a huge number of colors and finishes. The most common problems in a bathroom counter are chipping. Burns—just about impossible to repair—are much more common in kitchen countertop installations.

Post-form countertops, like the one with the vanity shown on pages 182 and 183, have the laminate preglued to a particleboard platform, complete with backsplash and a curved front edge. They save you a lot of finish work but might not fit your design. If not, you'll need to make your own countertop, and glue the laminate yourself.

Building the Countertop

To make underlayment for a laminate countertop, use two layers of ¾-inch exterior-grade AC plywood, or one layer of plywood and one layer of backer board. Never use interior plywood or particleboard. Include cross braces in the counter-base framing spaced a maximum of 36 inches apart. You can use 1×2s on edge or 2×4s laid flat for the braces. Make sure that a brace falls at the joint between plywood panels but that none fall at a sink or other fixture.

Measure, cut, and fit the plywood to provide the appropriate overhang on all open edges. After checking for level, fasten the underlayment to the braces from underneath with 1½-inch galvanized drywall screws.

Installing Laminate

You trim laminate to size by scoring the rigid material with a utility knife or a special laminate scoring tool. *(1)* To finish the cut, place the panel on a flat surface, and clamp a straightedge just past your score line. Snap the excess off the edge. *(2)*

Laminate is usually affixed to its substrate with contact cement. Always read adhesive label cautions before rolling onto sheets or brushing on edging. At minimum, open as many windows as you can for air circulation; you might even want to place a fan in a window to vent the fumes outside. Don't use contact cement in a windowless room or a basement.

Brush adhesive onto the edging with a sponge brush. *(3)* Position the strip over a double-thick plywood counter edge, and roll the strip firmly for good adhesion. *(4)* Trim the top edge using a router with a flush-cutting bit. For the countertop, brush a coat of adhesive on the back of the laminate and two coats on the substrate; then place lattice strips across the counter. After you position the sheet over the counter with a slight overhang, remove the strips one by one. *(5)* Use a router to trim the perimeter after the adhesive sets. Use a beveled bit with a ball-bearing guide to prevent scorching.

Caution

Use contact cement only in a ventilated area. Exposure to its fumes can irritate your nose, throat, and lungs. Wear eye protection and rubber gloves when handling it.

Installing a new laminate countertop

Difficulty Level: 🔨🔨

Tools & Materials: Laminate material ✧ Utility knife or laminate cutter ✧ Straightedge ✧ Bar clamps ✧ Paintbrush ✧ Contact cement ✧ Safety goggles, rubber work gloves & dust-mist respirator ✧ Lattice strips ✧ Laminate roller ✧ Router

3 Read adhesive label cautions (and note the caution box above) before rolling the adhesive onto the sheets and brushing it onto the edging pieces.

Cutting & Trimming Laminate

Laminate can be tricky to work with because of its hardness. You need this kind of durability on countertops, but the brittle sheets chip unless cut with very sharp tools. Laminate countertops and edgings are installed with a slight overlap, and then trimmed to a fine joint with a router. To avoid exposing dark substrate material under the color surface of inexpensive laminate, use slightly more expensive solid-color laminate. If your router bit does not have a ball-bearing guide, friction from the high-speed rotation is likely to scorch the laminate. If you push the router fast enough to avoid scorching, the joint is more likely to chip: it takes practice.

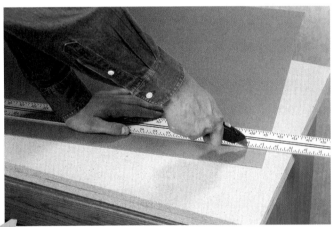

1 Trim the sheet of laminate to the size you need by scoring it with a utility knife or a special laminate scoring tool held against a straightedge.

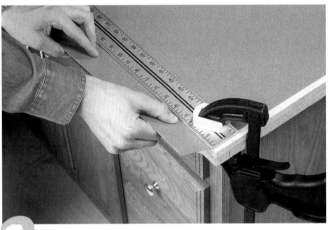

2 Clamp the straightedge on a sound, flat surface, such as a counter or workbench, with the excess hanging over the edge. Snap the laminate along the score line.

4 Position the edge strip over the double-thick plywood counter edge, and roll the strip firmly to ensure good adhesion.

5 Set thin lattice strips over the counter while you position the main sheet. When the sheet is on straight, remove the strips in sequence, and roll the sheet.

Ceramic Tile Countertops

The ideal substrate for a tile countertop is two layers of plywood or backer board. If you don't want to tear up the old countertop, you can also apply ceramic tile over old tile or plastic laminate countertops, but not over particleboard or fiberboard. Roughen old tile or plastic laminate by sanding the surface with 200-grit wet/dry sandpaper.

Preparation

If you are making a new countertop, build a base out of two layers of ¾-inch plywood—or one layer of plywood and one layer of cement-based backer board—that you have glued and nailed together.

Arrange the tiles on the countertop in the desired pattern. Be sure to use one of the edge tiles to establish a working line before setting the field tiles. *(1)* Try to position the field tiles so that the amount of cutting is minimized; avoid making narrow cuts. Also, if you intend to install a tiled backsplash with cove tiles, calculate the appropriate spacing.

If your tiles do not come with self-spacers, insert plastic spacers in each corner to set the proper grout-joint widths. Snap chalk lines near the center of the top, front to back, and side to side as reference lines. *(2)* Mark them in with a pencil, using a framing square for alignment.

Tiling a countertop

Difficulty Level:

Tools & Materials: Ceramic field & edging tile ❖ Pencil ❖ Tile snap cutter or wet saw ❖ Chalk-line box ❖ Thinset adhesive ❖ Notched trowel ❖ Plastic tile spacers (optional) ❖ Putty knife ❖ Grout ❖ Float ❖ Clean rag or squeegee ❖ Fiberglass mesh tape (optional)

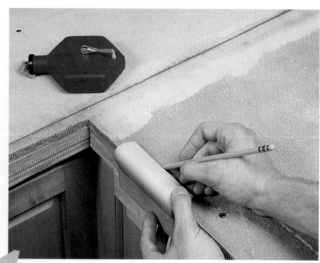

1 Use one of the edge tiles to establish a working line for the main field of full tiles. Mark the edge piece at several points along all counter edges.

4 Embed the first row of field tiles along your guidelines. Tile spacers will make setting subsequent courses easier. Set all full-size tiles before the edging.

5 Embed partial tiles in the adhesive with firm pressure. You may want to use a straightedge to be sure the cut tiles are flush with the field.

Installing the Tiles

Remove the dry-laid tiles. Apply thinset tile adhesive to the countertop using the notched trowel. *(3)* Take care not to spread adhesive over too great an area, so you have time to set the tiles before the adhesive begins to harden. Press each tile firmly in place with a slight wiggle to ensure a good bond. *(4)* Most DIYers find it helpful to use plastic spacers in the tile joints. They can be pulled out when the tiles are permanently set.

Cut partial tiles along the back edge using a snap cutter, and install them last. *(5)* For the technique for cutting border tiles, see "Resilient Floor Tiles," page 201, step 4.

Mix grout according to the directions (using a colorant if desired), and press it into the joints with a squeegee. When the grout is firm but not dry, clean the surface with a damp sponge. When the grout dries to a hazy residue on the the tiles, clean the haze off with a dry cloth. For more on grouting, see "Ceramic Tile on Floors," pages 205 to 207.

Installing Edge Tiles

If you used a wood guide to align the field tiles, remove it, and clear any excess adhesive. Fiberglass mesh tape will help adhesive stick to the counter edge, but you may find that it helps to butter the edge tiles before setting them in place. *(6–7)*

2 Snap chalk guidelines inset from the edges of the counters. Remember to allow for a grout joint between the field tiles and the edge tiles.

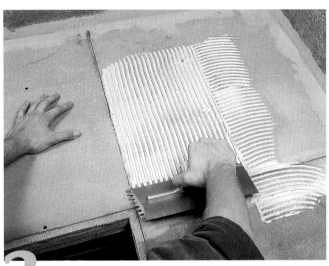

3 Spread thinset adhesive over the backer board with a notched trowel. Start at a point that controls the layout—for example, at an inside corner.

6 Butter the backs of V-caps or other edge pieces with adhesive. Fiberglass mesh tape on the counter edges will improve the bond.

7 Set the edge tiles to align with the grout joints of the field tiles. Work the edging pieces slightly side to side to embed them firmly.

Making a Backsplash

Apply the backsplash tiles the same way as the trim tiles. Before starting, make sure you turn off the power to any switch or outlet around which you need to tile.

First you need to establish the design of the backsplash. It may involve cove tiles (which curve at the bottom to meet the countertop tiles), trim tiles, and decorative tiles of a different size than your field tiles. Measure the total height of the design, including grout joints, and snap a chalk line along the top of your layout. You may want to mask any surrounding walls or surfaces that you want to protect from adhesive or grout.

Using a notched trowel, spread adhesive on the wall below your chalk line. *(1)* Place the bottom course of backsplash tiles on plastic spacers to keep them from resting on the countertop tiles. *(2)* This bottom joint will later be caulked rather than grouted. Thinset adhesive should have more than enough tack to keep the tiles in place while it sets. If your tiles won't stay on the wall, mix another batch of adhesive.

Finish the top edge of a backsplash with a cap tile or some other type of decorative trim tile. *(3)*

Once the adhesive has set, grout the backsplash tiles. (See "Ceramic Tile on Floors," pages 205 to 207, for more detail.)

Tiling a backsplash

Difficulty Level:

Tools & Materials: Ceramic field, cove & edging tile ❖ Snap cutter or wet saw ❖ Chalk-line box ❖ Thinset adhesive ❖ Notched trowel ❖ Putty knife ❖ Grout ❖ Float ❖ Clean rag or squeegee

1 Use a notched trowel to spread adhesive from the counter to a top guideline on the wall. If you want, add masking tape to keep a clean line on the wall.

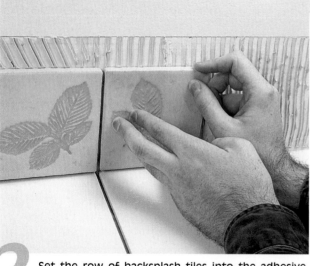

2 Set the row of backsplash tiles into the adhesive, but leave a standard seam along the bottom. Use spacers to keep the tiles from sagging.

3 Cover the top edges of full backsplash tiles with a cap tile. Another option is to use tile with a finished bullnose edge on top.

Sinks

Many bathroom vanity tops are made of solid-surface material and have integral sinks—the sink and the counter are cast in one seamless piece. Small half baths (which don't need much room for storage) usually have freestanding pedestal sinks. With other types of vanities—such as ceramic tile or the post-form laminate described in "Laminate Countertops," pages 184 to 185—you install a separate sink in an opening in the countertop. These sinks are held in place with clips or an adhesive applied under their rims.

Use the following guidelines for installing a sink into a vanity countertop. See "Faucets," pages 126 to 129, for help with the fittings and plumbing. If you must cut a hole in the countertop, it's usually easier to make the cutout before securing the countertop to the base cabinet.

For Solid-Surface Countertops

If the sink is not an integral part of the countertop, you can mount a self-rimming sink into the cutout. Order the countertop piece with the cutout already made, if possible. However, if you need to cut it yourself, mark the cutout, drill a pilot hole along the line, and cut the opening with a saber saw equipped with a carbide-tipped blade. Install the sink into the cutout as described in "Installing a Sink in a Laminate Countertop," page 191.

For Tiled Countertops

There are three ways you can install a new sink in a tile countertop:

• Over the tile by dropping the sink into the opening after tiling the countertop. Set the sink into a bead of caulk, and secure it with clips installed from below.

• Under the tiled surface by routing out a recess for the rim in the countertop. This allows you to set an unrimmed sink flush with the untiled surface. Install the sink in the countertop following the manufacturer's instructions before setting the tile. Then install bullnose trim tile over the edge of the sink.

• Flush with the tile by installing a self-rimming sink in the cutout before tiling, on top of a bead of caulk, and then tiling up to the sink's edge.

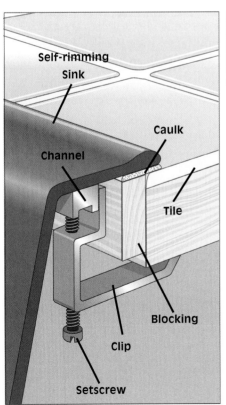 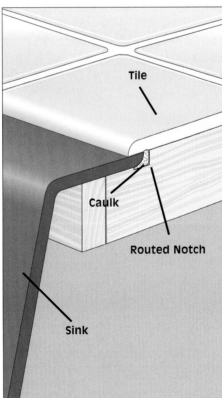 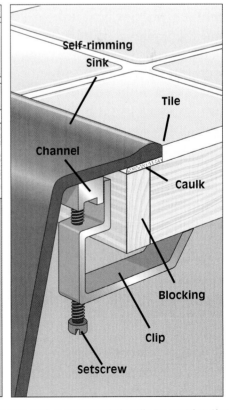

A sink set in a tiled countertop can be installed on a bead of silicone caulk set over the tile, left. If you want the tile to overlap the sink, rout out a notch or recess in the substrate so that the sink's edge is flush with the untiled surface, center. For a sink with a trimmed edge, you can install the sink first and then tile up to the rim of the sink.

For Laminate Countertops

Make a mark where you want the center of the sink to fall on the countertop. If your sink is self-rimming and doesn't come with a template to trace your cutout, place it upside down, center it over the line you drew, and trace around the outer edge of the rim. *(1)* Remove the sink, and mark the actual cutting line inside the outer line—usually about ½ inch in from the outer edge. If your sink is metal rimmed, lay the trim over the counter, and use it as a template to mark the cutout. Drill ⅜-inch holes at the corners (for a rectangular sink), at the wide and narrow points (for an oval sink), or at any point (for a circular sink). *(2)*

For support, install 2×4 braces in the vanity, one on each side of the sink, unless the countertop consists of two layers of ¾-inch plywood or solid-surface material. *(3)* Use a saber saw to make the cutout. *(4)*

The specific method of installation depends on the type of sink.

Self-rimming Sinks. To install a self-rimming sink, start by cutting a hole smaller than the outer rim. (See Steps 2 and 4.) Place a bead of caulk or plumber's putty where the sink rim will go and another around the underside of the sink's lip. *(5)* Then position the sink in the opening, and press it into the caulk or putty. Install the metal clips that come with the sink on the underside. Gradually tighten the setscrews enough to hold the sink firmly. Lastly, run your finger around the edge to shape the caulk and remove any excess from the countertop.

Metal-rimmed Sinks. Lay a bead of silicone caulk around the cutout, and place the metal rim onto the caulk. Have a helper push the sink up from below to meet the trim, allowing you to tighten the clips. If you have to work alone, suspend the sink in position. Hold it in place using a 2×4 across the top and another across the bottom, with a rope connecting the two. Before tightening the rope, place a bead of caulk between the sink edge and metal trim. Then tighten the rope by twisting it, to pull the sink up to meet the metal trim. Lastly, tighten the setscrews on the clips below, and clean off any excess caulk. (See the drawing above, right.)

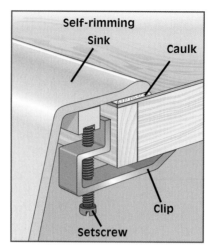 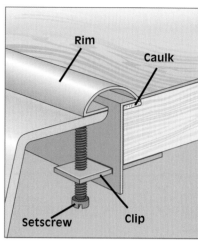

Self-rimming sinks are set in caulk and held with clips, left. Otherwise, first set the sink rim into sealant, and push the sink from below, right.

Vessel Sinks

For an arresting—and easily installed—addition to your bathroom, consider a vessel sink. A vessel sink is one step beyond a self-rimming sink—it's designed to sit on top of the counter rather than down inside it. A sink intended as a vessel sink must have finished surfaces both inside and out. They are available in cast iron, ceramic, and even translucent glass. They are plumbed the same as any sink, but remember that your faucet must be tall enough to curve over the top of the sink's edge.

Installing a sink in a laminate countertop

Difficulty Level:

Tools & Materials: Sink & laminate countertop
❖ Pencil ❖ Saber saw ❖ Power drill with ⅜" bit ❖ Adjustable wrench ❖ Basin wrench ❖ Spud wrench ❖ Screwdriver ❖ Utility knife ❖ Silicone caulk & caulking gun ❖ Masking tape ❖ Rope ❖ 2x4s for bracing

1 Make a line on the counter at the center of where you're placing the sink. If it is self-rimming, trace the sink's rim right onto the countertop.

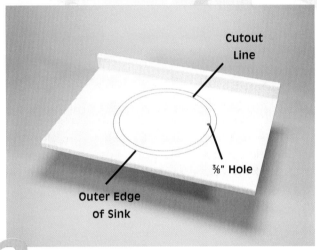

Cutout Line

⅜" Hole

Outer Edge of Sink

2 The instructions that come with the sink will indicate the size of the opening you need. Drill several holes along the cutout line for sawing.

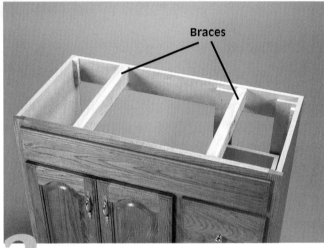

Braces

3 To support the weight of a heavy sink, add 2x4 braces flush with the countertop. Space them so that the sink's edges will rest on them.

4 Cut openings in plastic laminate countertops with a saber saw. (A keyhole saw is a possible but less desirable alternative.)

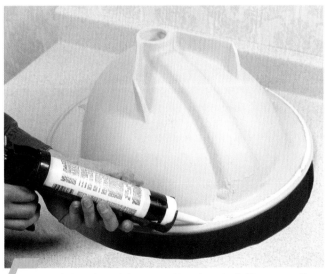

5 Self-rimming sinks are set in a bead of silicone caulk or plumber's putty. Some are also held in place with metal clips.

Medicine Cabinets

Medicine cabinets that stand out from the wall may not be as elegant as cabinets recessed into the wall, but hanging them is far simpler. If the wall contains pipes or wires, a surface-mounted unit may be the only practical option.

Surface-Mounted Medicine Cabinets

Use a spirit level to mark a line on the wall for the top of the cabinet. *(1)* For most people, a good height is 72 inches from the floor. Have a helper hold the cabinet up to the line while you mark its outline on the wall. If you can't use a pencil (such as on tile), use masking tape. Locate the studs within the area of the medicine cabinet. Use a magnetic stud finder, or drill small-diameter holes across the wall surface until you find a stud. *(2-3)* (You can fill in holes not covered by the cabinet.) Measure the positions of the studs from one edge, and transpose this to the back of the medicine cabinet. Drill holes through the back panel of the cabinet near the top.

Have your helper hold the cabinet while you mark the pilot holes. *(4)* Take the cabinet down, and drill the holes in the wall. If you're drilling through tile, use a carbide-tipped bit slightly larger than the screws to drill the tile, and then switch to a smaller bit. While your helper lifts the cabinet into position, insert the screws and tighten them.

Recessed Cabinets

Recessed medicine cabinets are sized to fit into walls framed with 2×4s. If you are lucky, the studs

Installing a medicine cabinet

Difficulty Level:

Tools & Materials: Cabinet ❖ Magnetic stud finder ❖ Pencil or masking tape ❖ Power drill with screwdriver bit, ¼" drill bit, & ¾" spade bit ❖ Keyhole saw ❖ Drywall ❖ Drywall tape ❖ Joint compound ❖ Drywall taping knife ❖ Sandpaper ❖ Paint ❖ Paintbrush ❖ 2x4s ❖ 3½ L-clip ❖ Hammer ❖ 3d & 6d nails ❖ Screws or nails for cabinet

1 Measure up from the floor (72 in. is a typical height), and mark the location of the top of the cabinet using a 2-ft. spirit level.

4 With a helper holding the cabinet in place, mark where the screws will go. Drill pilot holes into the studs, drive the mounting screws, and attach the cabinet.

5 For a recessed cabinet, mark the cutout size on the wall. Drill pilot holes at each corner of the cutout, and use a keyhole saw to cut out the opening between the studs.

will be just in the right position for you to insert a 14½-inch cabinet (or a double-width cabinet by removing a center stud). It's likely, however, that the studs will not be in the best place for the cabinet. Then you'll need to cut out some studs and add some new ones at the sides.

Locate the wall studs as described in steps 2 and 3. Unless you are certain that no wiring runs through the cutout area, shut off the circuit breaker that controls the electricity to that room. Drill a pilot hole ¾ inch or larger diameter at each corner of the cutout. Cut through the plaster or drywall with a keyhole saw. *(5)* If the wall is faced with ceramic tile, remove the tile in the area of the cutout with a hammer and chisel before sawing through the substrate.

Measure the exact distance between the studs (normally 14½ inches). Cut two pieces of 2×4 to this dimension; they will serve as blocking (head and sill) at the top and bottom of the opening. Attach a 3½-inch-long L-clip to the end of each 2×4 with 3d nails. Hammer two 6d nails partway into the studs below the sill to provide a temporary support. Then rest the sill piece on these nails, with the L-clips facing up, and attach the L-clips to the studs with three 3d nails. (Use screws for plaster-faced walls.) *(6)* Reverse the procedure at the top, except that you won't need the supporting nails.

Insert the cabinet into the opening, and screw it to the studs through the holes provided in the overlapping sides. *(7)* If there are no holes or they are poorly located, drill new ones.

2 You need to install surface-mounted cabinets onto the studs; a recessed cabinet between them. Locate the studs behind the wall with a magnetic stud finder.

3 To locate studs without a stud finder, you can knock on the wall, or drill small holes at 1-in. intervals until you hit a stud. Then measure 16 in. to find a second stud.

6 After removing the wall finish, install the head and sill blocking with L-clips attached to the exposed ends of each piece.

7 Once the rough opening is complete, install the cabinet into the opening. Screw the sides of the cabinet into the studs.

Cabinets That Span More Than One Stud Bay

Before beginning work, be sure to shut off the circuit breaker (or remove the fuse) that controls any wiring that may run behind the wall. Next, find the studs behind the wall in the location of the new medicine cabinet. Using a spirit level, mark the top line of the medicine cabinet. *(1)* This is generally 72 inches above the floor, but adjust this for your own comfort and use. Measure the height of the portion of the cabinet that will go into the wall, and add 3 inches to allow for header and sill blocking. Mark a horizontal line at the bottom of the cutout. Mark the outer studs, using a level held vertically as your guide.

Making the Opening. Drill a pilot hole at least ¾ inch in diameter at each corner of the cutout. Next, cut the drywall, using a utility or keyhole saw. *(2)* If the wall is faced with ceramic tile, strip it off before cutting through the drywall or plaster. After the studs have been exposed, determine which ones need to be cut. But before cutting, be sure the wall is not load bearing. If it is, you'll need to place a header above the remaining studs. (See "Enlarging a Rough Opening," page 103.) Use a backsaw to cut through the studs. *(3)*

Framing the Opening. Measure the horizontal distance between the edge studs, and cut two pieces of 2×4 to this dimension to serve as the header and sill. Drive pairs of 10d nails through the header and sill into the ends of the cut studs. *(4)* Then toenail the header and sill to the edge studs with 8d nails. You can also attach the header and sill to the edge studs with L-shaped framing hardware. If necessary, cut 2×4 trimmers to reduce one or both sides of the opening to the size required for the cabinet. You'll need to install one 2×4 next to the outside stud(s) to serve as blocking for the drywall patch. *(5)*

Cut strips of drywall to cover the exposed studs, leaving the recess for the cabinet open. Nail the drywall strips to the studs with drywall nails. *(6)* Then tape and finish the drywall joints, as described in "Finishing Drywall," pages 92 to 93. Then paint the new drywall to match the wall. *(7)* Insert the cabinet into the opening, and screw it to the edge framing through the holes provided in the sides. *(8)* Complete any electrical wiring if the unit comes with a lighting fixture.

Installing a cabinet that spans several studs

Difficulty Level:

Tools & Materials: Cabinet ❖ Magnetic stud finder ❖ Power drill with screwdriver bit & ¾" spade bit ❖ Utility or keyhole saw ❖ Wood chisel ❖ Backsaw ❖ Wood plane ❖ Rasp ❖ Drywall ❖ Drywall tape ❖ Joint compound ❖ Drywall taping knife ❖ Sandpaper ❖ Paint ❖ Paintbrush ❖ 2x4s ❖ 3½" L-clips ❖ 3d, 6d, 8d, & 10d nails ❖ Screws or nails for cabinet

3 Determine which studs need to be removed (here, just one). Cut through individual studs using a backsaw or reciprocating saw.

6 Finish the part of the wall that won't be covered by the cabinet with new drywall the same thickness as the old. Then tape and finish the seams with joint compound.

1. Measure up 72 in. from the floor, and mark the top of the cabinet, using a spirit level. Then mark the outline of the cutout on the wall.

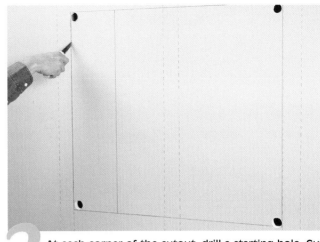

2. At each corner of the cutout, drill a starting hole. Cut out the drywall with a utility, keyhole, or saber saw, exposing the wall framing underneath.

4. Cut header and sill pieces to finish the opening. Face-nail the header and sill to the cut studs, and toenail them to the uncut ones at the side.

5. If the cabinet is smaller than the opening between the studs, use trimmer studs and blocking to reduce the size of the opening.

7. Once the final coat of joint compound has dried, paint over the patch to match the wall or repaint the entire room.

8. Place the medicine cabinet in the rough opening and securely fasten it in place following the manufacturer's instructions.

Finishing Floors & Walls
CHAPTER 14

The pipes are installed, the wiring is done. It's time to make the new bathroom beautiful by installing a finished floor and by finishing the walls and ceilings. In this chapter you'll learn to apply resilient flooring and ceramic tile, today's most practical and beautiful flooring options. You'll also learn how to repair walls and how to finish them with paint or ceramic wall tile.

Paint is the easiest finish for the do-it-yourselfer: it doesn't require a lot of measuring; it looks fine on uneven walls; and the preparation, while important, doesn't require special skills or expensive materials. Other finishes—such as tile, sheet flooring, carpet, and wallpaper—demand careful measurements and accurate calculations in order to achieve a balanced layout, especially on surfaces that are out of true.

It is best for the novice to plan a layout on paper. A scale drawing will enable you to visualize the room before you start, and it will help you estimate what you will need. It also will help you see any layout problems before you establish working lines on the floor.

Planning a Layout

Before planning a layout for new flooring, you will have to make sure that the floor is level and that the walls are straight and reasonably square.

Is the Room Square?

In small rooms, such as most bathrooms, you can check the squareness using a framing square positioned at each corner of the room, or by using the 3-4-5 triangle method: Measure 3 feet along one wall, at floor level; then measure along the other wall 4 feet. If the distance is between these two points is 5 feet, the walls are square. *(1)* For larger rooms, use a multiple of the 3-4-5 triangle (such as 6-8-10 or 12-16-20).

If the walls are less than ¼ inch out of square in 10 feet, it will probably not be noticeable. If they are is more than ¼ inch out of square, the condition will be visible along at least one wall, and you'll need to make angled cuts. (See the left half of the drawing below.) Try to plan the layout so that the angled tiles are positioned along the least noticeable wall. It may be helpful to snap a straight reference line (parallel with the opposite wall) along the this wall.

Is the Floor Level?

Use a 4-foot spirit level to check the floor along each wall. *(2)* An out-of-level floor does not present serious problems unless you plan to extend ceramic tile up the wall. If this is the case, consider using a continuous baseboard and a different type of wallcovering.

Are the Walls Wavy?

Bear in mind that even if the walls are reasonably square to each other, they may be bowed or wavy, which also may be noticeable after you install the tile. You can often detect a bowed or wavy condition by simply sighting down the wall at floor level. You can also screw two one-by blocks at the corners, and run a length of string between them. A third block the same thickness as the other two will show where the wall bows in and out.

Making Working Lines

Once you've established the pattern and selected the finish, you can snap the working lines used to guide the installation on the underlayment.

If you're installing any kind of tile flooring, plan the layout so that a narrow row of cut tiles does not end up in a visually conspicuous place, such as at a doorway. Often, the best plan is to adjust the centerline so that cut tiles at opposite sides of the room will be the same size. If you start by laying a full row of tiles along one wall or if you start laying tiles from the centerline, you can end up with a narrow row of partial tiles along one or both walls.

To correct this, shift the original centerline, or working line, a sufficient distance to give you wider cut tiles at both walls. Also, try to center the tiles across large openings, such as archways, or beneath focal points, such as picture windows or fireplaces. If the tiles extend into an adjacent room, lay out both floors so that the grout joints line up through the entryways.

In short, if you plan the layout carefully on paper, you will eliminate any unpleasant surprises once the project is well underway. Remember, once a few tiles are set, it becomes difficult to make changes in the overall layout.

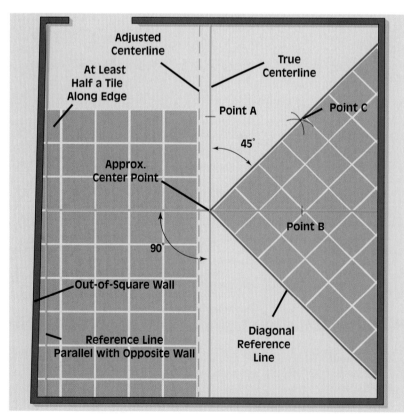

Carefully snapping chalk layout lines before you begin to install the flooring will help you to make a balanced, symmetrical layout. The blue lines indicate the lines for a standard layout; the red lines for a diagonal layout.

Working Lines for a Square Layout

If the room is relatively square, snap a chalk line along the length of the area down the center of the room. Then snap a second chalk line across the width of the room so that each chalk line crosses in the center of the room. Check the cross with a framing square to make sure the intersection forms a 90-degree angle. These will be your working lines, or layout lines, used to position the floor covering.

Working Lines for a Diagonal Layout

When laying tiles diagonally, a second set of working lines is required. You'll need to snap a chalk line at exactly 45 degrees from your vertical and horizontal working lines; you can't just snap a line from the center point to the corner.

From the center point, measure out an equal distance along any two of the lines, and drive a nail at these points, marked A and B on the drawing below left. Hook the end of a measuring tape to each of the nails, and hold a pencil against the measuring tape at a distance equal to that between the nails and center point. Use the measuring tape and pencil as a compass to scribe two sets of arcs on the floor. These arcs will intersect at point C.

Snap a diagonal chalk line between the center intersection and point C. Extend these lines in each direction. Repeat the process for the other two corners. Erase or cross out the original working lines, and lay the tile to the diagonal ones. Adjust the working lines, if necessary, to achieve the best pattern of partial pieces at all four walls.

14 *Finishing Floors & Walls*

Checking a room for square

Difficulty Level:
Tools & Materials: Measuring tape ❖ Chalk-line box ❖ 4' spirit level ❖ Long 2x4 ❖ String ❖ 3 one-by scraps & 3 screws or duplex nails

1 Use the proportions of a 3-4-5 right triangle to check corners for square. With legs of 3 and 4 ft., the diagonal is exactly 5 ft. if the corner is square.

2 Use a 4-ft. spirit level to check the underlayment for level. Set the level on a long, straight 2x4 to read the straightness of the floor over a large area.

3 To check for wavy walls, tie a string between two one-by blocks at opposite corners. Run a third block along the string; mark spots where the wall gaps or bows.

Resilient Floor Tiles

Installing resilient floor tiles is fairly simple and requires only a few tools. For a job to be successful, though, you'll need to plan the layout and prepare the substrate properly. Try to complete the installation all at one time when you won't be interrupted.

Most resilient floor tiles now come in 12-inch squares. Trim strips in various accent colors are available in ¼- to 6-inch widths. When ordering, figure the areas in square feet to be covered (length times width), and add 5 to 10 percent for waste.

Start with the Right Base

When you pick out resilient tiles, check the manufacturer's instructions for acceptable substrates. These include:

• Old resilient tile, sheet flooring, and linoleum. Must be clean, free of wax, and tightly adhered with no curled edges or bubbles.

• Ceramic tile. Must be clean and free of wax. If the surface is porous, be sure it is completely dry. Joints should be fully grouted and level.

• Concrete. Must be smooth and dry. Fill cracks and dimples with a latex underlayment compound.

• Wood flooring. Strip flooring will serve as an underlayment only if it is completely smooth, dry, free of wax, and all joints are filled.

• Plywood. Fir or pine plywood that bears the stamp "Underlayment Grade" (as rated by the American Plywood Association) provides the best underlayment for resilient flooring. Use only material of ½-inch or greater thickness. You can also use available lauan, a tropical hardwood, in ¼-inch-thick panels, but be sure you get Type 1, with exterior-grade glue. Firmly attach all plywood, and fill and sand smooth all surface cracks and holes.

Unacceptable Substrates. Never use particleboard for resilient flooring, because it will swell when moist. If you have particleboard on the floor now, remove it, or top it with underlayment-grade plywood. Though often used as a substrate, hardboard is specifically rejected by some manufacturers.

Preparing the Layout

Place a row of tiles along each of the chalk lines to check your layout. Test a diagonal pattern by first laying tiles down, point to point, along the perpendicular lines, then laying two rows along the diagonal line. *(1)*

Setting the Tiles

When you are satisfied with the layout, adjust your drawing so that you can remember how you placed the tiles; then remove them. Beginning at the intersection of the chalk lines, spread adhesive along one line with the smooth side of a notched trowel. *(2)* Then distribute the adhesive into even grooves by holding the trowel notched side down at an angle of about 45 degrees. Leave part of the line exposed for reference. Set a row of tiles into place; drop, rather than slide, the tiles into position. Starting at the center, set an intersecting row of tiles, and then fill tiles in the spaces between the two guide rows.

Begin a diagonal pattern at the intersection of the diagonal lines, and lay a row along one diag-

Setting resilient floor tile

Difficulty Level: ⚒⚒

Tools & Materials: Framing square ❖ Chalk-line box ❖ Measuring tape ❖ Resilient tiles ❖ Adhesive ❖ Solvent ❖ Notched trowel (notch size as specified for adhesive) ❖ Rolling pin or floor roller ❖ Utility knife

3 Cover that section of adhesive with tile, and embed all the tiles into the adhesive with a rolling pin (or a floor roller, if you have one).

onal. This row will serve as the baseline for the rest of the pattern. Use a rolling pin to apply pressure to each row of tiles as you set them. *(3)* To trim the edge tiles, place a dry tile exactly above the last set tile from the wall. Then put a third tile over these two tiles, pushed to the wall. Using the edge of the topmost tile as a guide, scribe the middle tile with a utility knife, and snap in two to make a trim piece. *(4)*

A diagonal pattern requires two different shapes of edge tiles, a small triangle and a larger five-sided piece, unless the wall line happens to fall exactly on a tile diagonal. Place a tile over the laid tiles with one point touching the wall. Mark off a line where the left side of the tile intersects the first joint line, and cut to make a triangle. Place another tile similarly, but mark where the right side of the tile intersects the joint. Cut this tile to give you a five-sided piece.

Trimming the Outside Corners

Put a tile directly above the last set tile at the left side of a corner. Place a third tile over these two, and position it ⅛ inch from the wall. Mark the edge with a pencil; then without turning it, align it on the last set tile to the right of the corner. Mark it in a similar fashion. *(5)* Cut the marked tile with a knife to remove the corner section. Fit the remaining part around the corner. After you set all the tiles, use the solvent recommended by the adhesive manufacturer to clean any adhesive from the top of the tiles.

1 Lay a row of tiles out on each of the working lines. If the tiles that abut the wall are much less than half a tile, adjust the first tile in the row so that the cuts are even.

2 Once you have adjusted the working lines, spread adhesive, beginning at the center. Work in small areas so that you can lay the tiles before it starts to dry.

4 To mark border tiles, place a tile over the last full tile, and place another tile on top of that but against the wall. Cut the first tile where the second tile meets it.

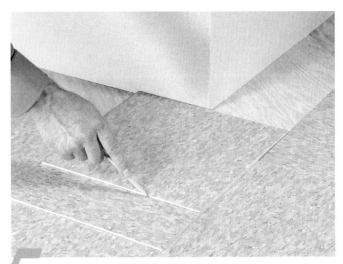

5 To cut the tiles at an outside corner, perform the same cut as in Step 4; then turn the corner and realign the pieces to make the second cut.

Sheet Flooring

Unlike setting tiles, putting down sheet flooring will require you to manipulate a large roll of material inside a small room—a challenge for anyone. So think twice about doing it yourself.

If you do decide you are up to the challenge, begin with a scale drawing of the room on graph paper, showing the exact outline of the flooring. Bring the roll into the bathroom, and let it acclimate to the room's temperature and humidity for at least 24 hours before you try to install it. Some resilient sheet flooring requires no adhesive, some requires adhesive around the outer edge, and some is stuck down with double-sided tape. The tried-and-true method described below is for adhesive-applied flooring. In any case, begin on a good substrate. (See "Start with the Right Base," page 200.) Remove the baseboard trim before you start.

Cutting & Fitting

Unroll the flooring in a room big enough to lay out the whole sheet. With a marker, draw the bathroom's edges on the flooring; add an extra 3 inches on all sides. Cut the flooring to the marks with a straightedge and a utility knife. Roll up the cut piece, and take it into the bathroom; then lay the longest edge against the longest wall. Position the piece so that about 3 inches of excess goes up every wall. *(1)*

If fixtures are not yet in place, roll the flooring out over the toilet flange, and cut the outline with

Installing sheet flooring

Difficulty Level: 🐦🐦🐦

Tools & Materials: 6'- or 12'-wide roll of resilient flooring ❖ Utility knife ❖ Straightedge ❖ Framing square ❖ Measuring tape ❖ Chalk-line box ❖ Handsaw ❖ Adhesive ❖ Solvent ❖ Notched trowel ❖ 2' long 2x4 ❖ Seam roller ❖ Rolling pin or floor roller

1 Make the rough cut with a knife and straightedge in an area where you can lay out the entire piece of flooring. Then lay the floor into position.

4 If you can't make the installation without a seam, roll out a second piece, and pull it over the first piece until the patterns match. Cut it to the approximate size.

5 At outside corners, slit the margin down to the floor using a utility knife. Be careful not to cut too far, or the mark will be visible on the finished floor.

a knife. *(2)* For fixtures already in place, precut a hole to match the outline of the fixture's base, but cut it smaller by 3 inches on all sides. You can trim it later. Then cut a slit from the cutout to the closest edge of the roll. *(3)*

Sometimes it isn't possible or practical to cover the floor with a single sheet. A deep jog in the wall may require seaming a second piece to the main piece. With the first piece in position, measure and cut the second piece as you did with the first one, leaving a 3-inch overlap at the seam. *(4)*

At the outside corners, cut a slit straight down through the margin to the floor. *(5)* Trim the inside corners by cutting the margin away with increasingly lower diagonal cuts on each side of the corner. Eventually you will have made a split wide enough to allow the flooring to lie flat. *(6)*

Crease the flooring into the joint at the wall with a 2-foot-long piece of scrap 2×4. Then place a framing square in the crease, and cut along the wall with a utility knife, leaving a gap of about ⅛ inch between the wall and the flooring. *(7)*

Completing the Operation

Use a handsaw to cut a recess in the wood door casing just above the underlayment and wide enough to slide the flooring beneath. Trim the flooring to match the angles and corners of the door casing; allow about ½ inch of the flooring to slip under the casing. *(8, page 204)*

14 *Finishing Floors & Walls*

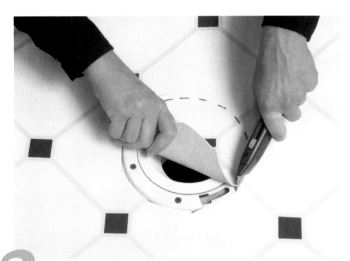

2 If the toilet isn't installed, cut around the toilet flange by pressing the floor covering down so that you can feel the edge. Cut as closely as you can to the edge.

3 If the toilet is in place, cut around the base, leaving a 3-in. margin. Cut a slit at the back of the toilet to the wall. Slit the 3-in. margin so that the flooring lies on the floor.

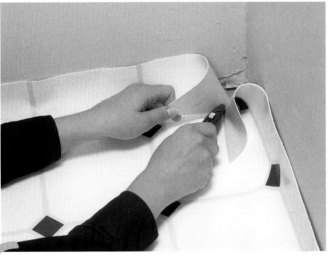

6 At the inside corners, cut diagonally through the margin until the flooring lies flat. Then trim the excess, as described in Step 7.

7 To trim along the walls, press a framing square tightly into the corner and cut away the excess using a utility knife with a fresh blade.

Continued on next page

Roll back the flooring to the center, and apply adhesive to the floor with the smooth edge of a notched trowel, following the manufacturer's directions. Comb out with the notched edge. *(9)* Push the flooring immediately onto the adhesive. Repeat for the other half of the flooring.

If a second or third sheet of flooring must join the first, stop the adhesive short of the edge to be seamed by 2 inches or so. Spread adhesive on the floor to receive the second piece, stopping 2 inches from the first sheet. Position and align the second piece carefully. With a straightedge and utility knife, cut through both sheets along the seam line. *(10)* Remove the waste. Lift up both edges and apply adhesive. Clean the seam, and use the seam sealer recommended for your flooring.

Clean excess adhesive off the surface with the solvent recommended by the manufacturer. Then roll the flooring firmly onto the adhesive with a roller, working from the center outward. *(11)* Last, you can replace the baseboard and shoe moldings. When replacing the shoe, nail it into the wall rather than the floor to allow the floor covering to expand and contract.

Installing sheet flooring, cont'd

8 To fit the flooring around doors or passageways with trimwork, you'll need to cut a recess in the door casing with a handsaw.

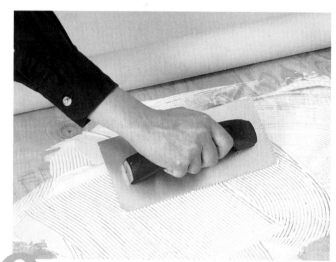

9 Roll half the floor covering back to the center of the room, apply adhesive, and roll it back down. Then repeat for the other half of the room.

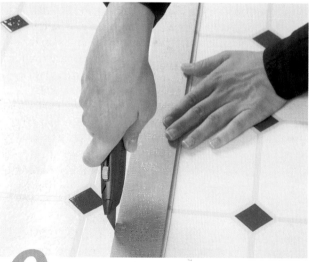

10 To make a seam, overlap the smaller piece with the first piece, matching the pattern. Cut through both pieces, and remove the excess.

11 Use a rented seam roller to force out any ridges and air bubbles in the flooring. Roll from the center to the edges.

Ceramic Tile on Floors

Setting ceramic and stone floor tile is similar to setting resilient floor tiles, described on pages 200 and 201. Ceramic and stone tile can be set into thinset adhesive over a plywood or cement-based backer board underlayment or over a smooth concrete slab using the guidelines that follow. Unlike floors, you set tiles for shower floors into a bed of thickset mortar over a rubberized plastic shower pan. However, this is a task that demands a high level of skill, and it is beyond the scope of this book.

Tile is an expensive finish that lasts for years, so choose your material carefully, and install it with patience and care. Sizes range from 1 to 12 inches square. You can choose from many shapes to create your own interesting patterns. Keep in mind, though, that cutting irregular tile shapes from square can be challenging and time-consuming.

Making a Layout

You can lay tiles starting from the center of the floor, following lines snapped on the underlayment using a chalk-line box, as described in "Making Working Lines," pages 198 to 199. If the floor is small and the tiles are larger than 4×4 inches, one way to lay out the design is to use the tiles as templates and mark each tile's position on the floor.

It is easier to have something other than the chalk line to keep the layout even. Some tiles have nubs on the edges that space the tiles for grout lines. Plastic spacers are available for tiles without nubs. Use the size recommended by the tile manufacturer.

Working Lines

To lay out the pattern from one corner of the room, you can make guide strips by temporarily nailing 1×2 or 1×4 battens to the underlayment, or just snapping chalk lines. Always check the layout with a test fit before laying the tiles.

Use tile spacers to indicate the width of the grout joint. If you're using mesh-backed tile sheets, you don't have to worry about joint spacing. Lay out the tiles to avoid narrow pieces of tile (less than 1 inch) abutting a wall. If this happens, adjust the centerline of your layout so that cut tiles on both sides of the room are the same size.

Cutting Tiles

To make straight cuts in most glazed tile, all you need is a conventional glass cutter or hacksaw, a short metal straight-edge or square, and a short length of coat-hanger wire or a thin dowel. Simply score the glazed surface of the tile with the blade and straightedge; then place the tile on the wire or dowel with the score mark centered directly above it, and press down on both sides of the tile to snap it.

Hacksaw

If you have many straight cuts to make, a snap cutter will speed things along considerably. Snap cutters are available at tool-rental shops. Some tile dealers loan out their tools if you purchase the tile from them. These tools are available in several sizes and variations, but most consist of a metal frame that holds the tile in position, a carbide-tipped blade or wheel to score the tile, and a device to snap the tile once scored. After positioning the tile, draw the carbide blade or wheel lightly across the tile to score it; then press down on the handle until it snaps.

Snap Cutter

Some snap cutters may not work on very large, thick tiles, such as unglazed quarry tiles or pavers. If you have just a few of these tiles to cut, use this variation of the score-and-snap method: equip a hacksaw with a carbide-grit blade; then cut a groove about $\frac{1}{16}$ inch deep in the face of the tile. (Very thick tiles may require a second cut on the back to get a clean snap.) Place the tile over a dowel, and press down sharply to snap the tile.

Wet Saw

If you have many cuts to make, have the tiles cut on a wet saw, a stationary circular saw with a water-cooled carbide-grit blade, used for cutting hard masonry materials. Most tile dealers have a wet saw and will make cuts for a small fee. You also can rent one at a tool-rental shop. Wet saws should not be used to cut floor tiles that are coated with a slip-resistant abrasive grit, because the grit will quickly dull the saw blade. Have your tile dealer cut these, or use the score-and-snap method, above.

Tile Nippers

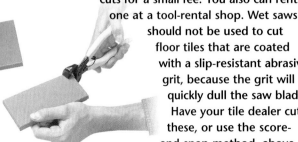

Laying the Tiles

Spread adhesive over a 24-inch-square area of the substrate with the smooth side of a notched trowel. Comb out with the notched edge. *(1)* Note that you may have only a limited time to work before the adhesive sets up. Take care not to cover the chalk lines with adhesive.

Press each tile or sheet of tiles into the adhesive. *(2)* Set mosaic tiles by rolling each sheet up loosely; then set one edge, and roll out the rest of the sheet. Insert a spacer (except with mosaics), and lay the next tile or sheet. If you notice that the tiles are getting out of line, wiggle them into position instead of lifting them out of the adhesive. Make frequent checks for alignment—every two sheets for mosaic tiles and every row for individual tiles. Before the adhesive dries, wipe off any excess on the tiles.

After laying several rows, embed them into the adhesive with a carpet-wrapped 2×4. As you move around the board, tap it firmly with a hammer. *(3)*

Grouting the Joints

Allow the adhesive to dry before filling in the joints with grout. Premixed grout is ready to apply. If you buy the grout as powder, mix it as directed. Spread the grout over the tiles, and press it into the joints using a rubber float held at a slight angle. Work diagonally over the tiles, taking care to fill all joints. *(4)*

After you cover the surface, remove excess grout with the rubber float. To avoid removing too much, work across the tiles diagonally. *(5)* Wipe the surface with a wet sponge, squeezing it out frequently in a pail of water. Get as much of the grout off the surface of the tiles as you can without eroding the joints. *(6)* Then wait 30 minutes until the residue dries to a haze. Wipe this off with a cloth.

For large tiles, you may want the joints to be smoother than they emerge after the grouting and cleaning steps. Tool these joints with a jointing tool you can obtain from your tile supplier, or use the end of a toothbrush or small brush. *(7)*

To prevent moisture from penetrating grout and unglazed tiles, seal the surface with a sealer recommended by your supplier. Some are applied with a roller; others come in a spray can. Allow two weeks for the grout to dry thoroughly, and then apply one coat of sealer. Apply another coat after the tiles have been in place for about two years. *(8)*

Setting ceramic floor tiles

Difficulty Level:

Tools & Materials: Measuring tape ❖ Chalk-line box ❖ 4' spirit level ❖ Framing square ❖ Ceramic floor tile ❖ Notched trowel ❖ Thinset adhesive ❖ Tile spacers ❖ Hammer & bedding block ❖ Snap cutter or wet saw ❖ Tile nippers ❖ Grout ❖ Rubber float ❖ Sponge or squeegee ❖ Pail ❖ Tile sealer & applicator ❖ Jointing tool

3 For each small section of tile you lay, embed the tiles into the adhesive by moving a padded board over the surface and tapping them with a hammer.

6 Wipe the remaining grout haze off the tiles with a dampened sponge. Once the grout has dried, go back and wipe off the remaining residue.

1 Spread the adhesive evenly with the smooth edge of a notched trowel, and then comb back over it with the notched edge. Be sure to leave your working lines visible.

2 Press tiles into the adhesive, making sure their backs are covered. Start your layout at the center point, and work your way along the working line toward the wall.

4 If you're using powdered grout, mix it according to the directions. Force the grout into the joints diagonally across the tiles with a rubber float.

5 Remove the excess grout by working the rubber float diagonally across the joints. You will leave a slight haze on the tiles.

7 For wide grout joints, you may want to smooth the grout with a jointing tool or the end of a brush, to make a slight depression.

8 Seal unglazed tiles with a sealer made for that purpose. For glazed tiles, apply sealer to the grout lines only, using a sealer with a brush applicator.

14 *Finishing Floors & Walls*

Tiling a Shower or Tub Enclosure

The first step in selecting wall tiles is to decide how much of the wall you want tiled and to plan a pattern. You can tile walls partway up or to the ceiling. You can develop patterns by mixing tiles of different colors and shapes. A trim band is useful to tie several features of the room together visually. When tiling walls you use the same tools and steps described for tiling floors on pages 206 and 207; lay a scrap piece of plywood to protect a newly tiled floor.

Before Tiling

A vertical line near the middle of the wall makes a convenient working line. Lay out a row of tiles on the floor in front of the wall, adjusting their position until you get the right spacing for even cut pieces in the corners. Be sure to allow for the width of the grout joints. Then use a chalk-line box to snap a vertical working line. *(1)*

Not all floors are perfectly level, so you'll need to check the floor with a spirit level. Use the highest point to measure up for your horizontal working line. *(2)* The caulk seam at the bottom will mask any discrepancy there. Measure up from the floor the distance of one tile, plus a grout joint at the top and caulk seam at the bottom. Use a level to establish the horizontal working line. Fasten 1×4 battens below the line to hold up the first course of field tile. Drive 2-inch drywall screws into the studs behind the cement-based backer board. *(3)*

Setting Tile

Using the smooth edge of a trowel, spread thinset adhesive over a small area: a square 2 or 3 feet on one side. Rake back over the adhesive with the notched edge of the trowel. *(4)* Set field tiles along the top of the batten, using plastic tile spacers to keep the grout joints even. *(5)* You can can use stack bond as shown here, or use a running bond or pyramid bond. Measure and set the partial tiles at the corners. *(6)* By the time you're done with this, the adhesive on the first course should be set up enough to set the bottom row. Remove the battens, and set the last row of field tiles along the floor, taping them to the course above to keep them from slipping. *(7)* Once the adhesive has fully cured, grout the tiles as described on page 207. *(8)*

Tiling a shower enclosure

Difficulty Level:

Tools & Materials: Measuring tape ❖ Chalk-line box ❖ 4' spirit level ❖ Framing square ❖ 1x4 lumber for battens ❖ 2" drywall screws ❖ Power drill with screwdriver bit ❖ Ceramic tile ❖ Accessories ❖ Thinset adhesive ❖ Notched trowel ❖ Tile spacers ❖ Snap cutter or wet saw ❖ Grout ❖ Float ❖ Sponge or squeegee ❖ Masking tape

3 Measure up the distance of one tile (plus grout joints on the top and bottom), and snap a horizontal line. Screw 1x4 battens to wall studs, to hold the field tiles in place.

6 To mark the corner tiles, set a full tile on the last tile in the field and then another tile on top of that flush with the corner. Mark the cut line on the first tile.

1 After finding the center, use a chalk-line box to snap the main vertical working line on the back, most visible wall. Lay plywood on the floor to protect it while tiling.

2 Check all sides of the base with a level. You need to find the high point before measuring up to establish the main horizontal working line.

4 Use a notched trowel to spread adhesive up to your working lines. For the best bond, spread adhesive with the flat edge before using the notched edge.

5 Set full tiles along the vertical working line, using spacers to maintain even grout seams. You can complete full rows or work in a pyramidal shape.

7 After removing the battens, rake out the adhesive for the bottom row, and set the tiles. Use tape and temporary spacers or tape to keep the tiles in place.

8 After the adhesive is set (usually overnight), use a rubber float to spread grout into the seams. Then follow Steps 5 to 7 on pages 206 to 207.

Soap Dishes & Grab Bars

Bar fixtures are installed two ways. One is to tile the wall completely and drill through the tile to surface-mount them with screws or wall anchors. The other, which generally looks better, is to use fixtures that match the tile color and layout. Because you'll set these accessories into areas of full tiles, you won't need to cut or trim any tiles.

Soap dishes are installed just like tiles; you butter the backs with thinset and set them in a space you have left untiled. The dish is then held to the surrounding tile with masking tape until the adhesive sets. Most bath-tile makers will have soap dishes that match the layout and decor of their tiles. Note that recessed soap dishes require extra work on the framing and substrate before you start filling in the tile. For safety, locate soap dishes where they will not be used as handholds.

Installing a Grab Bar

Unlike soap dishes, grab bars need strong fittings attached to the studs. Some tile makers may supply grab bars that fit in with tile grid; if not, you can drill through the tile and install one to the framing.

First, locate the studs: at least some of the anchors on each end of the bar need to be attached to a stud. Cover the tiles to be drilled with masking tape—it makes marking easier and keeps the glaze from cracking. Mark the fastener pattern on the tile, and drill the holes. *(1)* If some of the fasteners don't hit a stud, use hollow-wall anchors. *(2)* Tighten the fasteners carefully so you don't crack the tile. *(3)*

Installing a grab bar

Difficulty Level:

Tools & Materials: Power drill with carbide-tipped or glass-cutting bit ❖ Grab bar & fasteners ❖ Hollow-wall anchors or toggle bolts ❖ Screwdriver ❖ Masking tape ❖ 4' spirit level

1 Locate the wall studs, which will support the bar. Apply masking tape to the surface of the tile; trace on the holes of the bar; and drill with a masonry or glass-cutting bit.

2 You may not be able to hit a stud with every fastener. In these cases use heavy-duty hollow-wall anchors or toggle bolts.

3 Tighten all fasteners until the bar does not move when force is applied to it. Be careful not to over-tighten the screws and crack the tile.

Preparing for Painting

The economical finish for bathroom walls, ceilings, and wood trim, paint is also the easiest to apply. Unlike more-demanding finishes, paint is forgiving, allowing you to easily make corrections to mistakes or change the color with minimal preparation.

Added to all these pluses, paint provides a durable finish if you prepare the substrate properly and take measures to deal with the heavy amount of moisture in bathrooms.

Preparing Drywall

Before priming, check for nailheads that are protruding from the drywall. Drive new nails or drywall screws 1 or 2 inches above and below any popped nails. Then use a nail set to reset the popped nail, or pull it out using a claw hammer or pair of pliers. You then need to fill the new dimples (or the nail hole) with joint compound. Also fill any cracks, dents, or other surface irregularities before you prime. *(1)*

After the first coat of joint compound has dried completely, sand all filled areas completely smooth and flush with the surrounding wall surface using 100- or 150-grit paper. *(2)* For more detailed information, see "Finishing Drywall" on pages 92 and 93.

Spot-prime all filled areas and unpainted surfaces. *(3)* Use a latex-based primer if the top coats will be a medium to dark color. To ensure an even color for very light top coats, use a white-pigmented shellac primer.

Preparing drywall for painting

Difficulty Level:

Tools & Materials: Hammer ❖ Nail set ❖ Power drill with screwdriver bit ❖ Drywall screws or drywall nails ❖ 6" & 12" drywall taping knives ❖ Joint compound ❖ Sandpaper ❖ Primer ❖ Paintbrush

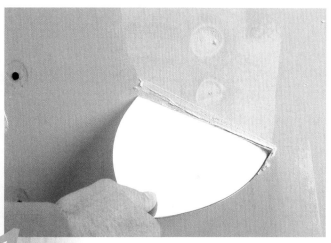

1 Fill the dimples above all the nails and screws you've pulled or reset with joint compound. Also fill any dents or irregularities in the drywall.

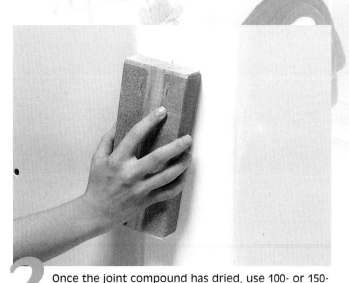

2 Once the joint compound has dried, use 100- or 150-grit sandpaper to sand each patch down until it is flush with the wall surface.

3 Spot-prime all patched areas and unpainted surfaces with a latex primer. Seal any mildew-stained areas with white-pigmented shellac.

Preparing Old Plaster

Before repainting old plaster, take a close look at its overall condition. If it has too many defects, such as being noticeably loose in spots and crumbling in others, you may be better off ripping it (and the lath underneath it) off and applying a new finish, such as drywall. This is, however, a very messy and labor-intensive job. (See "Stripping Down to the Studs," on pages 84 to 85.) If the plaster is basically sound, use the following steps to repair the imperfections.

Use a pointed tool such as a utility knife or even a can opener to enlarge hairline plaster cracks and provide a toothed base for the filler. Clean the joint with a dampened brush, and let it dry. Fill widened cracks with joint compound, leaving a slight hump. *(1)* Once the compound has dried, sand it smooth and flush with the rest of the wall surface using 100- or 150-grit sandpaper.

Larger plaster cracks often indicate a structure that is still settling; therefore, they are likely to reopen after patching. To prevent this, gouge out the crack with a pointed tool, fill it with joint compound, and let it dry. Then apply fiberglass mesh joint tape over the crack, and finish it with a second layer of joint compound. *(2)* The mesh tape will keep the crack from reopening longer than an unsupported patch.

Sand the patches smooth, recoat with a wider drywall knife, and sand again. *(3)* Spot-prime all filled spots as described under "Preparing Drywall," page 211.

Preparing plaster for painting

Difficulty Level:

Tools & Materials: Utility knife or can opener ❖ Small paintbrush ❖ Putty knife ❖ Joint compound ❖ Fiberglass mesh tape (for large cracks) ❖ 6" & 12" drywall taping knives (for large cracks)

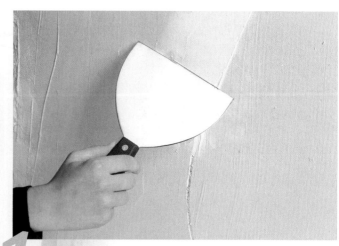

1 Fill any small cracks with patching plaster or drywall joint compound. Once the patches have dried, sand them smooth.

2 Fill deep or wide cracks with joint compound, and let dry. Then apply a piece of fiberglass mesh tape over the crack.

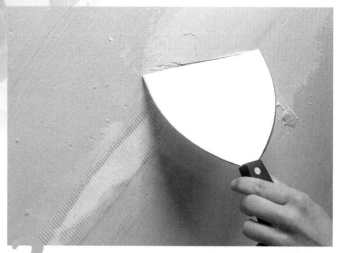

3 Cover the mesh tape with joint compound. When this layer has dried, sand it smooth. You may need another, wider coat to create an invisible patch.

Preparing Woodwork

How you prepare wood, plywood, particleboard, or any other lumber product depends on its current condition and what you want to end up with. You can repaint previously painted woodwork after repairing surface defects. To apply a natural finish, you need to start with raw wood or strip off any previous coating with a chemical stripper.

Use a hammer and nail set to drive nailheads slightly below the wood surface. Fill all holes and cracks with the appropriate filler. *(1)* Once the filler has dried, sand it smooth.

If the wood is to be painted (or repainted), use a powder-based or premixed wood filler. For naturally finished wood, you will want the filled spots to match the color of the wood when fin-ished. Select the premixed wood-filler color that is closest to the species of wood, and fill a hole in a scrap of the same color. When the patch is dry, apply the natural finish and evaluate the resulting color. Try a darker or lighter filler, as necessary, to get a close match.

Caulk joints between wood trim and walls with a high-grade flexible caulk, such as acrylic latex. Polyurethane is a good but messier choice. *(2)* To seal cracks between a finished floor and a wood baseboard, protect the floor with masking tape, and then use a flexible caulk, such as polyurethane or butyl, in the joint.

Prime the woodwork as required to achieve the desired finish. *(3)* Some of the options are listed under "Priming Wood," page 214.

Preparing woodwork for painting

Difficulty Level:

Tools & Materials: Hammer ❖ Nail set ❖ Putty knife ❖ Wood filler ❖ Caulk & caulking gun ❖ Primer ❖ Paintbrush

1 Fill all holes and cracks with the appropriate wood filler—your home center should have one that matches your wood. Once it dries, sand it smooth.

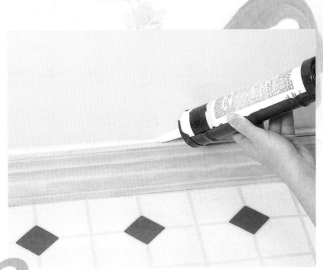

2 Seal the joints between the wood trim and walls with a high-grade flexible caulk. Press the caulk into the seam with a wetted fingertip.

3 Prime woodwork with the appropriate first coat for a natural or painted finish. (See "Priming Wood" on page 214 for the right primer.)

Painting Walls & Ceilings

Mildew affects even the best paint when walls are subjected to high humidity; a good first step to take before painting is to install an exhaust fan.

Choose paint with a high sheen. Gloss and semigloss paints resist moisture and are easier to clean than more porous flat or eggshell paints. Because oil-based paints are being phased out by antipollution legislation, the steps below apply to water-based latex paints.

You can paint intricate surfaces, such as wood trim or cabinets, and small wall areas using only a brush. If the project extends to larger walls or ceilings, you'll save time and effort by using a roller.

Preparing & Priming

The key to a successful paint job is what lies below the paint. Paints with a gloss or semigloss sheen reveal imperfections more than flat or eggshell paints, so begin with a good substrate. Wash previously painted surfaces with phosphate-free trisodium and water. If stains or marks remain after washing, brush white-pigmented shellac over them. To remove any adhesive that clings after stripping off an old wallcovering, brush on wallpaper remover solvent diluted with water (according to the instructions).

Remove switch and outlet cover plates, pipe escutcheons, and fixture trim strips. These items are

Painting Woodwork

Remove any knobs from doors and cabinets before painting woodwork. Unless you need to paint large surfaces, use a small sash brush to paint all wood in the bathroom. Paint the edges of doors first, ending with the larger surfaces. Use a paint shield to protect the floor while painting baseboards.

When painting the window sash, cut the trim as close as you can to the glass, but don't worry about paint that slops over onto the glass: you can scrape any spills off the glass with a razor blade. You can't remove paint quite so easily from tile, so if you are not confident of cutting a clean edge on wood trim next to tile, protect the tile with masking tape.

Priming Wood

Wood/Finish	Prime Coat(s)
Penetrating finish (oil)	Penetrating oil; one or more coats
Surface finish	Stain (if desired); two coats of clear surface finish
Bare wood, paint finish	Two coats latex wood primer or white-pigmented shellac
Prepainted wood, paint finish	Spot-prime filled areas with latex wood primer or white-pigmented shellac

usually easy to remove, and the result will be a much better job for your efforts. *(1)*

For the best results on new surfaces, use one coat of primer and two coats of semigloss or gloss enamel. Most paint covers about 400 square feet per gallon; estimate the amount you will need by determining the square footage of walls and ceilings, multiplying by the number of coats, and allowing for waste by rounding up. Before beginning, protect fixtures and floors with drop cloths. The usual sequence is to paint the walls first and do the wood trim later. But if all surfaces are to be painted with the same color and type of paint, it will be simpler to begin with the brushwork—trim, adjacent walls, and inside corners—and then do the walls with a roller.

Painting

Use a sash brush to "cut in," or trim around the walls and edges around fixture openings. Overlap the joint where the ceiling meets the wall. *(2)* Use a wide brush or roller to finish off the the ceiling, beginning at one wall and working across the ceiling to the opposite wall. An extension handle will allow you to paint the ceiling from a standing position. After dipping the roller in the pan, roll paint onto the surface in a zigzag pattern about two roller-widths wide and 36 inches long. Finish off by rolling the spots between with smooth, vertical strokes. *(3)*

Paint the corners and edges around open wall surfaces with a sash brush. If the wall color differs from the ceiling, let the ceiling dry completely; then cut the wall-ceiling joint carefully. *(4)* Use a roller to paint the wall field. Start at one corner and work across the wall, applying the paint to rectangular sections, as described in Step 3. *(5)*

Painting walls & ceilings

Difficulty Level:

Tools & Materials: Drop cloths ❖ Masking tape
❖ Insulated screwdriver ❖ Paint ❖ 1", 2" & 5" paint-
brushes ❖ Paint roller with roller sleeves & extension handle ❖ Paint tray ❖ Stepladder ❖ Paint shield
(for woodwork) ❖ Safety goggles

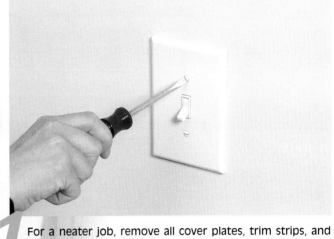

1 For a neater job, remove all cover plates, trim strips, and escutcheons before painting. Always shut off the electrical power before removing outlet and switch plates.

2 Begin by trimming the ceiling-wall joint with a sash brush. Don't worry about overlapping the wall—it's eas-ier to cut a finish trim line on the wall than the ceiling.

3 Begin rolling the ceiling at one wall, and work your way across the room to the opposite wall. Be sure to wear safety goggles to protect your eyes.

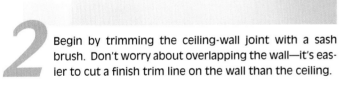
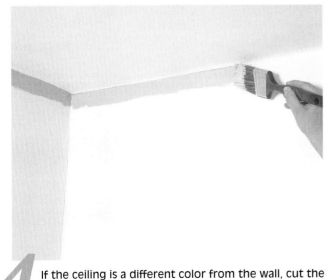

4 If the ceiling is a different color from the wall, cut the trim line on the wall with a sash brush, working the paint up against the ceiling line, as shown.

5 Use a roller for large areas. Paint each section in a zigzag pattern; then finish with up and down strokes until all spots are covered equally.

Resource Guide

American Standard
One Centennial Ave.
Piscataway, NJ 08855
732-980-3000
www.americanstandard.com
American Standard makes technologically advanced bathroom fixtures and fittings, among other products. Its brands include Trane, Armitage Shanks, and Dolomite.

Jacuzzi Whirlpool Bath
2121 N. California Blvd., Suite 475
Walnut Creek, CA 94596
925-938-7411
www.jacuzzi.com
Jacuzzi invented the whirlpool bath, and continues to be a leading manufacturer of whirlpools, indoor spas, pumping systems, luxury showers, and other fixtures.

BathEase, Inc.
3815 Darston St.
Palm Harbor, FL 34685
888-747-7845
BathEase designs bathroom products to meet the needs of those with physical challenges. Its products include a flat-bottomed bathtub unit with a watertight door that provides safer access.

Kohler Plumbing
444 Highland Dr.
Kohler, WI 53044
1-800-456-4537
www.kohlerco.com
Kohler is a leading manufacturer of plumbing systems, sold under more than a dozen brand names worldwide, including Kallista, Sterling, and Hytec.

Center for Universal Design
North Carolina State
University College of Design
Brooks Hall, Box 7701
Raleigh, NC 27695-7701
www.design.ncsu.edu
The Center for Universal Design is a national research and technical-assistance center that promotes universal design in housing.

National Association of the Remodeling Industry (NARI)
780 Lee St. Suite 200
Des Plaines, IL 60016
847-298-9200
www.remodeltoday.com
NARI represents thousands of home improvement professonalss. NARI certification provides the industry with a standard of expertise.

Ceramic Tile Institute Of America, Inc.
12061 W. Jefferson Blvd.
Culver City, CA 90230-6219
310-574-7800
www.ctioa.org
The Ceramic Tile Institute of America supports the expanded use of ceramic tile and is a good source of information about tiling.

National Kitchen & Bath Association (NKBA)
687 Willow Grove St.
Hackettstown, NJ 07840
908-852-0033
www.nkba.org
NKBA supplies design and planning information to professionals and homeowners involved with remodeling a kitchen or bath.

North American Insulation Manufacturer's Association

44 Canal Center Plaza #310
Alexandria, VA 22312
703-684-0084
www.naima.org
NAIMA, a trade association of manufacturers of insulation, promotes energy efficiency through the use of these products. Visit its Web site for publications on application and benefits.

Smedbo

1001 Sherwood Dr.
Lake Bluff, IL 60044
847-615-0000
www.smedbo.se
Smedbo, Swedish for "home of the blacksmith," is a manufacturer of quality decorative brass hardware for the home. Smedbo products—which include towel racks, grab bars, and decorative mirrors—are available worldwide.

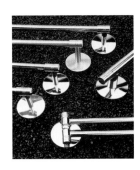

Plumbing Manufacturers Institute

1340 Remington Rd., Suite A
Schaumburg, IL 60173
847-884-9764
www.pmihome.org
Plumbing Manufacturers Institute is the voluntary, not-for-profit trade association for makers of plumbing products. Member companies produce a substantial quantity of the nation's plumbing products.

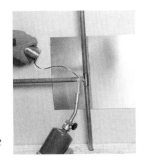

Tile Council of America, Inc.

100 Clemson Research Blvd.
Anderson, SC 29625
864-646-8453
www.tileusa.com
This trade group represents hundreds of tile companies and offers a variety of information on tile, including Handbook for Ceramic Tile Installation. Visit its Web site for technical assistance regarding tile installation.

Saunatec

575 Cokato St. East
Cokato, MN 55321
800-882-4352
www.helosaunas.com and
www.finnleo.com
Saunatec, founded in Finland in 1919, is now North America's largest manufacturer of saunas, steam baths, sauna heaters, and steam generators, under the brand names Helo and Finnleo. Its products are available worldwide.

Underwriters Laboratories

333 Pfingsten Rd.
Northbrook, IL 60062
847-272-8800
www.ul.com
UL is an independent, not-for-profit product safety testing and certification organization. Each year, more than 14 billion familiar UL marks are applied to products worldwide. Since 1894, UL has the reputation as the leader in product safety for electrical products.

Sloan (Flushmate Division)

30075 Research Drive
New Hudson, MI 48165
800-533-3450
www.flushmate.com
Flushmate is a pressure-assisted flushing system for low-consumption toilets, available through leading toilet manufacturers worldwide.

Velux

450 Old Brickyard Rd.
P.O. Box 5001
Greenwood, SC 29648
800-888-3589
www.velux.com
Velux makes roof windows and skylights, as well as such supplemental products as sunscreens, roll shutters, and flashing.

Resource Guide

Glossary

Accent lighting Spot lighting that focuses on decorative features.

Ampere (amp) The unit describing the rate of electrical flow.

Anti-scald valve Single-control fitting that contains a piston that automatically responds to changes in line water pressure to maintain shower temperature. The valve blocks abrupt drops or rises in temperature.

Backsplash The tiled wall area behind a sink, countertop, or stove.

Barrier-free fixtures Fixtures specifically designed for people who use wheelchairs or who have limited mobility.

Base plan Scale drawing made by using the rough measurements of an existing room. A convenient scale for planning a bathroom is to have ½ inch equal 1 foot.

Bearing wall A wall that supports the floor or roof above it.

Bidet A bowl-shaped bathroom fixture that supplies water for personal hygiene.

Blanket insulation Flexible insulation, such as fiberglass or mineral wool, that comes packaged in long rolls.

Blocking Small pieces of wood used to reinforce framing members.

Bridging Lumber or metal installed in an X-shape between floor joists to stabilize and position the joists.

Cable One or more wires enclosed in protective plastic or metal sheathing.

Cement-based backer board A rigid panel designed for use as a substrate, or underlayment, in wet areas.

Cleanout A removable plug in a trap or drainpipe, which allows easy access for removing blockages.

Cleat A piece of lumber fastened (for example, to a joist or post) as a support for other lumber.

Closet bend A curved section of drain beneath the base of a toilet.

Closet flange The rim of a closet bend used to attach the toilet drainpipe to the floor.

Code The rules set down by local or county governments that specify minimum building practices.

Double-glazed A window consisting of two panes of glass separated by a space that contains air or argon gas. The space provides most of the insulation.

Drain Any pipe that carries wastewater through a drainage network and into the municipal sewer or private septic system.

Dry run The process of placing the tiles to check the layout before applying grout; usually tile spacers are used to indicate the width of the grout joints.

D-W-V Drain-waste-vent: the system of pipes and fittings used to carry away wastewater.

End-of-run Outlet or switch box at the end position of a circuit.

Escutcheon A decorative plate that covers a hole in the wall in which the pipe stem or cartridge fits.

Fish tape Flexible metal strip used to draw wires or cable through walls and conduit.

Fixed Windows that do not open. They come as glass sheets to be installed into a finished opening or as ready-to-install units enclosed in wood, metal, or plastic frames.

Flux The material applied to the surface of copper pipes and fittings when soldering to assist in the cleaning and bonding process.

Full bath A bathroom that contains a sink, toilet, and tub/shower.

Furring Wood strips used to level parts of a ceiling, wall, or floor before adding the finish surface. Also used to secure panels of rigid insulation. Sometimes called strapping.

Ground The connection between electrical circuits and equipment and the earth.

Ground-fault circuit interrupter (GFCI) A safety circuit breaker that compares the amount of current entering a receptacle with the amount leaving. If there is a discrepancy of 0.005 volt, the GFCI breaks the circuit in ¼₀ of a second. GFCIs are required by the National Electrical Code in areas that are subject to dampness, such as bathrooms.

Grounding screw Terminal screw to which a bare or green grounding wire is connected.

Grout A binder and filler applied in the joints between ceramic tile.

Half bath Bathrooms that contain only a toilet and a sink.

Hardboard Manufactured pressed-wood panels; hardboard is rejected by some manufacturers as an acceptable substrate for resilient and tile floors.

Junction box Electrical box in which all standard wiring splices and connections are made.

Luxury bath A full bath with a bidet and/or second sink.

Middle-of-run Electrical box with its outlets or switch lying between the power source and another box.

Nonbearing wall A wall that does not support a load from above.

On center A point of reference for measuring. For example, "16 inches on center" means 16 inches from the center of one framing member to the center of the next.

Overflow An outlet positioned in a tub or sink to allow water to escape if a faucet is left on.

Particleboard Reconstituted wood particles that are bonded with resin under heat and pressure and made into panels. Particleboard has a tendency to swell when exposed to moisture.

Pigtail Short piece of wire that connects an electrical device or component to a circuit.

Resilient flooring Thin floor coverings composed of materials such as vinyl, rubber, cork, or linoleum. Comes in a wide range of colors and patterns in both tile and sheet forms.

Rigid foam Insulating boards composed of polystyrene or polyisocyanurate. Rigid insulation offers the highest R-value per inch of thickness.

Riser A supply pipe that extends vertically, carrying water, steam, or gas.

Roughing-in The installation of the water-supply and D-W-V pipes, before the fixtures are in place.

Rubber float A flat, rubber-faced tool used to apply grout.

R-value A number assigned to insulation to measure the insulation's resistance to heat flow. The higher the number, the better the insulation.

Sister joist A reinforcing joist added to the side of a cut or damaged joist for additional support.

Soil stack The main pipe that carries waste from the waste pipes and drainpipes to the sewer or septic tank.

Spa A bathtub-like unit, usually with a high, round shape that is deeper than a whirlpool tub. Unlike whirlpools, spas are not usually drained after each use.

Spud washer On a toilet that has a separate tank, the large rubber ring placed over the drain hole. The tank is placed over the spud washer.

Stops On doors, the trim on the jamb that keeps the door from swinging through; on windows, the trim that covers the inside face of the jamb.

Stub-out The end of a water-supply or D-W-V pipe extended through a wall or floor.

Stud Vertical member of a framed wall, usually 2×4s or 2×6s installed every 16 or 24 inches on center.

Subfloor The surface below a finished floor. In newer homes the subfloor is usually made of sheet material such as plywood; in older houses it is usually diagonally attached boards.

Switch loop Installation in which a switch is at the end of a circuit with one incoming cable, and the neutral wire becomes a hot wire.

Terminal The place in a circuit or device where an electrical connection is made.

Thickset A layer of mortar more than ½ inch thick that is used to level an uneven surface for tiling.

Thinset Any cement-based or organic adhesive applied in a layer less than ½ inch thick and used for setting tile.

Three-quarter bath A bathroom that contains a toilet, sink, and shower.

Toenail Joining boards together by nailing at an angle through the end of one and into the face of another.

Tongue-and-groove Boards milled with a protruding tongue on one edge and a slot on the other for a tight fit on flooring and paneling.

Top plate Horizontal framing member, usually consisting of 2×4s, that forms the top of a wall and supports floor joists and rafters.

Trap A section of pipe that is bent to form a seal of water against sewer gases.

Tripwaste A lever-controlled bathtub drain stopper.

Vent stack The main vertical vent pipe.

Volt The unit of electrical force.

Watt The unit of measurement of electrical power required or consumed by a fixture or appliance.

Wax ring A wax seal used to seal the base of a toilet so it won't leak.

Whirlpool A tub that contains a pump that circulates water through jets around the sides of the unit.

Wire connector A small cap used for twisting two or more wires together.

Wire shield Metal plate nailed to a framing member to protect wiring behind a wall from nails and screws.

Index

Metric Conversion

Length

1 inch	2.54 cm
1 foot	30.48 cm
1 yard	91.44 cm
1 mile	1.61 km

Area

1 square inch	6.45 cm²
1 square foot	929.03 cm²
1 square yard	0.84 m²
1 acre	4046.86 m²
1 square mile	2.59 km²

Volume

1 cubic inch	16.39 cm³
1 cubic foot	0.03 m³
1 cubic yard	0.77 m³

Common Lumber Equivalents

Sizes: Metric cross sections are so close to their nearest U.S. sizes, as noted below, that for most purposes they may be considered equivalents.

Dimensional	1 x 2	19 x 38 mm
lumber	1 x 4	19 x 89 mm
	2 x 2	38 x 38 mm
	2 x 4	38 x 89 mm
	2 x 6	38 x 140 mm
	2 x 8	38 x 184 mm
	2 x 10	38 x 235 mm
	2 x 12	38 x 286 mm
Sheet	4 x 8 ft.	1200 x 2400 mm
sizes	4 x 10 ft.	1200 x 3000 mm
Sheet	¼ in.	6 mm
thicknesses	⅜ in.	9 mm
	½ in.	12 mm
	¾ in.	19 mm
Stud/joist	16 in. o.c.	400 mm o.c.
spacing	24 in. o.c.	600 mm o.c.

Capacity

1 fluid ounce	29.57 mL
1 pint	473.18 mL
1 quart	1.14 L
1 gallon	3.79 L

Temperature

(Celsius = Fahrenheit – 32 x ⅝)

°F	°C
0	–18
10	–12.22
20	–6.67
30	–1.11
32	0
40	4.44
50	10.00
60	15.56
70	21.11
80	26.67
90	32.22
100	37.78

Index

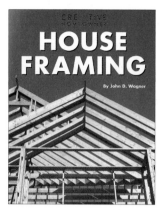
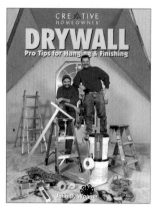
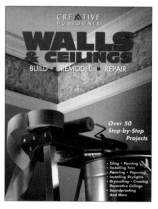
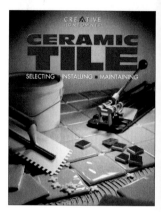
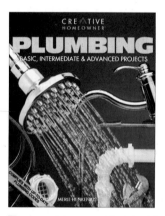
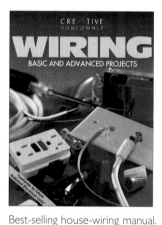
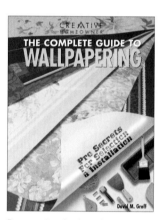

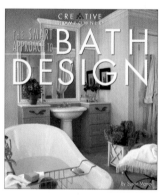